# 'GIRL POWER'

mediated
youth

Sharon R. Mazzarella
*General Editor*

Vol. 4

PETER LANG
New York • Washington, D.C./Baltimore • Bern
Frankfurt am Main • Berlin • Brussels • Vienna • Oxford

Dawn H. Currie, Deirdre M. Kelly, Shauna Pomerantz

# 'GIRL POWER'

## Girls Reinventing Girlhood

PETER LANG
New York • Washington, D.C./Baltimore • Bern
Frankfurt am Main • Berlin • Brussels • Vienna • Oxford

**Library of Congress Cataloging-in-Publication Data**

Currie, Dawn.
Girl power: girls reinventing girlhood /
Dawn H. Currie, Deirdre M. Kelly, Shauna Pomerantz.
p. cm. — (Mediated youth; v. 4)
Includes bibliographical references and index.
1. Teenage girls—Social conditions. 2. Girls—Social conditions.
3. Identity (Psychology) in adolescence. 4. Feminism.
I. Kelly, Deirdre M. II. Pomerantz, Shauna. III. Title.
HQ798.C87    305.235'2—dc22    2008043863
ISBN 978-1-4331-0571-5 (hardcover)
ISBN 978-0-8204-8877-6 (paperback)
ISSN 1555-1814


Bibliographic information published by **Die Deutsche Bibliothek**.
**Die Deutsche Bibliothek** lists this publication in the "Deutsche
Nationalbibliografie"; detailed bibliographic data is available
on the Internet at http://dnb.ddb.de/.

Cover art by Nora Kelly


The paper in this book meets the guidelines for permanence and durability
of the Committee on Production Guidelines for Book Longevity
of the Council of Library Resources.

*To the girls who*

*participated in our study*

# CONTENTS

# SERIES EDITOR'S PREFACE

Underage Lolitas! Teen Pregnancy Pacts! Girls Gone Wild! Growing Up Too Fast! Starving to be Thin! Girl Gangs! Girl Lured by Online Predator! Mean Girls! Pick up any newspaper, and these are the kind of headlines one is likely to find announcing yet another facet of the perceived crisis facing this generation of North American girls.

Such cultural constructions of girls tend toward the sensationalistic and essentializing, often indicating North American culture's obsession with girls' bodies—whether used to define ideal female beauty, to sell products, or as fodder for the latest media-fueled moral panic. John Hartley (1991) labels this phenomenon as "juvenation"— a pervasive, bipolarity in news coverage of girls in which young female bodies are celebrated and flaunted to attract adult consumers while simultaneously offered up as evidence of youthful transgressions, flaws, and missteps. Such representations, Dawn Currie, Deirdre Kelly, and Shauna Pomerantz argue in *"Girl Power": Girls Reinventing Girlhood*, provide evidence of "a narrative that is symptomatic not of girls, but of social investments in girlhood." (p. 184)

Rather than seek to understand the broader social investment in girlhood, *"Girl Power"* undertakes to understand how girls themselves construct girlhood(s), in particular as this construction relates to the contested concept of "girl power." Unlike mainstream cultural representations of girls—representations constructed by adults, for adults, and featuring a noticeably silent *girl object* (Mazzarella, 2008; Mazzarella & Pecora, 2007), Currie, Kelly, and Pomerantz. see girlhood as an "embodied presence." While the objectified youthful female body at the center of many mainstream media representations of girlhood is an adult construction, Currie, Kelly, and Pomerantz's concept of embodied presence is situated in girls' own *identity practices, agency, subjectivity, and communities of practice.* This conceptual framework, along with the authors' ethnographic methods, enables *"Girl Power"* to explore the ways in which girls themselves "do girlhood." The book's title is telling—girls are not so much "inventing" girlhood as they are taking it back—"(re)claiming" it, as the title of Chapter One announces.

While girls' voices play a prominent role in this interview-based book, the authors caution readers not to expect to find in the book "a girlhood that was waiting to be 'discovered' by our research" (p. 65). Such an erroneous belief puts the power to define girlhood(s) in the hands of the researchers instead of the girls themselves. Moreover, there is no one, singular, monolithic girlhood, and the authors are careful to point out that "any of the girlhoods discussed in this book are snapshots of ongoing projects of becoming" (p. 114). Doing girlhood, they argue, is a process, not a static state, and certainly far different from adult, mainstream constructions.

*"Girl Power"* is now the fifth book published in the "Mediated Youth" series. Interestingly, while not a series focusing specifically on girlhood(s) or Girls' Studies, all five books thus far have been about girls, each in its own way adding something to the dialogue on girlhood; each including the voices of girls themselves; and each positioning girls as active agents. While Susan Driver's *Queer Girls and Popular Culture: Reading, Resisting, and Creating Media* (2007), Shayla Thiel Stern's *Instant Identity: Girls in the Culture of Instant Messaging* (2007), and Kathleen Sweeney's *Maiden USA: Girl Icons Come of Age* (2008) focus primarily or in part on the relationship between girls and technology, specifically girls making their own media content, *"Girl Power"* focuses less on technology/media and more on communities of practice. Ruth Nicole Brown's *Black Girlhood Celebration: A Hip Hop Feminist Pedagogy* employs a hip hop feminist perspective to demonstrate how Black girls and women can come together to celebrate Black girls—again, raising the

point that there is not one, singular "girlhood." Like Brown and Swee-ney, the authors of *"Girl Power"* reject the notion that adult women can "save" girls. Rather, all three books advocate girl-positive programs in which girls themselves play an active role. In all five of these books, we are introduced to girls who are actively engaged in constructing their identities (e.g., through instant messaging), safe spaces (e.g., the SOLHOT program in Brown's book), a sense of community (e.g., online communities created by queer girls), mediated images of themselves (e.g., filmmaking initiatives for girls), and girlhood itself.

What *"Girl Power"* contributes to the series is not an understanding of skater girls, or online girls, or any of the other girlhoods discussed in the book. Instead, *"Girl Power"* is a theoretically grounded exploration of feminism ("girl power") as it is currently practiced by some girls and young women in North America. While too many adult feminists dismiss the lived experiences of girls by labeling them as "postfemi-nists," Currie, Kelly, and Pomerantz provide a glimpse into how some girls are creating *their own* definitions of what it means to be a feminist. Whether girls themselves accept that label is certainly an issue under contestation, and it makes for some of the most interesting discussions in this groundbreaking book.

Sharon R. Mazzarella
Series Editor
October 31, 2008

## REFERENCES

Brown, R. N. (2008). *Black girlhood celebration: A hip hop feminist pedagogy*. New York: Peter Lang.

Driver, S. (2007). *Queer girls and popular culture: Reading, resisting, and creating media*. New York: Peter Lang.

Hartley, J. (1998). Juvenation: News, girls and power. In C. Carter, G. Branston, & S. Allan (Eds.), *News, Gender and Power* (pp. 47–70). London: Routledge.

Mazzarella, S. R. (2008, May). *A Growing Concern: U.S. Newspaper Coverage of "Early Puberty" in Girls*. Paper presented at the Annual Meeting of the International Communication Association, Montreal, Canada.

Mazzarella, S. R., & Pecora, N. (2007). Girls in crisis: Newspaper framing of adolescent girls. *Journal of Communication Inquiry*, 31(1), 6–27.

Stern, S. T. (2007). *Instant identity: Girls and the culture of instant messaging*. New York: Peter Lang.

Sweeney, K. (2008). *Maiden USA: Girl icons come of age*. New York: Peter Lang.

# PREFACE

These days in movies, pop songs, news stories, video games, magazines, and maybe around your dinner table, you are likely to encounter any one of a number of common stereotypes about teen girls. Who are the powerful teen girls today? They're mean, Machiavellian, and wield their style savvy as a weapon. Who are the ones we are told to worry about even more? They're wild, acting out their opposition to the adult world through sexual exhibitionism, drug use, and promiscuity. Mean girls. Wild girls.

While in the middle of trying to make sense of these various meanings attached to girls and girlhood, one of us, Deirdre, had googled the lyrics to Pink's song *Stupid Girls*, which mocks female celebrities who play dumb and obsess about being thin, blonde, and buxom. Deirdre also viewed the *Stupid Girls* video, which contains scenes showing the harmfulness of bulimia and cosmetic surgery. This prompted her eleven-year-old daughter, Nora, to ask a seemingly straightforward question: "Mom, why do you like *Stupid Girls* and not *Mean Girls*?" Deirdre recalls the question much more vividly than her on-the-spot answer, but thinks she managed to say something about how *Stupid Girls* takes society to task for glamorizing such a narrow, demeaning image of young women and, instead, encourages girls to reject it. "Outcasts and girls with ambition, that's what I wanna see," sings Pink, and on the video, we see a young girl click off the TV in disgust and grab a ball to go outside and play.

By contrast, the movie *Mean Girls*, arguably, stays focused on girls—and girls' friendships—as the problem, rather than as symptoms of deeper concerns. Questions, such as why attracting a boyfriend by being thin and pretty is still the main way for girls to attain status and popularity within high school, are glossed over. The movie describes girls' meanness as "girl-on-girl crime." Toward the end of the film, the principal asks a woman teacher to meet with all junior girls in the school gym to speak "lady-to-lady" in an attempt to resolve the "lady problem." After confirming that all girls present have experienced the cruelty of other girls, the teacher admonishes them, "You guys have got to stop calling each other sluts and whores. It just makes it okay for guys to call you sluts and whores!" In other words, it is not the boys who are to blame for the smearing of girls' reputations; it is the girls. And if only the girls would stop doing it, the boys would, too.

In this way, the movie *Mean Girls* presents female "bullying" as a closed loop that does not implicate society or boys and men in any way. It does not open up for critical discussion the still prevalent sexual double standard, where girls—but not boys—are judged harshly for moving on from an intimate relationship too quickly or too often. Nor does the film make visible how girls are pitted against each other for the attention of boys, or boys' complicity in this process. Many adult viewers can take heart that the movie's main girl character ultimately rejects mean-spirited name-calling and sneakiness in favor of personal achievement; she joins the school math team and declares, "All you can do in life is try to solve the problem in front of you." And yet, because the film does not so much as hint at the links between girls' sexual competitiveness, heterosexism, and the fostering of competition by the school and the wider society, we see this pop culture text as one more call for girls to conform to an inequitable adult world.

The images of girls in movies like *Mean Girls* and songs like *Stupid Girls* exist in complex relationship to real girls, as we explore in *"Girl Power": Girls Reinventing Girlhood*. We set out to talk to girls between the ages of twelve and sixteen on the many meanings of "girl power" and how they made sense of what it means to be a girl today. Ultimately, we interviewed seventy-one girls from a variety of neighborhoods in and around Vancouver, BC. From those conversations emerged a very different picture of young female identity than is often reflected in consumer culture or in conventional psychology textbooks. Femininity, we will argue, is not a pre-given identity that simply emerges in young women as they age; neither is it imprinted on them by outside forces. In other words, girls are not just slaves to consumer fashion or status competition. Girls' identities are shaped as they try out different ways of being girls in various social settings. They are active in this process; they are "doing" girlhood.

During our fieldwork, we met girls who consciously rejected the culturally valued, all-too-familiar form of femininity that is sexy, coy, vulnerable, and oriented toward accommodating the needs and desires of men. These girls acknowledged that this more traditional femininity had made their classmates popular, but they were also aware that it has been blamed for girls' lowered self-esteem, dissatisfaction with their bodies, and disordered eating. These girls were engaged in activities like skateboarding and online gender bending. They took on unconventional monikers, alternative identities, and embraced the risk of being labeled unusual.

Girl skateboarders, as we document in the book, forged an alternative identity as *sk8ers* through audacious physical feats (nothing dainty!), risk-taking, androgynous dress, and a willingness to claim public space and show off. They used their skateboarding skills to challenge the male-dominated pecking order in skate parks. In one case we learned about, the girls' skating convinced the boys to question their sexist assumptions about girls being unable to skate.

Yet other girls enjoyed being *online gender benders* by switching gender or sexuality in role-playing games; a few used Internet chat rooms to challenge "girly girls" and "macho boys" and perform a rebellious femininity. These efforts by girls to reinvent girlhood did not, of course, go unchallenged. The online gender benders created powerful female characters. They got expelled from or ignored in chat rooms, flamed or insulted, and labeled as inauthentic. One girl, for instance, went into the online Vampire Desecrated Cathedral and posted a picture meant to represent her in the chat room, which got her kicked out. Why? Her chosen avatar self wasn't sexy enough.

So, there are social constraints on girls' ability to reconfigure their identities, even in cyberspace. This means that reinventing girlhood cannot be done by girls in isolation; neither can this reinventing happen one person at a time. The girls in our study talked about the importance of support from friends and others practicing their form of alternative girlhood. Whereas, according to Kate (age fifteen), "guys expect you to wear like really tight clothes and like dress the sexy way, our group of friends, we wear what's comfortable." Grover and Gracie (both fifteen years old and interviewed together) explained that they chose their friends "carefully," because they didn't want to hang around people who were "close minded to things and less likely to just let loose and have fun." In these words and practices, we discerned girls to be doing girlhood differently, in ways that gave them a sense of agency—and sometimes power—in their lives.

"Girl Power": Girls Reinventing Girlhood is part of a book series called *Mediated Youth*. To mediate is to make something happen or to bring something about through an intervening agent. This idea of mediation captures a number of important contributions and themes of "Girl Power". Unlike more conventional empirical investigations, we spotlight rather than obscure the mediated analytical process whereby what the girls told us in interviews is transformed into what we as researchers claim that they said (see, especially, Chapter Three).

Throughout the book, we assume that the girls' ways of making sense of each other and themselves is mediated through talk and interaction with other people. For the girls in our study, peer group cultures were particularly important in their identity-making practices. We view such youth cultures as a key arena mediating between girls' personal views and ideas about themselves and the belief systems, values, and knowledge of extra-local culture expressed in adult talk, commercial culture, corporate news media, public debate, and research reports. Peer group cultures can be seen as in the middle between the girls and various adult-led and adult-maintained institutions such as schooling, family, paid work, and organized religion; they are spheres where young people creatively re/invent themselves, albeit within limits and with uneven results.

We have already seen how commercialized pop culture often reinforces constricted and disparaging images of femininity that can fuel feelings of insecurity and inadequacy. In addition, girls' identities are continually mediated by inequalities of gender, class, race, sexuality, and ability. While it is currently fashionable to believe that girls are becoming emblematic of individuals who are confidently preparing for a lifetime of continual self-invention, ready to seize opportunities when and where they crop up, the reality is quite different. This belief may describe a small group of white, upper- to upper-middle-class, heterosexual, able-bodied girls, but most girls will not be so privileged. Women heading lone-parent families, immigrant women, women with disabilities, and aboriginal women are at much higher risk of poverty, unemployment, and poor housing than are other Canadians (Status of Women Canada 2005). The life expectancy of aboriginal women, for example, is more than six years shorter than that of Canadian women in general, and they are more likely to live in poverty—36.4% as compared with 17.7% (Status of Women Canada 2005: 7, 9). Even among the relatively privileged, a Statistics Canada study shows only a moderate decline during the 1990s in the earnings gap between young men and women, despite a dramatic increase in the proportion of young women holding university degrees. An important reason for this continuing disparity is that female-dominated fields such as health and education suffered wage declines in the latter part of the twentieth century, while male-dominated fields such as engineering, commerce, and computer sciences enjoyed wage gains (Frenette and Coulombe 2007). And despite mainstream media stories to the contrary, gender explains relatively little about who performs well academically when compared with race and class (Bouchard, Boily, and Proulx 2003; Corbett, Hill, and St. Rose 2008; Francis and Skelton 2005).

Framing and guiding our analysis are several concepts that mediate between the broad social structures just mentioned, on the one hand, and girls' identity-making practices, on the other. These concepts are "agency," "subjectivity," and "community of practice." By *agency*, we mean the conscious, self-directed actions of girls—what girls say and do to accomplish girlhood within limits. We use the term *agency* rather than *choice*, because the word *choice* tends to be equated with entirely self-generated and intentional actions. The common understanding of the word *choice* tends to mask the circumstances under which people make decisions; particular material conditions, cultural practices, and social networks influence individuals and shape their decision-making. The word *choice* does not draw attention to the fact that more powerful and privileged people command a broader range of choices than those less advantaged. By contrast, the word *agency* spotlights human actors and social forces simultaneously; it encourages us to situate individuals in their historical context.

Because of our interest in agency, the notion of "subjectivity" is important in our work. *Subjectivity* refers to how girls think and feel about their worlds, what they value, and what they believe to be true. Subjectivity thus helps us look at the world from the standpoint of the girls who participated in our study rather than from the standpoint of the adult researchers. While subjectivity may appear to be a very individualistic way of looking at the world, we understand subjectivity as a social and not personal point of view. Among other processes, subjectivity is socially constructed through the language that we use to describe the social world and the frameworks we use for thinking about this world—what academics refer to as "discourses." By focusing on the discourses that shape the way we think and talk about the world, subjectivity mediates the individual and the collective; while we may experience our understandings of ourselves and our world as personal, language and discourse are vehicles of communication. They belie the social nature of our existence. Given the way they can shape decision-making, we view them as vehicles of power.

In this way, although we organized interviews around girls' talk about their personal experiences and understandings, our analysis of these interviews directs attention to what girls share as members of a socially significant group—"girls." In order to explore the social nature of girls' subjectivity—hence agency—our third mediating concept is "community of practice." *Community of practice* acknowledges the same-sex peer groupings that emerge in the informal spaces of the school as important—but often overlooked—contexts within which girls learn "who they are" and how to "become someone." In Chapter Four, and again in Chapter Eight, we discuss why we prefer this term over approaches used by other researchers who explain youth practices in terms of peer pressure or in the context of friendship networks. A community of practice draws attention to the way that groups of people, united by shared practices, engage in collective meaning making. In our work, the meaning making that interests us concerns "girlhood." Specifically, what does it mean to be a "girl" in today's society? How do girls learn to become participants in the social world beyond their families and their lives at school, a world, we argue, that continues to be highly gendered? While much attention has been given to the formal curriculum of the school, "community of practice" spotlights the way in which much of the learning by youth about "who they are," "how they want to be seen by others," and "who they might become" takes place informally in school-based peer groups. As we shall see in Chapter Four, membership in these groupings has significant implications for young people. As a consequence, inter-group dynamics can be competitive. One of our tasks is to understand how this competition plays out in the lives of girls, and how, as teachers and as interested adults, we can foster the kind of cooperative behavior that is more typical of egalitarian practices. In this spirit, our concluding chapter moves from an analysis of girls' agency and debates over "girl power" to a discussion of the practical implications of our research.

Finally, this book is mediated by feminism. Each of us identifies as feminist, and we believe in feminism for girls. Born twenty-two years apart from one another, we bridge second- and third-wave feminism. At a minimum, the three of us agree that feminism means challenging the subordination of women and girls in society and disrupting cultural resources that are unequally distributed and differentially valued by virtue of class, race, gender, and sexuality and that are used in the ongoing construction of femininities (and masculinities).

As the oldest author, **Dawn** was born in 1948. *One of four daughters, I grew up in a military family, which meant that I attended small schools. More importantly, given that such families are relocated on a regular basis, my experiences of high school were not characterized by the kinds of cliques discussed in our book. Being among the "new kids" at the beginning of the school year was a recurring experience; in retrospect it enhanced my self-confidence—and optimism—about meeting new people and adapting to new social settings. On the other hand, growing up in a military community during the 1950s meant that I had limited ideas of what women could accomplish. Like other military wives, my mother gave up any chance for a meaningful career (until her 50s) in order to be a full-time wife and mother. I cannot remember a time when I did not hold what became later identified as a "feminist sensibility." Until recently, I would have described myself as a "tomboy," only because there was no language for "alternative" femininities until the establishment of women's studies. In my late teens and early twenties, I devoured books that became designated as "classics" of feminist scholarship. Sociology as a discipline attracted me when I returned to university in my late twenties, primarily because it was among those fields that embraced feminist scholarship. My interest in world politics made London School of Economics and Political Science a "natural"* *choice for my doctoral studies, and is reflected in my ongoing work in Viet Nam. Although married twice, I have no children. But as a lifelong equestrian, I continue to encourage the involvement of girls in outdoor pursuits and physical activities that enable them to experience what their bodies can "do" rather than how their bodies "look."*

**Deirdre** was born in 1959, the same year that Mattel introduced Barbie to the world. *Barbie and I grew up together. The girls in my neighborhood would gather and pool together all their Barbies and Barbie friends to create stories—soap operas, really—that would last for days. It was not until I was much older that I felt concerned about the effects of Barbie's outlandish measurements on girls' unhappiness with their own bodies. Later, I derived subversive pleasure from stories of girls giving their Barbies Mohawks or otherwise treating Barbie irreverently. I was an early beneficiary of second-wave feminism. My mother subscribed to Ms. magazine not long after it hit the regular newsstands in 1972, so I read it in my teens. In 1975, Title IX came into effect, so while I was still in high school, I heard more talk about supporting girls' sports teams, and my public school did not automatically kick pregnant girls out. I feel I belong to wave 2.5: I never attended a consciousness-raising group, and although inspired by the second wave of the women's movement, I did not participate directly in it. My early activist concerns involved protesting the Viet Nam War draft, US imperialism in Central America and the Caribbean, and the ill treatment of women on the global assembly line. My interest in feminist postcolonial writing and my desire to critically engage, while still having fun, with popular culture perhaps mark me as a third-wave feminist.*

**Shauna** was born in 1970, smack dab in middle of the second wave. *For me, there was always feminism. It was in the air that I breathed and the water that I drank. I grew up with all the privileges that second-wave feminists fought for, but I also knew that the struggle was not over. In junior high school, I was excluded from playing the drums in band class because I was a girl. In high school, I waited patiently for topics that featured important female historical figures and authors, only to be disappointed. And in the labor market, I experienced the sexual harassment that was a ubiquitous and tacitly accepted part of minimum-wage culture. I think that it was music that saved me, offering both comfort and power. My detailed knowledge of Pink Floyd, the Doors, the Violent Femmes, and the Cure generated respect from boys in high school. But in the 1990s, when women rockers became much more* *prevalent, a whole new world of female experience opened up to me. When Hole lead singer, Courtney Love, shrieked into her microphone, I felt satisfied. When Madonna sang "respect yourself," I nodded in ardent agreement. When Alanis Morissette belted out her critiques of the male establishment in rock music, I was electrified. When Gwen Stefani hypnotically chanted, "I'm just a girl," I understood her ironic girlie playfulness as a major assault on dominant culture. My feminism was strengthened by these influences, marking me as part of the third wave. For me, third-wave feminism is a continuation of the second wave but with more attention to difference, sexuality, popular culture, postcolonialism, and postmodern multiplicity. While I grew up thinking that I could do and be anything I wanted, I also grew up knowing that the world did not favor girls and women. Privileged optimism coupled with everyday reality is the complex juncture at which my feminism sits. Now, as a new mother of a daughter, I know that while much has improved for girls today, feminism is still as relevant and crucial as it was in 1970.*

The media pundits would have us—feminists spanning more than one generation—at war with one another and unable to bridge the divide, but for us, the reality of feminist politics has always been more dynamic, multifaceted, and full of many voices than it has been represented within the mainstream. To the extent that people do not understand this, to the extent that they believe the hype that feminism is a set of fixed rules and dictums, then—and only then—is feminism in danger of becoming a spent force. As we argue in this book, girls are in the process of reinventing girlhood, and therefore feminists—young and old—need constantly to be reinventing feminism. Only a feminism that moves at the speed of girlhood—at the speed of girls' lived, daily experiences in the hallways at school, dances, the playground, the mall, community centers, skate parks, and online—can be useful and relevant to girls. Feminism is a politics that must stay on the move if it is to remain attuned to girls' on-the-ground grappling with inequities and contradictions generated by oppressive conditions and a significant force for localized and social change. In short, feminism must move as quickly and bravely as a girl on a skateboard.

# ACKNOWLEDGMENTS

We thank the Social Sciences and Humanities Research Council of Canada for providing generous support for the research on which this book is based. *"Girl Power"* has been an arduous journey; we are bound to forget many of those who inspired, encouraged, and supported us along the way. These individuals include colleagues and students, partners and children, friends and relatives. We have also been excited by the growing body of scholarship dedicated to improving girls' lives and opportunities. To them we owe our gratitude. We also thank series editor, Sharon Mazzarella, for her interest, enthusiasm, and support for the field of girls' studies, as well as other folks at Peter Lang Publishing (Sophie Appel, Mary Savigar, and others). We are grateful to Alexis Roumanis for the creativity and care he brought to the preparation of the manuscript for printing.

We especially thank Nora Kelly for her wonderful cover design. We are encouraged by her creative vision about what girls like her "can be" and "might become." In many ways, her contribution represents what we imagine "girl power" embodies.

Aftab Erfan, Lori MacIntosh, Abby Wener Herlin, and Caroline White provided excellent research and clerical assistance on the research project. A special thanks to Lori, who conducted some of the interviews for the group we have come to call the "online girls."

Dawn thanks a range of people who, over the past many years, have steadfastly supported her sociological curiosity about the social world and belief that, as individuals, together we can "make a difference." These people include her parents (Margaret and Herbert Wiesenberg), her sisters (Joan, Faye and Sara), and—as always—her long-term companion Brian. She also wants her graduate students—especially those in her graduate seminar—to know how valuable their interest in her research has been over the years.

Deirdre expresses her everlasting thanks to Dave Beers, partner and soul mate, for his unflagging support, his sharp wit and political acumen, his invaluable editorial suggestions, and his companionship. Thanks, too, to Nora and Quinn Kelly—your sense of fun, your amazing drawing abilities and comic artistry, and your imaginations have nurtured her belief that girls and boys can, indeed, reinvent girlhood and boyhood.

Shauna would like to thank Jon Eben Field for his deeply felt encouragement, his endless patience, his superb suggestions, and his unconditional love. She would also like to thank her daughter, Miriam Field, for arriving at just the right time and for giving "girl power" a dazzling new meaning. Thanks to Hart and Nancy Pomerantz, who made it clear right from the start that girls can do and be anything they want. And finally, thanks to Dawn and Deirdre for their friendship and for making this experience so rewarding.

We would also like to express our gratitude to the many girls who generously gave of their time to participate in the study, as well as the community workers, teachers, and other adults who brought the study to the attention of young people and thereby helped in the recruitment phase of the study. Although we have used pseudonyms in order to protect the privacy of all the research participants, most of you selected your own "fake names." We dedicate this book to you.

# 1

# (RE)CLAIMING GIRLHOOD

G iven the current "cult of the individual," it may be difficult to recognize the historically specific nature of our identities. The emphasis we place in this book on girls' construction of their identities as young "women"[1] reflects its importance to feminism; at the inception of the "second wave," Betty Friedan (1963: 63) lamented that, historically, women have been encouraged to ignore the question of their identity as individuals. What she called "the feminine mystique" instructed women "to answer the question, 'Who am I?' by saying 'Tom's wife... Mary's mother...'. An American woman no longer has a private image to tell her who she is, or can be, or wants to be." Along with postcolonial writers,[2] feminists have shown how the meaning of "personhood" corresponded to characteristics of the socially dominant group who (mis)took their social identity for a naturally occurring "norm" for humanity. It has been primarily those designated as "other" — women, people of color, sexual "deviants" — who have interrogated how we become "who we are."

Simone de Beauvoir (1953) inspired such an interrogation when she pointed out that women are made, not born. Within this context, gender was identified as a site of potential agency for women. Through a "liberation movement" in the West,[3] women began (and continue) to ask, "Who am I?" and, on that basis, "Who can I become?" Their necessity to do so reflects Beauvoir's claim that what it means "to be a woman" historically has been authored by male "experts." Women themselves were denied control over the production of their identities "as women." Because this denial robbed women of self-determination, second-wave feminists argued that they have been denied the exercise of what makes us Subjects in liberal western democracies.[4] Thus the movement for Western women to claim Selfhood began (and continues) to raise questions about the nature of the social world. Claiming Selfhood challenged "femininity" as a seemingly naturally occurring identity by drawing attention to the power for men, as the dominant group, to name our identity as women.

Understanding "Selfhood" as a social project is a central task of *"Girl Power"*. In our work, "Selfhood" refers to a culturally and historically specific form of social identity; it captures the meaning that our social presence has for us and for others. The challenge we face is to theorize Selfhood in a way that does not naturalize what Cronin (2000) calls "compulsory individualism" (see Skeggs 2004, Chapter Two). This challenge requires us to theorize gendered Selfhood as necessary to reconstitution of a social order in which individuals must "claim" their "proper" place. In our study, girls claim a place by participating in systems of meaning and identity practices that define them, socially, "as girls." As we shall see, not all identity practices by female adolescents earn membership in socially recognized girlhood. In our study, those labeled by classmates as "slut," "butch," or "lesbian" are positioned outside normative girlhood. As Gonick (2003: 5) argues, this positioning is implicated in projects of Selfhood; by delineating others as "not normal" we locate ourselves among the socially accepted "normal." While we agree with postmodern writers that our identities are constantly shifting as we negotiate multiple and often contradictory roles throughout our lives, Selfhood sustains a degree of predictability in social life. Moreover, our sense of "who we are" for the moment shapes our thinking about "who we can become"; the identity practices of girls thus tell us a lot not only about their potential futures "as women,"[5] but also about the current status of women's and girls' liberation.

While much of the routine "work" entailed in continually reconstituting an adult Selfhood occurs at a level below ordinary consciousness, figuring out "who" we are and "who" we want to be is an urgent task as young people move from family-based to peer-oriented identities. As a time of physiological maturation, adolescence[6] overlaps with heightened awareness of the gendered and sexualized nature of our social identities. Thus puberty is a time when the cultural inscription of gender and sexuality are readily observable. This awareness is not limited to young people themselves, however; much public concern is directed toward the gendered and sexualized self-expression of teenagers, especially schoolgirls. What is lost in much of this adult attention is the meaning of often extravagant displays of Selfhood to youth themselves. In order to address this omission, *"Girl Power"* explores the identity practices of seventy-one girls between twelve and sixteen years of age. Because we attend to girls' active role in creating their social presence, we refer to their identity practices as "doing girlhood."[7]

By using the term "doing" we draw attention to girls' agency. While an extensive body of research implies that gender is passively learned through venues such as popular culture, we view girls as creators (as well as inheritors) of their identities. Such a view requires us to understand agency, defined in our work as self-directed activity in pursuit of a conscious goal. That is not to say that girls are rational actors, but implies intention and reflexivity. At the same time, we acknowledge that processes below the ordinary level of everyday awareness shape our sense of "who we are" and "who we can become." We thus distinguish between girls' agency and social power as those processes that make specific performances of gender (as well as class and racialized identities) possible. In other words, no matter how seemingly creative, girls' identity practices are mediated by the sociocultural conditions of their "doing." Because we support projects that have the potential to enlarge girls' beliefs in what is "do-able," our goal is to bring the operation of power into view. In thinking about girls' identity practices in this way, our research necessarily raises questions about girls' relationship to feminism, as a discursive and political movement for gender equality.

To focus our exploration on the identity practices of girls is not to deny the importance of understanding the social life of boys. While we did not ask girls specifically about their relationships with boys, boys play an important role in the social life of girls at school. As we shall see, girls' identity practices cannot be understood apart from those of boys; we hope our study of girlhood will inspire further work on how boys "do" masculinity.[8] But this is not to say that boys have been neglected by social scientists. On the contrary, until recently, social scientists used boyhood as a "generic" paradigm for "adolescence" (and later "youth"), paying little attention to the ways that girls negotiate their gendered identities (see Erikson 1950, 1968). Even when developmental psychologists and sex role researchers raised questions about girlhood, for the large part girls have been treated as passive "recipients" of feminine identities.

One goal of our work is to challenge this characterization of girls as passive. As others have noted, the "invisibility" of girls' agency reflects the way in which much of their doing girlhood (until fairly recently) occurs as "bedroom culture" (see McRobbie and Garber 1976, but also Lincoln 2004), out of sight of adult researchers. We build on Hey's (1997: 30) observation that "It is between and amongst girls as friends that identities are variously practiced, appropriated, resisted and negotiated." Our focus on girls also reflects interest in how feminism informs young people's understanding of gender, especially as these understandings influence girls' negotiations of Selfhood. We ask "how" rather than "whether" feminism shapes the identity practices of young women, because many girls are now growing up in a context where feminism is a household word. Whether one is supportive or dismissive of "women's liberation," feminism has become a common sense explanation for changes ranging from the "demise" of the traditional family and increased public expressions of sexuality, to demographic shifts in the workforce (see Marshall 2000).

## FROM "WOMEN" TO "GIRLS": THE EMERGENCE OF GIRLS' STUDIES

Given the way that feminism has been associated in public consciousness with broadening the options available to young women today, it is interesting that, until recently, girlhood has been "the other" of feminism's womanhood: girlhood was defined negatively, against womanhood. By drawing attention to the way in which femininity is an accomplishment rather than a destiny, Beauvoir's work initiated a view that the "problem" of womanhood begins in adolescence. Beauvoir herself devoted large sections of *The Second Sex* to a discussion of girlhood as "the formative years" of bourgeois womanhood. Characterizing the adolescent boy as actively moving toward adulthood, by contrast the young girl's youth "is consumed in waiting, more or less disguised. She is awaiting

Man… Marriage is not only an honorable career and one less tiring than many others, it alone permits a woman to keep her social dignity intact and at the same time find sexual fulfillment as loved one and mother. It is thus that her entourage envisages her future, as she does herself" (1953: 307). Following Beauvoir's lead, much feminist research on girlhood throughout the 1970s focused on ways in which adolescence prepares girls for subordinate roles in their adult life.

Beauvoir's work was highly influential among feminist social scientists into the 1980s, inspiring a new field of "sex role" research. Adapting socialization theory,[9] girlhood was cast as preparation for womanhood rather than an identity in its own right. Female adolescents were referred to as "young women" rather than "girls." Because men used the term "girl" to infantilize adult women, feminists consciously distanced themselves from association with this category, which invoked immaturity and the depoliticization of women (see Leonard 1997). In fact, Friedan chastised women to "grow up" because "they have become dependent, passive, childlike, they have given up their adult frame of reference to live at a lower human level" (1963: 307). While she linked women's "immaturity" to the work that they carried out as housewives and mothers, socialization theory signaled to women that other "scripts" are possible. "Assertiveness training" and self-defense courses flourished as ways to help adult women unlearn much of what they had internalized during girlhood about being "women." As a virtual "industry" during the 1970s, sex role research enabled adult feminists—including the two older authors—to better understand aspects of their gendered lives: everyday experiences of subordination were seen to lie in our indoctrination into roles requiring compliance and service to others while denying our "inner voices." This denial gave rise to what Friedan (1963: 15) called "the problem with no name": "a sense of dissatisfaction, a yearning… [making each woman] afraid to ask even of herself the silent question: 'Is this all?'"

While we include ourselves among its critics, we recognize that socialization theory gave feminists a way to discuss the socially constructed nature of femininity as a compulsory identity for women. It thus opened up discursive space for the eventual emergence of Girls' Studies. One problem is that the study of girlhood in much of the pioneering feminist scholarship was at the expense of the study of girls. As Ward and Benjamin (2004: 23) note, adult feminists tended to trace the genesis of women's problems backward, toward girlhood. As a result, feminist "truths" about "girlhood" were often informed by adult reflections on the traumas of growing up "as a girl" during the 1950s and 1960s (see, for example, Johnson 1993; Douglas 1994; Pipher 1994). While we acknowledge that this re/construction of girlhood has benefited many women, this kind of thinking gave rise to a troubling theme that gained widespread acceptance among academic and nonacademic audiences alike: the notion of girlhood as a "time of crisis."

Given the tenet that adolescent femininity teaches girls to accept a subordinate status, the emerging field of Girls' Studies characterized adolescence as a time of "risk" for girls.[10] Gilligan, Lyons, and Hanmer (1990) described adolescence as a "crossroads" for girls, a time between childhood and adulthood when girls enter into a period of danger and loss of Self. While girls before the age of eleven or twelve were characterized as boisterous and self-confident, after this age they were typified as withdrawn and negative about their futures. Feminist research on girls associated adolescence with girls' "loss of voice" (Brown and Gilligan 1992), a lowering of their self-esteem (Orenstein 1994), and a culture that "poisons" girls toward their female bodies. This view that girls "lose" an authentic Selfhood in order to become what our culture dictates was popularized by the bestselling *Reviving Ophelia: Saving the Selves of Adolescent Girls*. Written primarily for parents, Pipher (1994) asks why so many American adolescent girls are prey to depression, eating disorders, addictions, and suicide attempts. Her goal was to "offer parents compassion, strength, and strategies" with which to revive their daughters' lost sense of Self (book cover).

Reflecting the popular appeal of Pipher's book, psychologists and journalists scrambled to listen in on the lives of girls in order to engage in a form of "girl advocacy" (Brumberg 2000). Gaining an audience among concerned parents and teachers, and promoted through popular media such as *The Oprah Show*, girl advocates warned that "without a strong sense of self, girls will enter adulthood at a deficit: they will be less able to fulfill their potential, less willing to take on challenges, less willing to defy tradition in their career choices... They will be less prepared to weather the storms of adult life and more likely to become depressed, hopeless, and self-destructive" (Orenstein 1994: xxviii). By the end of the millennium, one prevailing discourse about girlhood signaled that "girls are in trouble."[11]

Within this context, the appearance of what many call a "girl power" movement may be puzzling. While debate still surrounds exactly when and how such a movement emerged, there is agreement that "Riot Grrrl" bands of the 1990s were an important influence.[12] These bands challenged the sexism and racism of punk rock, expressing a general desire to make things better for girls (see Hancunt 2001). Their lyrics reclaimed not only the word "girl" but also words that, traditionally, have been used to keep women "in line" — "slut," "cunt," and "dyke" (see Scott-Dixon 2001). Stylistically, Riot Grrrl bands combined an "innocent" girlish aesthetic with what is most threatening to adults: youthful rage and bitterness about the adult world. Musically, Riot Grrrl bands are credited with popularizing the term "girl power," initially appearing as "Grrrl Power" on the cover of a Bikini Kill fanzine in the early 1990s. Bikini Kill released both an album and a single entitled "Girl Power" in 1995 (although it was the Welsh indie band, Helen Love, which first recorded the words "girl power" in their 1993 debut single, *Formula One Racing Girls*).

While taken up by a number of female musicians, "girl power" had various meanings within girl-positive music. For the female pop duo Shampoo, it signified "coming home drunk in the midnight hour," signaling how their music was not for "girls" per se but rather teen and twenty-something university women. It was a British all-girl band, the Spice Girls, who promoted girl power among girls. As commented by Press (1997):

> The Spice Girls' official book, *Girl Power!*, is plastered with slogans like "Girl power is when… you believe in yourself and control your own life." Pushing sisterhood ("You stick with your mates and they stick with you") and equal rights ("I expect an equal relationship where he does as much washing up as I do"), the Spice Girls have done the seemingly impossible: they have made feminism, with all its implied threat, cuddly, sexy, safe, and, most importantly, sellable.

Press opines that, however compromised, the Spice Girls have given many prepubescent girls their first taste of feminism. She concludes that although girl power "may turn out to be fleeting… chances are that… it will expand society's ideas about what is acceptable and what's possible for young women."[13] Perhaps as testament to Press's prediction, "girl power" became a household word: the 2001 edition of the

*Oxford English Dictionary* included a "girl power" entry. Specifically, *OED* defines "girl power" as "a self-reliant attitude among girls and young women manifested in ambition, assertiveness and individualism" (page 3).

The term "girl power" soon became associated with a range of adult-initiated projects intending to "save" girls "at risk." In the United States, for example, the Department of Health and Human Services offers a *Girl Power!* website alongside a nongovernmental *Girlstart* that provides resources to help girls become "smart from the start" (Harris 2004: 75). These types of initiatives promote what Harris (2004) calls "can-do" feminism: a movement emphasizing that success is the result of personal effort and spurring girls on with messages that "girls rule" and that "girls can do anything" if they put their minds to it. Unlike girl-oriented music of the Riot Grrrl bands, adult-initiated projects of "girl power" construed the relationship between girls and feminism as "top down," with the goal of feminism to "save" girls from girlhood.[14] As Gonick (2001) notes, however well intentioned, the impetus to save girls in their time of trouble assumes that we have already "gotten it right" through a version of feminism [read "second wave"] that is non-negotiable; it fails to consider the ways in which feminism is an object of young women's consciousness (Frith 2001: 148–9).

More recently, a body of work has emerged in Canada, the United States, Australia, and other parts of the English-speaking world that allows for the possibility that, as "daughters of feminism" (see Henry 2004), girls are coming into their own. Girlhood is recognized as an important social category in its own right, and girls are characterized as agentic. Influenced by British cultural studies,[15] "girl power" has been the subject of much research, in terms of cultural production both *for* girls and *by* girls, through what girls consume and what they produce (Driscoll 1999). Girl power culture produced *for* girls is evidenced by hugely successful commercial ventures: beyond the Spice Girls it includes popular TV programs featuring female heroines such as Powerpuff Girls, Buffy the Vampire Slayer,[16] Xena the Warrior Princess, and Sabrina the Teenage Witch, as well as an endless array of clothing, makeup, and adolescent magazines promoting commodities for a growing girl-oriented market, appropriating the kinds of feminine symbols that Riot Grrrls parodied, but without their political irony. While Riot Grrrl culture emerged as consciously anti-consumerist, its originally political slogans—such as "Girls Rule" or "Girls Kick Butt"—are being spread through mass production of goods bearing these claims.

Girl power culture produced *by* girls came in the form of self-styled "zines" and websites made possible by household access to the Internet and technologies of textual production, as well as from girls' bodies. Through inexpensive tabletop production and access to cyberspace, a genre of writing took up girl-oriented themes. This writing was simultaneously angry, supportive, and advice-giving on topics ranging from sexual abuse to discrimination. In contrast to the adult-initiated message that girls are "in trouble," one lasting representation that emerged is powerful girls who "kick ass" and engage with boys on their own terms. In celebration of girls' agency, today a generation of young women revel in their femininity through a distinctive "girl power style": sexually provocative clothing, wildly sculpted and dyed hair, body piercing, and publicly displayed tattoos.

Dubbed "lipstick liberation" (Abraham 1997) and derided as "self-obsession" (Bellafante 1998), these expressions of girl power were quickly pronounced as a rejection of feminism.[17] Ignoring contested meanings of "girl power" as it gained popular momentum, media commentators evoked commercialized constructions in order to mock the view, promoted by aging feminists, of young women as oppressed victims of a male-centered culture. Instead, they characterized young women's (hetero)sexualized agency and girl-oriented culture as evidence of female power, a power glorified in toys such as *Bratz* and television shows such as *Sex in the City* or the more brazen *Girls Gone Wild*. In the face of these displays of feminine sexual power, second-wave feminism pales as an outdated and restrictive orthodoxy. As pronounced by one of the "daughters" of feminism: "be[ing] feminist in the way we have seen or understood feminism is to conform to an identity and way of living that doesn't allow for individuality, complexity, or less than perfect personal histories" (Walker 1995: xxxiii).

Within this context, the relationship between young women and feminism is not so clear. Public disagreement among feminists themselves about what constitutes a feminist issue or feminist identity has not only fueled a common sense claim that we have reached a "post-feminist"[18] era; as we explore in the next chapter, it has contributed to hostile depictions in the media of feminism as no longer the solution to girls' problems, but rather as contributing to these problems. If we take girl power culture at face value, equality has been achieved, and young women should be encouraged to take advantage of women's liberation by pursuing individual rather than collective goals (Budgeon 2001, 2003). If a third (or fourth) wave of feminism is seen to exist, it is being characterized by some commentators as informed by "individualism" rather than collectivism: the value of feminism is seen to lie in its potential to help individual women make their own choices without judging what these choices may be (see Lorber 2005). In a less sympathetic vein, the blatantly commercial and celebrity-oriented nature of much girl power culture has been interpreted as evidence of the manipulation of girls by marketing interests and the commodification of feminism (see Goldman 1992; Driscoll 1999; Riordan 2001).

To be sure, the implication of feminism in young women's lives is much more complex than characterized here. Adding fuel to debates is the way that competing positions are often based on a caricature of opponents, obscuring the situations of "ordinary" girls. As noted by Bettis and Adams (2005: 2), what is missing in public debate over the meaning of "girl power" are the experiences and concerns of girls themselves. Our book is an attempt to address this gap by exploring how girls produce themselves as social Subjects in a context of ambiguity and intense public struggle over what it means (more often, *should* mean) to "be a girl" today. How do girls themselves take up the contemporary mandate for young people to fashion a Selfhood and, in so doing, their futures? How does feminism, as a discourse with a vested interest in how girls think about "who they are" and imagine "who they can become," figure into girls' performances of girlhood? Within the context of a current girl power culture, these types of questions concern girls' agency, subjectivity, and empowerment.

## STUDYING GIRLS AND GIRLHOOD

In her genealogy of girlhood, Driscoll (2002: 4) shows how competing knowledges work to shape what it means "to be a girl" at any one moment and how girls experience their own positioning in the world. What we have tried to convey in this introduction is the complexity of that positioning. As sketched out above, girlhood today is signified through a number of competing, often contradictory, discourses about what it means "to

*[handwritten marginalia: cultural producers, blogs, zines, poetry, music]*

be a girl." These discourses testify to the way in which girlhood is never predetermined; girlhood is not a stage of maturation fixed by biological imperatives and necessary stages of psychological development. Following Butler (1990), we view adolescent femininity as an identity that must be brought into existence through what one "does" to be a girl. *(connect to project)*

To view gender as performative is to recognize that doing Selfhood gives our presence only provisional meaning within any immediate social context. This is not to imply, however, that people are chameleons; particular ways of doing girlhood are fixed within specific discourses that institutionalize various subjectivities about appropriate ways of being a girl. However temporary, we will see how this fixity imparts a sense of "real" Selfhood. It allows us to differentiate "performativity" from the everyday notion that gender is a "performance." When "doing" a particular social presence does not align with our sense of authentic Selfhood, we may experience ourselves as "performing" an identity, as "getting by." Performativity, on the other hand, refers to processes that usually operate below the ordinary level of consciousness.

The hidden processes that interest us are discursive: they are the unspoken discourses that work to regulate our sense of what is appropriate, what is "say-able" and what makes sense in specific places and times. Because these processes tend to work below everyday awareness, one task of our research is to make the operation of these discourses visible, hence open to critical inspection.[19] While we do not deny that young people often "perform" an identity by consciously choosing how they dress, talk, and present themselves to others, we are interested in how institutionalized power operates to fix girlhood through the mundane ways in which girls experience "Selfhood." Thus, while our study focuses on girls' identity practices, we hope to show how their agency, hence power, is gendered. Our interest in the social rather than personal nature of power does not deny individual agency: as Nelson (1999) argues, analyzing Selfhood as socially constructed does not mean that people do not have the capacity for critical reflexivity. For us, feminism invites critical reflexivity by drawing attention to the ways in which particular performances of femininity work to enlarge the field of possibilities for girls,[20] while others subordinate girls' interests to those of boys.

In the final analysis, we found Butler's notion of performativity a useful reminder that identities are nonfoundational and processual: in her work, gender is not "a stable identity or locus of agency from

which various acts proceed; rather, it is an identity tenuously constituted in time—an identity instituted through stylized repetition
of acts" (2003: 415). As Bettie (2003: 52) notes, while girls might consciously express particular ways of "being girls," the performativity
of gender is found in "unthought" displays that are inherited from
the specific historical configuration of social relations. As we shall
see, it is unthought displays that tell us the most about how power
operates through discourse. Material relations of race, class, sexuality, able-bodiedness, and so on mean that both experiences of girlhood and available ways of "doing girlhood" are always mediated
by processes that position various girls in sometimes complementary,
sometimes competing, identity discourses. Despite this complexity of
gender, adolescence is a time when the explicitly sexualized nature of
gender becomes apparent. Within this context, it made sense to talk to
participants about "being girls."[21]

Like Nelson (1999), we recognize that while "coming into being" is
shaped by unconscious processes, it is never unmediated by an actor's
meanings and intentions. Our analytical attention, therefore, is directed to girls' subjectivities as those processes through which our participants make sense of their "doing" and of the world around them, albeit
not through the kind of reasoning implied by notions of "choosing"
specific identities. Drawing on Adams (1999; also see Weedon 1987: 32)
we employ "subjectivity" to include both conscious and unconscious
aspects of the way we understand "who we are" and "our place" in
the world. Discourse provides one avenue of exploring these conscious
and unconscious negotiations. Knowing our place in the world comes:

> ...not through the revelations of our "true selves," but via our negotiations
> through and within discourse—regulated systems of what can be expressed
> and said. Our discursive attachments let us bring meaning to the world
> around us and to our place within it. They offer us subject positions through
> which we come to understand who and what we are. Our location at the con-
> fluence of a variety of discourses makes possible the range of ways we have
> of expressing ourselves, as well as the meanings we assign to our expressions.
> It makes it possible to resist what some have called "discourse determinism"
> (Adams 1999: 15–16).

In *"Girl Power"*, the power of discourse lies in its ability to facilitate,
but also circumscribe, subjectivity, hence our performances of gender.[22]
Although individual girls can—and often do—resist being positioned

in prevailing discourse, we question how power operates to make specific girlhoods more available (to specific girls) and more durable than others without making these girlhoods "inevitable." Drawing on Gee (2002), we are interested in discourses that emerge among a local community of speakers but question how these discourses are mediated by dominant culture. Our focus is on ways in which the discourses employed by individual girls to sustain particularized, local meaning systems are connected to school-based peer cultures as the actionable contexts of their performances (Fraser 1992b: 185). Thus, we see the subjectivities that are expressed in girls' talk as properties of social organization rather than of individual subjects, as what Valverde (1991) calls "social subjectivities" (also see Smith 1987: 3).

## THE POWER OF DISCOURSE

As noted above, the study of discourse can make visible the:

> ...particular, limited set of concepts, images, metaphors, ways of speaking, self-narratives and so on that we take on as our own. This entails both an emotional commitment on our part to the categories of person to which we are allocated and see ourselves as belonging... Our sense of who we are and what it is therefore possible and not possible for us to do, what it is right and appropriate for us to do, and what it is wrong and inappropriate for us to do thus all derive from our occupation of subject positions within discourse (Burr 1995: 145–146).

In our work, we explore what girls' subjectivities tell us about negotiation through and within discourse. Like Hall (1996) we treat identity as a "meeting point":

> The point of suture, between on one hand the discourses and practices which attempt to "interpellate," to speak to us or hail us into place as the social subjects of particular discourses, and on the other hand, the processes which produce subjectivities, which construct us as subjects which can be spoken (1996: 5).

In our work, this interpellation corresponds to the way discourse can be what we call a "vehicle" of power. As we shall see, embodiment cannot be ignored in understanding how this power of discourse operates. This is because, as Weedon (1987: 112) notes, to "be effective, they [discourses] require activation through the agency of the individuals whom they constitute and govern, in particular ways, as embodied subjects." As we explored how discourses sustain girls' performances of girlhood, the embodied nature of gender practices became increasingly apparent. In Chapter Four, we will see how girls' embodiment is sexualized through discourses of heteronormative femininity, in particular, that position girls socially in specific ways, even while remaining unspoken. Exploring how power works in this way helps us understand what we refer to as the performative nature of gender.

We begin our exploration with an interrogation of those discourses through which girls spoke their world into existence during interviews. The discursive positioning that interests us in this talk occurs through identity labels used by girls to locate both themselves and others in their social world.[23] This analysis of doing girlhood, while informed by poststructuralism, is not as determinist as some accounts; we do not see the Self or subjectivity as mere "effects" of discourse (on this point see Nelson 1999: 338). We assume, as practice theorists do, that human beings act within particular contexts created by past actions and decisions and that, while "bound by the conditions of their political, economic, and cultural circumstances" (Dillabough 2004: 498), we have some room to improvise "on materials provided by the gender order" (Connell 2002: 23). As D. Holland and colleagues (1998: 18) argue, these improvisations contain the potential beginnings of an altered subjectivity, thus an altered girlhood. Nevertheless, there is a felt moral imperative to get gender "right." Our work explores how "getting it right" renders girls accountable to other girls in particular. As Bettis, Jordan, and Montgomery (2005: 69) point out, peer groupings are about "where to sit at lunch, what to wear, where and with whom to hang out with between classes," and, in general, "how to be." In recognizing how girls in groups construct collective female identities, they can be considered as "co-learners" in what Paechter (2003a) and others call "communities of practice." As we explore in Chapter Four, a community of practice refers to "an aggregate of people who, united by a common enterprise, develop and share ways of doing things, ways of talking, beliefs, and values—in short, practices" (Eckert and McConnell-Ginet 1999: 186). Locating girls' identity practices within such communities, we are able to explore the kinds of discourses that shape girls' sense of what is "right." However, it is not the content per se of girls' talk that interests us in this book.

Following Foucault (1972: 49), discourses are not merely "groups of signs (signifying elements referring to contents or representations) but practices that systematically form the objects of which they speak." Thus we are interested in how the meanings sustained by the local communities of practice inhabited by the participants in our study bring girlhood into existence by coordinating their talk "with ways of acting, interacting, valuing, believing, feeling, and with bodies, clothes, non-linguistic symbols, objects, tools, technologies, times, and places" (Gee 2002: 23). Understanding this coordination will help us understand what we refer to as the "power" of discourse. It takes us beyond (simply) attempting to capture what meanings any individual girl gives to her identity project; it requires investigation of the social nature of girls' meaning-making practices.

Central to these practices is what Foucault (1977) calls subjectification: a twofold occurrence that both shapes the Subject through interpellation *and* enables the possibility for the Subject to reshape her own subjecthood. Subjectification simultaneously forms and enacts the Subject, allowing for what Gonick (2003: 10) calls a "double movement between a subject speaking/writing her way into existence by using the stories or discourses that are made available and in the moment of doing so, also subjecting herself to the constitutive force and regulative norms of those discourses."

As elaborated in Chapter Two, "girl power" is a discursive field within which competing meanings associated with "being a girl" are made available within popular culture. Within this field, discontinuous and constantly changing subject positions are offered through systems of stabilizing, but at other times disorienting, discursive elements. The result is that not simply different, but contradictory, discourses can coexist within the same discursive domain with unpredictable effects (Foucault 1990). Thus we cannot know in advance whether taking up an available position in any specific discourse will reinforce power or, alternatively, "undermine, expose, thwart, or render power fragile" (ibid.: 102). In other words, although contextualizing girls' agency within "discourses of girl power," we cannot simply read this agency off discourse. Our investigation must attend to the ways embodied girls actively engage with the various discursive elements through which their identities "as girls" are accomplished. As noted by Weedon (1987: 109), when speaking "in her own right," the female subject can disrupt

*[handwritten margin note:] speak back through zine, blog, writing*

discourses by "talking back." Since discourses are vehicles of power, we are interested in how girls' talk might do so as a challenge to established ways of speaking and being in the world.

Despite the apparent malleability of gender implicit in this approach, certain ways of being girls are socially sanctioned by adults as "inappropriate" or by peers as "weird" (Jones 1993). The girls in our study referred to this negative sanctioning as "pressure" to perform girlhood in specific ways. In Chapter Four, we explore how this pressure operates to reconstitute femininity as compliance to a male-oriented culture; Chapter Four thus explores the power of discourse to reconstitute dominant definitions of girlhood. It shows how some identities are more durable than others (see McNay 2000). However, a central concern of *"Girl Power"* is how girls extend or transgress the boundaries of girlhood by taking up femininities that are devalued or repressed within discourses of hetero-normative girlhood. Our purpose in doing so is not to celebrate the heterogeneity of girls' identity practices. Rather, we look for discourses that encourage girls to challenge and rewrite girlhood in ways that foster greater equality between girls and boys. In this sense, our central concern is the power of discourse to support social justice through the feminist empowerment of girls. By *feminist* empowerment, we critique the sloganeering of popularized girl power and advocate, instead, the need for girls to understand how various discourses that operate to position them in specific ways can be taken up strategically or resisted. As Cook and Kaiser (2004: 206) note, while girls may have little control over representations of girlhood in mainstream culture, they do exercise agency in the representations they create every day, through acts such as contemplating and dressing their bodies. By looking for what we call emergent feminisms in this agency, however, we do not want to replay what Frith (2001: 147) describes as a dichotomy between "old" (which we read as "second-wave") and "new" (which we read as "third-" or "fourth-wave") feminisms (also see Eisenhauer 2004). Rather, like Frith, we are interested in connections and continuities that are missed by claims that second-wave feminism is not relevant to young women or that the next generation of feminism must define itself against established feminism. As will be evident in our concluding chapter, while we support feminism by girls and for girls, we do not see this feminism as somehow distinct from what has gone before it.

## A GIRL'S WORLD?

Ebert (2005) maintains that the "cultural turn" in feminism has isolated issues of gender and sexuality from their material conditions of possibility. Her criticism is directed toward the treatment of culture as an autonomous zone of signifying practices (page 33). We share Ebert's worry about the "dematerialization" of feminist theorizing that can take place when discourse becomes its problematic, and agree that it can lead to the depoliticization of feminism. Although focusing on the discursive constitution of girlhood, we do not want readers to lose sight of its broader material and sociocultural context. As noted above, we view the central categories of this book—"Selfhood" and "girlhood"—as expressions of the way power works to naturalize historically and culturally specific ways of doing a social presence. Indeed, the very fact that our research takes "girlhood" as its problematic is symptomatic of its historical context. Until the emergence of Girls' Studies in the early 1990s, the kinds of issues and questions we raise in *"Girl Power"* were not seen as topics worthy of scholarly investigation. Within cultural studies generally, and youth studies specifically, "adolescent" and "youth" were signifiers for boys; girls were either missing or portrayed as "incidental" in research texts about boys' lives (see Hebidge 1979, 1988; Willis 1977). While this neglect reflected the way that girls, in general, were not legitimate occupants of the kinds of public spaces accessible to especially male researchers, it also signals a more general cultural devaluation of girls and young women.

The consolidation of feminist scholarship through the establishment of Girls' Studies has been important in changing the marginalized status of girls among youth researchers. In popular consciousness, their status is being challenged by a new, neoliberal economic and cultural order. Girls— read: middle-class white girls—are beginning to challenge the gender gap in public school performance as educators prepare them for careers rather than domestic roles. However optimistic, jobs for life are being replaced by part-time, casual laborers employed under the kinds of conditions that historically have been typical of distinctly "women's work." In the industrialized world, this shift reflects the decline of primary industries where men have dominated and the expansion of the service sector (Bakker 1996; Walby 1997). This increased demand for workers who now deal with people rather than with "things" can give both women and conventional femininity a competitive market advantage (Lovell 2000). While women's employment has thus climbed during the past several decades, male managers and executives are now being trained in "people-oriented" styles of communication and "worker management." Within this context, values historically confined to the domestic arena where women dominate are spilling over into other areas of social life. The 1990s witnessed movements to help men, particularly middle-class professional men, "reclaim" the experience of "being in touch" with their inner Selves (see McLeod 2002). While advertising historically signified consumption as leisured self-indulgence by bourgeois women, the "aestheticization" of Self (Featherstone 1991; also Bowlby 1993) is now a mandate for "successful" men and women alike. It is not surprising, therefore, that a period characterized by political conservatism has also been marked by considerable transformation of the cultural values surrounding gender.[24] The effect of such changes on young people generally has been education oriented to continual self-invention and transformation, a skill necessary for survival within the new economic, social, and cultural order. What remains unaddressed is the way that girls live this necessity in particularly gendered ways. These kinds of changes can foster new subjectivities for girls. As noted by Francis and Skelton (2005), individualism, choice, and self-realization—as historic markers of masculinity—now interpellate female Subjects, along with discourses of conventional femininity that orient adult women's identities towards the needs of others.[25]

As a number of writers have noted, Girls' Studies emerged in this context that they claim has had the effect of constructing women as "the vanguard of a new subjectivity" (see Harris 2004: 1; Walkerdine, Lucey, and Melody 2001). Within mainstream academic discourse, this subjectivity signals the emergence of the "reflexive individual" (Giddens 1991, Beck 1992). Flexible and self-actualizing, the individual of the twenty-first century (purportedly) has been freed from the constraints of tradition and positioned by an information age to manage their own life choices. One of the most influential ideas is the notion that because of the (apparent) demise of social structures that historically regulated identities through the institutions of gender, class, family, and so on, our biographies are increasingly under individual control. The ideal subject of late modernity is individualized, flexible, resilient, self-driven, and self-made (Harris 2004: 16). While theorists tend to ignore the way in which some people (especially privileged white males) are more able to construct their futures than others (working class women, people of color, disabled persons), within popular culture young women—read: white, heterosexual and able-bodied—have been portrayed as being advantaged by this new, idealized Subject.

Reflecting the visible changes in women's lives, in popular consciousness girls are now favored over boys. Various media have created concern over the way that girls are outperforming boys academically, and highlight women who delay or avoid motherhood altogether by making marriage a secondary life interest in order to seize new employment opportunities and achieve once unimaginable goals. As a result, girls have replaced "youth" as a cultural metaphor for social change (McRobbie 2000: 201). Power, opportunity, and success are all modeled by what Harris (2004: 1) calls "future girl." With the world at their feet, young women have come to symbolize hopes for the new millennium. The concept "girl power" has come to signify young women as the independent inheritors of a new world order. As a household word, "girl power" constructs:

> …a generation of young women as a unique category of girls who are self-assured, living lives lightly inflected but by no means driven by feminism, influenced by the philosophy of DIY (do it yourself), and assuming they can have (or at least buy) it all. The evidence for these new ways of being is drawn from a wide range of areas: girls' educational success; their consumption, leisure, and fashion practices; apparent rejection of institutionalized feminism; sexual assertiveness; professional ambitions; delayed motherhood; and so on. Nowhere is girl power more evident, though, than in popular culture, particular in the promotion of certain pop stars, comic book heroes, TV and film characters, and advertising icons (Harris 2004: 17).

One goal of our work is to interrogate the notion of "future girl(s)" through an exploration of girls' lived experiences of "girl power" culture. If the claims of popularized girl power are correct, and young women indeed are the beneficiaries of the new world order (Aapola, Gonick, and Harris 2005: 12), why do women still rarely reach the highest positions of decision-making in society, and why do so many occupy some of the least desirable positions in the labor market? In considering these kinds of questions we ask: How much individual control do embodied girls exercise over "who they are" and "who they might become"? Which girls are the beneficiaries of a transforming world order? What happens to the others? What kinds of discourses support girls' resistance to an order based on gender subordination? How does feminism enlarge the future for all girls?

## ABOUT *"GIRL POWER"*

We chose *"Girl Power"* as the title of our work precisely because the meanings of this phrase are so contentious. In the following chapter, we explore the diverse and contradictory meanings of "girl power" that circulate through popular culture. Here, "girl power" has come to signify the personal power of individual girls to pursue an unlimited future and, perhaps as a consequence, also to signal anxiety that girls are now being favored over boys, at the neglect of boys' potentials. In Chapter Two, we explore how these competing discourses construct everyday knowledge about girlhood. We also explore the messages about feminism implicit in these discourses (also see Taft 2004). Whether structured by liberal feminist aspirations for girls, antifeminism, or the notion that feminism is no longer relevant or needed, popularized discourses of girl power position girls in relation to feminism as an equality-seeking movement. This positioning is at the heart of our inquiry, because it tells us a lot about the transformative agency of girls, hence potential futures for girls and women.[26]

We recognize that by locating our work among these competing discourses, *"Girl Power"* is among the now many texts that contribute to the construction of girlhood as an object of adult concern. As outlined in the preface, our concern centers on girls' subordination in an antifeminist context that makes it difficult to raise issues of gender inequality. This concern leads us to question girls' relationship to, and interest in, feminism. Rather than stipulate what we believe this relationship *ought* to be, our task is to understand what girls' identity practices tell us about the place of feminism in everyday contexts. We hope to contribute to the growing body of work that attempts to understand how power operates to construct gendered identities in historically specific ways. By focusing on discourses that support girls' identity practices, our investigation is not an attempt to "culturalize" feminist politics; we are interested in how the cultural realm of "girl power" connects to the material, embodied world of lived experience. In doing so, we do not "judge" girls' self-expressions; rather we aim to advance at least one of the central goals of feminism—to enlarge the possibilities for girls' thinking about "who they are" and "who they can become."

In closing this chapter, we emphasize that our understanding of girlhood and of the relationship between girls and feminism changed during the fieldwork and intense discussions that accompanied our analysis of interviews. While the representation of research is always retrospective, and thus tends to portray the endeavor as linear and perhaps "self-fulfilling," to the extent possible we have tried to make it apparent how our thinking changed as we listened to girls. What we have learned through our work with girls is that feminism must be open to new and diverse possibilities that will bring new and diverse Subjects to the fore, thereby continually reconstituting feminism. We see "everyday"[27] girls who do "everyday" things as a good place to start (see McRobbie 1999: 72).

NOTES

1   At the same time that we focus on "identity," we problematize this
    focus; specifically, we do not intend to advance a view of feminism
    as a "variant" of identity politics that diverts attention away from
    "structural" inequalities. Rather, like Young (2000: 89) we acknowl-
    edge that any group—such as "girls"—consists of a "collection of
    individuals who stand in determinate relations with one another
    because of the actions and interactions of both those associated
    with the group and those outside or at the margins of the group.
    There is no collective entity, the group, apart from the individuals
    who compose it."

2   Postcolonial writers include Fanon (1967, 1986) and Said (1985,
    1993). However, we do not want to imply that postcolonial writers
    are nonfeminists; see for example Spivak (1985, 1987); Anzaldua
    (1987); Mohanty, Russo, and Torres (1991); McClintock (1995); Na-
    rayan (1997).

3   By West we refer to the post-war industrialized world; feminism
    during other times and in other parts of the world did not focus on
    women's identities as "individuals." See for example Bulbeck 1998.

4   We acknowledge Skeggs' (2004) claim that such a Subject is the ba-
    sis for the kind of self-governance required by liberal democracies.
    Also see Walkerdine and Lucey 1989.

5   However, we are not claiming to theorize what has not yet come
    into existence.

6   We do not mean to imply that there are fixed "developmental stag-
    es" for young people. Overall, we share Bucholtz's (2002) injunc-
    tion to expand the scope of research from "the teen years, puberty,
    or other chronological or biological measures of adolescence in or-
    der to incorporate the full range of ways that youth may be defined
    socioculturally." She rejects the concept of "adolescence" because
    it contrasts and connects—etymologically as well as socially—with

adulthood. Specifically, "adult" connotes "completeness" and "adolescence" "growth and transition." In contrast, "youth" foregrounds age not as trajectory, but as identity as "agentic, flexible, and ever-changing" (page 525). Following Bucholtz, we prefer the term "youth" but employ the term "adolescent" (reflexively) when used by other scholars.

7   While we do not follow their methodology, here we acknowledge that West and Zimmerman (1987) first introduced the phrase "doing gender" (for criticisms see Collins 2002 and Deutsch 2007). Below we clarify how we employ the notion of gender as "performative." Although we draw on Butler (1990), what we find missing in much writing on the performativity of gender through discourse is a reminder that "performance" presupposes an audience. Like West and Zimmerman (1987) we see gender performances as "accountable" to their audience. See Moloney and Fenstermaker 2002.

8   For work on how boys "do" masculinity, see Kehler and Martino (2007), Kehler (2007), Connolly (2006), Renold (2003), Bamberg (2004), and Martino (2003).

9   Within socialist and Marxist feminism, a focus on the sexual division of labor as the fundamental "causal factor" supporting women's oppression contributed to this view.

10   We do not deny the existence of the kinds of gender-specific issues facing girls; in fact, our interest in feminism for girls is based on that recognition.

11   Here we note that this concern was directed primarily toward the "risks" facing girls from white middle-class families.

12   Aapola, Gonick, and Harris (2005: 33) draw attention to the roots of Riot Grrrl culture in African American women's culture; it is not the white punk music scene as much as Black hip-hop music that spawned and supports the changing modes of femininity understood as "girl power."

13   What Press (1997) wants to see is similar to what we would like: not a celebration of apolitical girl power or feminism with "all the struggle and critique removed."

14   For an example of girl power programs that promote feminism for girls rather than attempt to "save" girls, see Pamela Millar and Sher Morgan (1998) or Stephanie Higginson (2006).

15   In particular, the work of Angela McRobbie (1978).

16   Produced originally for male audiences, the show was not initially intended to be marketed as a "feminist" production (see Riordan 2001: 292).

17   This claim ignores the origin of girl power culture in a grrrl movement inspired by radical, pro-feminist Riot Grrrl music.

18   By *postfeminism*, we refer to the view—sometimes expressed by girls in our study—that, because gender equality has been accomplished, feminism is no longer politically relevant.

19   Furthermore, the performativity of gender helps us avoid the problems common in some feminist interpretations of socialization theory that associate "ideology" with the distortion of "truth." The search for an authentic voice of girlhood, for example, replays the binary of true/false Selfhood. As well, this way of thinking has encouraged feminists to see agency only in terms of resistance to dominant ways of being. As we explore in Chapter Four, girls can be "agents" in the reconstitution of girls' subordination to boys.

20   As we elaborate in Chapter Nine, we emphasize possibilities for *all* girls, not simply those advantaged by their class location, racialized identity, or embodiment that conforms to idealized cultural standards.

21   While we accept Eckert and McConnell-Ginet's (1999: 186) criticism of analytically separating "gender" from other aspects of our identities, being "girls" and "boys" is among the primary divi-

sions used by the school system to classify and "manage" students (along with age and academic performance). Students are not similarly identified and divided according to racialized identities, for example. Here we simply recognize how different our research would be if we had talked to girls about "being white" or "being Asian," for example. See Kruger, Lezard and Easterson 1994; Pantin 2001; Eisenhauer 2004; Jiwani 2006; Lee 2006.

22  While we treat discourse as a process that mediates between lived experience and the meanings used to make sense of those experiences, we do not mean to advance what Adams (1999: 16) calls "discourse determinism." As we discuss in Chapter Three, girls can have experiences that affect them even though they cannot "name" these experiences because they lack access to a relevant discourse.

23  Girls and not discourses are the producers of identities. In our view of how discourse works, a person expresses agency "even if" they position themselves in a discourse of victimhood, for example.

24  Of course, we point out that the liberalization of gender is an "uneven" phenomenon. Breazeale (1994) documents how *Esquire* had to reshape its representations of masculinity in order to market to men as consumers of "style." We also point out that contemporary styles of masculinity (such as metrosexuality) and the increased visibility of transgendered identities are more likely to be "tolerated" in urban than rural settings, for example, and "accepted" among younger rather than older segments of the population. However encouraging, these transformed cultural expressions of gender have not led to widespread transformation of the gendered division of domestic labor (Neft and Levine 1997), hence the basis for Ebert's (2005) worry that the cultural turn that encourages "identity politics" has "depoliticized" feminism.

25  The extent to which girls represent the idealized Subject of neoliberalism is a matter of debate among Girls' Studies scholars. For example, see Francis and Skelton's (2005) critique of writers like Walkerdine, Harris, and others who claim that girls (and women)

are now portrayed in public discourse as the archetype for either the "ideal learner" or the "ideal subject" (pages 124–126).

26 To this we add the transformative potential, hence potential futures for "boys and men."

27 We do not intend to construct a monolithic category but rather, following Smith (1987), we use "everyday" to signal the importance of local, "ordinary" contexts where the majority of people interact in ways that generally escape the interest of researchers or media commentators.

# 2

# "HARDLY INNOCENT"

## POPULAR MEANINGS OF GIRLHOOD

The word *girl* had formerly seemed to me innocent and unburdened, like the word *child*; it now appeared that it was no such thing. A girl was not, as I had supposed, simply what I was; it was what I had become. It was a definition. Always touched with emphasis, with reproach and disappointment.
—Alice Monro, 1968, page 118

Within everyday thinking and talking about girls, "girlhood" appears to be a naturally occurring category, signaling a temporary period in women's lives that has always existed across time and place. Indeed, the visible presence of embodied "girls" reinforces this ready apparentness of girlhood. Despite appearances, however, exactly what it means to be "a girl" has a long history (see Driscoll 2002). Historically speaking, the meaning of girlhood in Western culture has been the subject of intense debate among "experts" for several centuries and, since the nineteenth century, has reflected adult concern over the "innocence" of childhood. Rousseau, for example, regarded children as being born "naturally innocent" (Gittins 1998: 151) but corrupted by society. In contrast, Locke argued that the child is neither good nor bad, but a tabula rasa, an empty slate upon which parents, society and culture construct his or her personality: "Innocence, in the sense of not-knowing, is therefore innate" (page 150). While both accounts emphasize "innocence," neither recognizes how the innocence of childhood is gendered. In patriarchal cultures, where girls' virginity and adult women's chastity are prized, "not-knowing" takes on specific meaning. Girls, more so than boys, are expected to remain "sexually innocent" until marriage.[1]

Reflecting this legacy, within Westernized cultures, schoolgirls in particular are idealized as the repository of purity through the rhetoric of their "vulnerability" and need for "protection."[2] As Jackson (2006: 251) argues, this thinking is not necessarily helpful to children or young people, because these notions do not increase children's abilities to understand their worlds. In other words, while adults have shown a tendency to romanticize girlhood in particular with innocence, this is a double-edge sword in that it becomes a way of curtailing girls' self-determination. In this chapter, we see how "girl power"—as a feminist-inspired discourse that has been taken up within popular culture—challenges the idealization of girlhood. While we give emphasis to commercial culture—film and television in particular—we include academic work as contributing to common-sense understandings of what it means today to be "a girl." By locating our work within public debates and popularized understandings of girlhood and girl power, this chapter helps explain the questions that we raise throughout *"Girl Power"*. Furthermore, popular culture is the context within which *"Girl Power"* will be read; this chapter invites readers to reflect upon the socially constructed nature of much popular knowledge about girls and the state of girlhood. Hopefully readers will see that our goal is not to contribute a new, competing "truth" about girlhood; our motivation is much more practical. As teachers of young women and of teachers, our hope is to contribute to the development of critical literacy for youth, an issue we elaborate in Chapter Nine.

Critical literacy includes the ability to recognize the constructed nature of our social world and of competing knowledge claims about it. Incorporated into public school curriculum, critical literacy can help both girls and boys interrogate how gendered, classed, and racialized constructions, in particular, position them in specific ways while at the same time invoking personal responsibility for the outcome (see Walkerdine, Lucey, and Melody 2001). While such an interrogation is typically associated with social research, we equate it with feminist empowerment that is connected to political movements for social justice. After all, the constructed nature of the world is what makes its reconfiguration possible. Because we see girls as social Subjects, we are interested—theoretically and practically—in their constitution as historical agents.

In advancing this goal, it was necessary to include in our study of girls' subjectivities and everyday agency an interrogation of popularized understandings of the state of girlhood. What cannot be ignored is the way in which "girl power," as an everyday expression, has become a shorthand way to explain dramatic changes that characterize the state of girlhood today. Although a contested term, it implies that girls have been "liberated" from the kinds of constraints identified by second-wave feminists. Within popular consciousness, girl power positions girls as ambitious, success bound, and independent, and thus celebrates both youthful femininity and individualism.

Girl power rhetoric was peaking when we interviewed the girls in our study between 2000 and 2003. Two out of every three girls whom we asked about "girl power" said they associated the term primarily with the Spice Girls, who rose to fame in the mid- to late-1990s, and whose image was deliberately aimed at young girls. As we have seen in Chapter One, the Spice Girls have been credited with making "girl power" a household word. Our interviewees would have been in elementary school during this time, and a number of them mentioned being avid Spice Girls fans when younger. Nina, for example, described herself as having grown up "in the Spice Girls era. My favorite was Sexy Spice or Ginger Spice... I grew up thinking that a guy would do anything for sex and therefore women ruled them." None of the girls admitted to still liking the Spice Girls, and, in fact, quite a few expressed disdain for their message of "liberation." Jessica disapproved of the Spice Girls' use of the term *girl power* because they weren't powerful "in the right way. They were too showy with their bodies. I think that [the term girl power] belongs to a person that's really accomplished something that's worth remembering." As Jessica's assessment suggests, girls are not uncritical consumers of popular culture.

The social significance of the Spice Girls remains a matter of debate among Girls' Studies scholars. Because their blatantly commercialized girl power culture sustains normative femininity, like Jessica, many feminists reject the Spice Girls as proponents of feminism for girls.

While Adams (2005: 110, 111), for example, acknowledges that girl power can be seen as a positive move away from an earlier discourse of "girls in crisis," she concludes that it sells many girls short—particularly working-class girls and girls of color. The flexibility it allows in reconstituting youthful femininity remains bounded by patriarchal power and privilege. Girls today are being urged to be independent, assertive, and achievement oriented, but they are still encouraged to be "demure, attractive, soft-spoken, fifteen pounds underweight, and deferential to men" (Douglas 1997, cited in Adams 2005: 110). Although sharing many of these views, Fritzsche (2005: 160, 161) argues that while feminist critiques are useful in pointing out that the Spice Girls sustain normative expectations for teenage girls, they help (some) girls find their own way in dealing with these expectations. In her study with young Spice Girl fans, Fritzsche found a culture that offered an opportunity for girls to take a playful approach toward questions of self-representation, self-confidence, and heterosexuality. She interprets the phenomenal success of the Spice Girls as a reminder of the absence of empowering symbols in the lives of young women. She also reminds feminists that "empowerment" is not a word that we can simply "explain" to girls; empowerment is a practice learned, in part, through the kind of playful, body-oriented practices encouraged by girl power culture.

The goal of *"Girl Power"* is to take up questions raised by these kinds of debates. While we look for answers through interviews with embodied girls, in this chapter we focus on representations of girlhood and girl power found in commercial film and the work of journalists and professionals writing mainly for adult audiences (e.g., parents and teachers who work with girls), and academic researchers who have helped to produce and circulate these representations in the wider public realm. Our review is not meant to be exhaustive. As much as possible, we highlight popular representations of middle-school and high-school-aged girls, as the girls in our study ranged in age from twelve to sixteen years old.

What we present in this chapter is not so much a celebration of girlhood in the way that girl power culture might lead us to expect. Rather, we found a range of representations of girls—as overpowered "bitches" who rule the social scene at school, as sexual exhibitionists out of control, and as overachieving girls in the misguided, relentless pursuit of excellence in academics, athletics, and community service. Less frequent but potentially more positive themes concern girls as new superheroes or rebels with a (feminist) cause. Taken together, these images naturalize largely negative behavior as a normal part of girlhood. Moreover, whether claiming that girls are wildly out of control or simply the "victims" of celebrity-oriented consumer culture, the general message is one of postfeminism.

For some commentators, the term "postfeminism" is used to mean antifeminism, while others employ the term to say that feminism as a movement is no longer necessary, and still others use it to signify the emergence of a new, third-wave feminism (for a discussion, see Hawkesworth 2004). We follow Judith Stacey (1990: 339) in defining postfeminism as "the simultaneous incorporation, revision, and depoliticization of many of the central goals of second-wave feminism." Or, as Angela McRobbie (2004: 255) elaborates in a critique of popular culture, "Postfeminism positively draws on and invokes feminism as that which can be taken into account, to suggest that equality is achieved, in order to install a whole repertoire of new meanings which emphasize that it [feminism] is no longer needed, it is a spent force." As we will show, the prevailing discourses on girl power appear largely to share the common sense assumption that—as the June 29th, 1998, cover of *Time* magazine implied—feminism is "dead," and girls today, although in trouble, are without politics and without the need for collective deliberation, evaluation, or action to solve problems.[3] Such a discourse works to limit girls' access to feminism as a discourse that names their experiences and links these experiences and feelings to the ongoing quest for social justice.

In what follows, we showcase some of the ways in which professional, academic, news media, and popular narratives feed into each other and mediate public knowledge about teenaged girls, girlhood, and girl power. Within each discourse, we highlight the main dimension of female power that girls are said to enact, as well as the discourse's post/feminist subtexts. We foreground some of the dominant messages that girls and adults might take from these representations and identify points of commonality and contradiction within and across the various discourses.[4]

## RULING THE SOCIAL SCENE: GIRL POWER AS MEANNESS

"Power Play: Welcome to the Subtle But Cruel World of Schoolgirl Aggression"
—Reich, 2003, p. 37

"In middle school, girls have the only power that counts at that moment, social power."
—Stepp, *Washington Post*, 2002, p. C1

The turn of the new millennium witnessed a virtual explosion of mainstream books and movies portraying girls as schoolyard bullies and backstabbing competitors for popularity: clinical psychologist Sharon Lamb's (2001) *The Secret Lives of Girls*; Rachel Simmons's (2002) exposé, *Odd Girl Out* (later made into a TV movie); Rosalind Wiseman's (2002) parental help guide, *Queen Bees and Wannabes*; Lynn Glazier's (2004) insider documentary, *It's a Girls' World*; and Mark Waters' (2004) blockbuster movie, *Mean Girls*. *Mean Girls*, written by former *Saturday Night Live* comedian Tina Fey (based on Wiseman's nonfiction book), did much to popularize the notion of the "Mean Girl": catty, without scruples, shallow, and sexually aggressive. Fighting the sneaky way grants girls in the movie access to the highest reward: popularity at school. The most popular girls in the film are "the Plastics," led by Regina, the Queen Bee; the Plastics are rich, thin, "hot," have popular boyfriends, wear sexy clothes, drive cool cars, and follow the rules of "Girl World" without seeming to follow any rules at all. Regina's power stems from her ability to do and be all of these things, while she continuously undermines other girls and regulates a highly heterosexualized femininity in the school.

*Mean Girls* continually invites viewers to draw parallels between "Girl World" and—as one scene is entitled—"Jungle Madness." Girls fight over boys like prey. Rules must be followed or else severe punishments are doled out, such as social exclusion ("you can't sit with us") and humiliation. Even the "nice" girls are shown to be spiteful. Outcast Janis Ian masterminds a plan to take the popular Plastics down by tricking the Queen Bee Regina into getting fat, making sure she gets caught cheating on her boyfriend, and tearing her friendship group apart. The film shows girls to be the makers of their own misery and does not situate girlhood in relation to boyhood, dominant masculinity, patriarchy, status or class competition, or compulsory heterosexuality. Girls are mean to each other simply because they are "natural" bitches.

This portrayal might seem perplexing, given that its context includes a decade of writing about girls as "victims" rather than perpetrators of aggression. Books such as the bestseller *Reviving Ophelia* (Pipher 1994) portrayed girls as suffering from lowered self-esteem as they navigate adolescence, fueling concern about girls as vulnerable "saplings in a hurricane" of a "girl-poisoning culture" (13, 22). The sad and drowning Ophelia has been usurped by these new versions of girlhood, fueling anxieties about girls' "over-empowerment." In the early 2000s, as Chesney-Lind and Irwin (2004) note, the moral panic over gang-girl violence among Latina and African American inner-city girls shifted to highlight the nonphysical fighting of white, middle-class suburban girls. Rooted in studies on bullying, psychologists and journalists identified "relational aggression" among girls as a form of bullying that is invisible, specifically feminine, and particularly devastating. As Simmons (2002: 3) writes, "There is a hidden culture of girls' aggression in which bullying is epidemic, distinctive, and destructive." Such a culture is said to be pervasive among teenage girls, where gossip, backstabbing, manipulation, the cold shoulder, and other forms of indirect aggression are the norm.

Academic, professional, journalistic, and pop culture texts alike have offered in-depth examples of how girls are mean to each other: three-way phone calls where one girl is tricked into saying bad things about another; boyfriend stealing; excommunication where a girl is frozen out of her friendship group without so much as an explanation; verbal punches about weight, style, and looks; accusations of lesbianism, sluttiness, and "dirty" behavior; and intricate hierarchical structures where girls control the activities of others through Machiavellian means. While much of the initial flurry of books and media stories was aimed at anxious parents, this discourse was fed back to girls themselves through "empowerment" programs, TV shows, and popular novels. Naomi Wolf reviewed three recent best-selling young fiction series—"Gossip Girl," "A-List," and "Clique"—finding that these books encourage girls to conform to a corrupt, banal adult world rather than question or criticize it. The girls in Lisi Harrison's "Clique" series, for example, "...are empowered. But they are empowered to hire party planners, humiliate the 'sluts' in their classes ('I'm sorry, I'm having a hard time understanding what you're saying,' Massie snapped. 'I don't speak Slut.') and draw up a petition calling for the cafeteria ladies serving their lunch to get manicures" (Wolf 2006: para. 3).

Explanations for mean girl behavior coalesce around the idea that meanness is a "girl thing" (Bright 2005) and that it is "what girls do" (e.g., Wiseman 2002: 4).[5] Like the expression "boys will be boys," the expression "what girls do" suggests that girls have the tendency to perform certain negative behaviors as a part of "who" they are—naturally—"rather than seeing them [these behaviors] as strategies for negotiating the particular times and place in which some girls are living" (Gonick 2004: 397). As the logic goes, because girls are denied access to typical "masculine" aggression, such as fighting or other straightforward ways of dealing with a problem, teenage girls are relegated to the use of relational aggression, where they can carry out their dirty deeds in secrecy. According to Simmons (2002: 3), "Unlike boys, who tend to bully acquaintances or strangers, girls frequently attack within tightly knit networks of friends, making aggression harder to identify and intensifying the damage to the victims." Ironically, this analysis sets up a binary opposition between physical and relational aggression, where the physical violence of the boys is viewed as better—a more honorable way of dealing with social problems in the school, as opposed to the vicious way in which the girls deal with problems.[6]

Simmons and other authors suggest that relational aggression is the ultimate form of power, making girls much more brutal in their punishments than boys. But, as Chesney-Lind and Irwin (2004: 51) point out, alternative forms of aggression are typically "weapons of the weak" and actually reflect girls' relative powerlessness in the wider social world. Furthermore, making meanness a "girl thing" ignores what Gonick (2004: 397) calls the "sociohistorical, material, and discursive contexts which actually produce social categories like 'girls' and the processes which render them intelligible." By ignoring the social and institutional contexts of girls' mean behavior, then, regardless of intentions, this discourse reflects an ideology of postfeminism and implies that relational aggression expresses immutable traits inherent in girls by virtue of nature, nurture, or both.

## FLAUNTING SEXUAL MORES: GIRL POWER AS HYPERSEXUALITY

"It's a cramped vision of girlhood that enshrines sexual allure as the best or only form of power and esteem."
—Downes, *New York Times*, 2006, para. 8

"I have the girls being more aggressive, they set things up and instigate. They're excited with their new sexual power."
—Catherine Hardwicke, director and co-writer of *Thirteen* (in Fuchs, 2003, para. 38)

Without much explicit discussion, the girls portrayed as mean are implicitly white, middle to upper class, and heterosexual. In the movie *Mean Girls*, for example, the popular Plastics are all white but have their racial counterparts in the school: in an early scene in the cafeteria, the audience is briefly introduced to the "Cool Asians" (who are contrasted with the "Asian nerds") and the "unfriendly Black hotties." All three groups of popular girls are portrayed as rich, thin, and glamorous, but the dramatic action quickly focuses on the Plastics. In an accompanying but distinct discourse, hyperheterosexuality is central to the production of this form of femininity. Within this discourse, girls' aggression is anything but covert. Girls are loud and bawdy sexual exhibitionists. Although they may in fact be middle class, the behavior and style associated with hypersexualized girlhood is coded as working class and racialized as nonwhite.[7]

In the 1990s, the British media dubbed these girls "ladettes." A ladette is a young woman who has adopted behavior typically associated with working-class young men or "lads," such as drinking, smoking, swearing, fighting, engaging in vandalism, and mouthing off to authority figures (Muncer et al. 2001; Jackson and Tinkler 2007). Media attention inspired Jackson, a social researcher, to query teachers and students in various high schools around England on their perceptions of the "schoolgirl ladette." Schoolgirl ladettes were said to "act hard, smoke, swear, fight occasionally, drink, disrupt lessons"; they "are cheeky and/ or rude to teachers, are open about (heterosexual) sex, and are loud or 'gobby'" (2006: 346). While a few women teachers saw some aspects of the ladettes' behavior as positive, such as their assertiveness and confidence, most others, like media pundits, viewed ladettes as going too far, with (liberal) feminism portrayed as ultimately to blame.

In North America, the stage for this sexually aggressive, rude, and otherwise out-of-control version of girl power was also set throughout the 1990s, in part by the hypersexualized teen-girl (and, increasingly, preteen-girl) consumer marketplace, which incited parents to fear that attire formerly associated only with prostitutes and porn stars was forcing "an insidious form of premature sexual awakening" on girls as young as ten years old (Overbeck 1993: para. 4). Suddenly, the midriff became a regular feature of girls' style, as did low-rise jeans with visible underwear. In the late 1990s, the specter of Monica Lewinsky fueled concern about the sexual attitudes and behavior of the new generation of ambitious young women (just how many were flashing their thong underwear and baring their breasts to male superiors at work?).

In response, a number of popular nonfiction books—written by journalists and based on interviews and reporting—appeared. These books focus primarily on college-age women, albeit they incorporate some examples drawn from recent headlines or a few interviews with high school-age girls. Nevertheless, the way these books get taken up in the popular press is misleading and without nuance, with arguments applied to girls as well as young women. In *Her Way: Young Women Remake the Sexual Revolution*, Paula Kamen (2000: 17) identifies what she calls "superrats," "an emerging breed of sexually aggressive women" whose sexual behavior is "male-like," "including having casual sex and challenging old sexual scripts in bed." Monica Lewinsky, according to Kamen, is a superrat; so are the mostly thirty-something, sexually liberated professional women in the popular TV show *Sex in the City*. While these real and fictional superrats are supposedly no longer constrained by the sexual double standard, Kamen does acknowledge that the same does not hold true for real teenage girls (citing the journalistic research of Tanenbaum 1999).

Ariel Levy's (2005) *Female Chauvinist Pigs* is an examination of what she calls "raunch culture." For example, she followed the *Girls Gone Wild* video team (a franchise started in 1993 by Joe Francis, whose soft-core porn is marketed primarily to young men) to Florida, where young college women flash their breasts and buttocks in exchange for souvenir T-shirts and trucker hats. Levy also interviewed high school girls who competed with each other to look and act as "slutty" as possible in order to attract boyfriends. Similar to Kamen's superrats, the women Levy calls "female chauvinist pigs" (FCPs) have taken on the worst stereotypes of male sexual behavior. Also like superrats, FCPs are postfeminists. And while Levy is clear that she does not equate sexual raunchiness with women's liberation, she argues that it no longer makes sense to blame men for objectifying women, because FCPs encourage each other to be raunchy, in an effort to distance themselves from anti-porn, second-wave feminists. In other words, women only have themselves to blame, and, in particular, certain feminists whom Levy deems to be antisex.

Concern over the sexual aggression and exhibitionism reportedly being displayed by younger women reached a fever pitch around publicity for the movie *Thirteen* (2003), in which the two girl protagonists engage in disordered eating, tongue and belly piercing, self-mutilation, self-harm, drinking, drugs, giving boys oral sex, shoplifting, swearing, cutting classes, and academic failure—in other words, they enact parents' worst nightmare for their daughters. One episode of *The Oprah Show* (which aired in 2003) featured Nikki Reed, the young star and co-writer of the film based on her life story. Reed's appearance drew out similar tales of woe from audience members with "troubled" teenage daughters. In the second part of the show, Oprah featured a journalist from her *O Magazine* who had done some "research" into the lives of real teenage girls. The teens described for the journalist something that has since become infamous in the imaginations of parents throughout North America—the "rainbow party." Rainbow parties, the journalist explained, are events where girls line up to give boys blow jobs, each wearing a different color of lipstick, thus creating a rainbow effect on the boys' penises. This notorious television moment spawned a fictional account of such an event in the Simon and Schuster teen novel, entitled *Rainbow Party* (Ruditis 2005). Subsequently, it became difficult to determine fact from fiction, as art—having imitated life—suddenly turned into life imitating art.

Sensing a profit to be made, toy and clothing manufacturers have tried to sell the image of "girls gone wild" to younger and younger girls (see Cook and Kaiser 2004) who want to emulate pop stars like Britney Spears, Christina Aguilera, Fergie of the Black Eyed Peas, and Paris Hilton. For example, Bratz dolls came onto the market in 2001; journalist Margaret Talbot (2006: 74) dubbed them "Little Hotties—Barbie's New Rivals": "They look like pole dancers on their way to work at a gentlemen's club." Bratz dolls are "shorter and less busty" than Barbie, wear lots of makeup, sport revealing party-girl fashion, and "look ethnically indeterminate" (page 76). Positioning itself against Bratz dolls, the very expensive American Girl (Mattel) line of dolls launched a campaign in 2005 to "save girlhood," with the website motto, "Save unicorns. Save dreams. Save rainbows. Save girlhood" (quoted in Talbot 2006: 82).

Many experts, from various ideological directions, have concluded that sexually aggressive girls are ultimately in danger of losing themselves, a theme replayed from the Ophelia discourse. From a conservative perspective, Caitlin Flanagan, writing about the "teenage oral-sex craze" in the *Atlantic Monthly*, concludes that girls today are literally and figuratively "on their knees": "experienced beyond their years, lacking any clear message from the adult community about the importance of protecting their modesty, adrift in one of the most explicitly sexualized cultures in the history of the world" (2006, para. 63). Flanagan blames girls' plight partly on feminists for encouraging girls to be aggressive in order to level "the playing field in a male-dominated world" (para. 48) but also for encouraging girls to "think of themselves as victims of an oppressive patriarchy" (para. 62). From a feminist perspective, Jean Kilbourne, maker of the documentary series *Killing Us Softly* (about the harmful representations of gender in advertising), argues that the references to porn stars and strippers on products being sold to younger girls convey a "very narrow, clichéd version of what's sexy as opposed to any kind of authentic sexuality," a sexuality that "has to do with attracting men, and has nothing to do with a girl being the agent of her own sexual desire" (quoted in Pollet and Hurwitz 2004: para. 3, 17).

Still other pundits, usually pro-feminist, are less likely to see girls' inevitable downward spiral in recent trends. In a cover story for the Vancouver-based weekly, *The Georgia Straight*, writer Pieta Woolley (2006) argued that just because young women pole dance does not mean they are promiscuous. The young people she interviewed saw pop culture as "one of the only open forums for talking about sex and making it acceptable for talking about sex" (page 46). While some might see pole dancing as misguided by encouraging girls and women to see themselves as (simply) objects of desire for men, others say they are discovering their own desire and expressing their sexuality in fun, safe ways.

Although popular analysts have thus described wild girls, variously, as postfeminist pole dancers, ladettes, female chauvinist pigs, and superrats, we believe the terrain of competing meanings that this discourse seeks to fix is decidedly more complex. Kamen, for example, argues that "Although superrats have absorbed the individualistic advances of feminism, such as sexual self-determination and control, they have left aside the parts about political awareness, organizing, and making a connection to other women" (2000: 22). Against this view, she cites a number of examples of high school girls, supposedly postfeminist superrats, who took on the establishment at various schools across the United States by filing lawsuits to protest the banning of gay/straight alliances, failure to protect them from sexual harassment, and discrimination on the basis of pregnancy and unmarried motherhood (pages 35, 36). Kamen mentions eighteen-year-old Amanda Lemon, of Xenia, Ohio, who filed suit against her school; it revoked her membership in the local chapter of the National Honor Society because she was an unmarried mother. A similar lawsuit was filed by Somer Chipman (age seventeen) and Chastity Glass (age eighteen) in Williamstown, Kentucky.

What interests us is the fact that Chipman and Glass were represented for free by lawyers from the American Civil Liberties Union and the National Organization for Women, while other feminist groups made their support of the girls public. Chipman and Glass, as well as Lemon, were not afraid to explain their cause to the mainstream media and in ways that made clear the interests they felt they shared with other girls and women. They saw what they were doing as, in part, standing up so that other young women would not have to face similar discrimination. In short, the practices do not strike us as postfeminism, but rather as de facto feminism, which we discuss in Chapter Five.

## EXCEEDING EXPECTATIONS: GIRL POWER AS THE PURSUIT OF PERFECTION

"Girl power is dominating in the classroom."
—Alphonso, *Globe and Mail*, 2003, p. A3

Partly in reaction to the alarm and negativity of the above discourses, some journalists, popular writers, and pop culture texts have begun to point out that "the girls are all right" (for example, Pikul 2005). A staff writer for the *Washington Post*, Laura Sessions Stepp, coined the term "gamma girl" to describe "a girl who rules based not on what she appears to be but on what she does," a girl who engages in "productive and task-oriented relationship building" (2002: C1). Gammas differ from "alphas" (think: really mean girls) and "betas" (think: wannabe mean girls). The gammas are on student council, taking science, doing sports, and not caring (too much) about being popular or dressing sexily. Inspired by Stepp's Greek-alphabet typology of girls, *Newsweek* carried a story on them, filling out the portrait of gamma girls as "emotionally healthy, socially secure, independent minded, and just plain nice" (Meadows 2002: para. 3).

In this discourse, girl power means deftly pursuing middle-class avenues and definitions of success, namely conventional forms of academic, athletic, artistic, and interpersonal achievement as well as community service. Television has featured some overachieving girls. There was *Sabrina, the Teenage Witch*, an attractive, well-balanced girl, often forced to deal with the cheerleading mean girl, Libby, in her high school but excelling in math and science, serving as school newspaper editor, and grappling with her amazing powers as a half-witch in a mortal realm. Television also offered Rory Gilmore of the *Gilmore Girls* as a representation of clever girlhood. Rory is someone who studies all the time, reads obsessively, and still attracts boyfriends who are both alternative and "cool." Eventually, she graduates from high school as valedictorian, turns down offers from Harvard and Princeton, and attends Yale University. In short, Rory "has it all."

Popular commentators have portrayed overachieving girls as both cause for concern and reason to take heart. In one version, there are undertones of worry that girls might be over-empowered and poised to take over the world (the flip side of this, of course, is a portrait of boys as victims or slackers). A cover story for *BusinessWeek online* (Conlin 2003) was entitled "The New Gender Gap—From Kindergarten to Grad School, Boys Are Becoming the Second Sex." In this story, Conlin refers to the "alpha femmes" (para. 3) taking over schools: "Today, across the country, it seems as if girls have built a kind of scholastic Roman Empire alongside the boys' languishing Greece" (para. 5). Girls as Roman alpha warriors marks the coming together of the mean girl (that is, aggressive and domineering) and overachieving girl discourses. In a related vein, child psychologist Dan Kindlon's book aimed at parents is entitled, *Alpha Girl: Understanding the New*

*American Girl and How She Is Changing the World*. An "alpha girl," according to Kindlon, is "a young woman who is destined to be a great leader. She is talented, highly motivated, and self-confident" (2006: 1). Promoting his book on NBC's *Today Show* (2 October 2006), Kindlon described alpha girls as taking for granted the achievements of the women's movement; their declared postfeminism is in keeping with his own view that today "society is relatively equal" for men and women. In a liberal feminist vein, however, *New York Times* columnist Maureen Dowd notes that while alpha girls may rule the school, when it comes to corporations and politics, "Professional alpha women are an endangered species" (2002: para. 19).

Almost by definition, overachieving girls are middle to upper class, usually white, and destined for top-notch universities. Some see this achievement path to girl power as better, because gamma girls supposedly "don't have to manipulate and posture to acquire [influence]" (Stepp 2002, "A Better Letter": para. 3)—"They're not mean. They like their parents. They're smart, confident, and think popularity is overrated" (Meadow 2002: para. 1). However, others point to harmful side effects. An early warning came in 2003, when Duke University released a study of the status of women on its campus, which reported undergraduate women to be feeling pressured to be "smart, accomplished, fit, beautiful, and popular, and that all this would happen without visible effort" (quoted in Lipka 2004: A35).

Reporting from an affluent suburb of Boston seemed to bear this out. *New York Times* journalist Sara Rimer (2007) hung out with a group of elite, mostly white, university-bound teenagers she described as "amazing girls": "Girls by the dozen who are high achieving, ambitious, and confident (if not immune to the usual adolescent insecurities and meltdowns). Girls who do everything: Varsity sports. Student government. Theater. Community service. Girls who have grown up learning they can do anything a boy can do, which is anything they want to do" (para. 7). The problem—as the Duke University report emphasized—is that hyperachievement and multitasking are not all that is required. Girls must strive for perfection without appearing to work too hard, and they must still be pretty and thin—a recipe, as Rimer argues, for stress.[8] Writer Emily Martin is even more worried, based on research for her forthcoming book *Perfect Girls, Starving Daughters*; she sees in the overachieving girl a "trend in outwardly high-achieving and inwardly self-hating young women. ...these girls are obsessed with recognition. As opposed to being equal and free, as 1970s feminism envisioned, these girls are better than and ensnared in an unenlightened more, better, faster ethos" (2006: para. 10).

The discourse of overachieving girls encompasses what Anita Harris (2004) has called the "can do" or "future girl." As we discussed in more detail in Chapter One, feminist sociologists and social psychologists such as Angela McRobbie and Valerie Walkerdine claim that, in the current neoliberal social and economic order, young women are being constructed to signal freedom, personal choice, and self-improvement, with little to no attention being paid to persistent gender and other inequalities. In their work, upwardly mobile, middle-class, often white girls are portrayed as the neoliberal subject par excellence (McRobbie 2004; Walkerdine 2003; Walkerdine, Lucey and Melody 2001; but also see Francis and Skelton 2005).

## KICKING BUTT: GIRL POWER AS NEW FEMININE TOUGHNESS

"Brave New Girls—These TV Heroines Know What Girl Power Really Means"
—Stoller, *On the Issues*, 1998, p. 42

The new millennium saw a confluence of tough girls appear in the movies, video games, comic books, and television, leading commentators to wonder if these female action heroes were serving as role models of physically formidable, brave girls who stand up for themselves and the greater good. Whereas the mean girls are bullies, the butt-kicking girl has a moral compass and is trying to do the right thing. At the same time, these tough girls are usually portrayed as scantily clad, sexy "babes" (think: videogame *Tomb Raider*'s Lara Croft, TV's *Xena: Warrior Princess*, or Hollywood's remake of *Charlie's Angels*) or cute (think: Cartoon Network's *Powerpuff Girls*, who, when they are not fighting crime, attend kindergarten). So, as in the case of the sexually aggressive wild girls, popular culture does not seem to generate or embrace images of physically and emotionally powerful women unless they are also conventionally beautiful and sexualized, not to mention white, slim, heterosexual, able bodied, and middle class. This discourse raises the question: "Can female power truly be respected if it's consistently packaged as supernaturally sexy or freakishly cute?" (Havrilesky 2002: para. 6).

The butt-kicking girl par excellence is perhaps *Buffy the Vampire Slayer* (which initially aired on TV from 1997 to 2003). *Buffy* featured a teen-age girl (played by Sarah Michelle Gellar, a brown belt in tae kwon do) who fights evil and rescues men as well as women. While tough, Buffy is conventionally attractive, petite, and blonde. Her mission as humanity's protector—a mission more important, ultimately, than hav-ing a boyfriend—requires that she kill as many demons as possible, and she carries out this mission with displays of physical and mental strength as well as personal sacrifice. Buffy does have a close gang of friends, including her best friend, Willow, who is a witch and a lesbian. Some feminist cultural studies scholars have seen in this an alternative to the stereotype of the male action hero as independent and autono-mous. According to Sharon Ross, Buffy often consults with her friends before taking action and sometimes must let Willow make decisions and take action, thus sharing power (2004: 240–241). Further, Willow shows Buffy "that emotional knowing is critical to being effectively tough" (page 247). Nevertheless, Buffy's role as slayer makes her dif-ferent from everyone in her friendship group. Many episodes show her to act independently, away from the gang, as a way of protecting them. She is a martyr to the core and twice "dies" to save humanity, leaving her friends to mourn her loss.

Similarly, the lead character in the noirish TV drama *Veronica Mars* (first aired in 2004) is a high school (later, college) student—white and middle class—who moonlights as a skilled private investigator. Like Buffy, Veronica is depicted as a tough, independent loner who helps others because she is driven to do so from within. Both young wom-en, while ensconced in a friendship network, choose to bear the brunt of their "destiny" alone and on the outskirts of mainstream society. Operating as powerhouses of individualism, these fictional characters come to signify the "cool" female hero. Thus, as appealing as Veronica, Buffy, and older female action-adventure heroes can be, and as much as they build from a feminist consciousness, they nevertheless under-pin an ideology that is decidedly individualist and postfeminist (see Helford 2000).

By portraying a (fantasy) world where girls can do or be anything, butt-kicking girl icons fail to question the prevalence of violence in both entertainment media and real life. Moreover, they imply that gender justice has been achieved and that feminism as a collective project in social change is no longer necessary. Alternatively, or additionally, many women may relate to the avenging female action hero because they are only too aware of—and angry about—gender injustices such as (still) pervasive male violence against women. Certainly, many plots on *Veronica Mars* and *Buffy* revolve around sexual harassment and sexual aggression, including date rape. As Dawn Heinecken (2003) points out in *The Warrior Women of Television*, "the endangered state of the female hero [such as Buffy] is a way of criticizing male violence as well as justifying the use of female violence" (page 153).

These fantasy heroines seem to have created a demand for information about real-life butt-kicking girls. For example, a new magazine aimed at young people, *niNe*, featured a profile of Bethany Hamilton, "the young surfer who lost her arm to a shark in 2003 but continues to compete" (Campbell 2006: A19). What is new about the recent generation of tough girls, and what distinguishes them from "tomboys," is that they do not necessarily eschew all things feminine as inferior. As Ross (2004) argues, *Buffy* in fact re-signifies (or at least attempts to re-signify) emotional intelligence and female friendships as sources of toughness. In other words, girls who kick butt cannot be dismissed as simply "tomboys," the rare girl who sees herself as one of the boys.

## QUESTIONING THE MAINSTREAM: GIRL POWER AS REBELLION

"Outcasts and girls with ambition, that's what I wanna see."
—Pink, lyrics to *Stupid Girls* (2006)

Across North American schools and other public gathering places, it is not hard to find a minority of girls who bond through alienation with others who share a subcultural style and disdain for—or, at a minimum, a questioning of—the mainstream, whether that be consumer culture, the dominant high school status system, electoral politics, or conventional standards of femininity. Sporadic academic studies exist

on these groups (punks, Goths, etc.), and Riot Grrrls generated popular media attention for a time in the 1990s. But the discourse of girls'
rebellion has not been popularized in the same way that the above discourses have, perhaps because of its (barely submerged) politics. One
can hear echoes of it, however, in pop singer Pink's recent hit, *Stupid
Girls*, a spoof of celebrity consumer culture: "I'm so glad that I'll never
fit in; that will never be me. Outcasts and girls with ambition, that's
what I wanna see."

Drawing on her own experience as well as ethnographic interviews
with forty girl punks in three major North American cities, sociologist
Lauraine Leblanc (1999) theorized that the punk subculture provides
(typically white) girls "a place to be assertive and aggressive, to express
[themselves] in less 'feminine' ways than other girls" (page 6). The typical age for girls to enter the punk subculture is thirteen years, or around
the onset of puberty (page 102), when girls face the femininity trap. Punk
girls try to avoid the trap by combining plaid skirts and retro dresses
with combat boots, lipstick with "kicking some ass" (page 134). Riot
grrrls comprise a faction of punk that can be traced back to the early
1990s. Fed up with the male-dominated punk scene, a group of young
women, partially inspired by feminist themes, began making their own
music and accompanying cultural, do-it-yourself scene. Riot grrrls were
angry about sexism and alienated from corporate consumer culture (see
Kearney 1997; Leonard 1997; Wald 1998), and in their DIY zines, they
wrote about music as well as stereotyping and injustice, sexual abuse,
self-mutilation, going through puberty, and sexual harassment (Shilt
2003; see also Harris 2003). At times, girl zinesters wrote about such
topics in ways that pointed a finger directly at dominant groups.

With the increasing access of youth to the Internet, girls today are
using websites to express their rebellion. Some have a cause, others do
not—at least not yet. Some websites encourage girls to become critics
of consumer culture and take on the identity of *culture jammer*. Merskin (2005) examines About-face.org, a website launched in 1997 that
explains, exemplifies, and encourages girls and women to engage in
"subvertising" and "culture jamming." A well-known Canadian culture
jammer is Carly Stasko, who began publishing the zine *uncool* at age 16
and is featured in the documentary film *Culture Jam* (2001). Other girls
use the relative safety of Internet sites to perform queer identities and
connect with other youth. As Driver, who studied queer youth online

practices, argues: "DIY practices of self-expression and self-publication are key to the empowerment of queer young people who are largely invisible within mass media and who actively distance themselves from mainstream messages" (2005: 112).

While nonconforming or rebellious teen girl heroines have not exactly taken Hollywood by storm, *Six Feet Under* (originally broadcast on HBO from 2001 to 2005 and meant for an adult audience) offered the intelligent, sardonic character of Claire Fisher, who resists various efforts to label her and ultimately finds a way to express herself through photography and other art. In the critically acclaimed art-house film *Ghost World* (2001), the two main characters, Enid and Rebecca, are smart and angry misfits who disparage conformity to the mainstream and draw power from their refusal to surrender willingly to consumer culture. On her first day of paid work, Enid is chastised by her manager at the multiplex movie theatre candy counter for not "pushing the bigger sizes." Enid follows his advice with a vengeance:

> Customer:  Hi, can I get a medium 7-Up?
> Enid:       Medium? Why sir, did you know that for a mere twenty-five cents more you can purchase a large beverage? And you know... I'm only telling you this because we're such good friends: Medium is really only for suckers who don't know the concept of value.

Enid repeatedly enacts this kind of rebellious girl power. In this scene, she uses the techniques of a culture jammer (in this case, lampooning and using an advertising gimmick against itself) but without necessarily any hope for a better world or a sense of effective spheres of action (for further analysis, see Kelly and Pomerantz in press).

Rebellious girls are perhaps as close as contemporary popular culture gets to a representation of young feminism. The fictional world inhabited by girls like Claire, Enid, and Rebecca presents postfeminism as a given. Second-wave feminism is caricatured as monolithic, passé, and ideologically rigid. Roberta, the only openly feminist character in *Ghost World*, is ridiculed for her overwhelming emotion, her victim feminism, and her inability to effect any real change. In the film, feminism is coded as earnest and no fun in moments like the one where Rebecca sees a rental ad for an apartment that interests her but then notices: "Oh, but you need to share with a nonsmoking feminist and her two cats." Yet Rebecca and, especially, Enid seem close to a feminist (third-wave) consciousness without identifying as such. Their style seems calculated to please themselves above all, and their combat posture signals a readiness to fight back if need be. Enid is vocal in her critique of most boys (who, in her opinion, seem to care about only guitars and sports) and men out "trolling for chicks." In *Six Feet Under*, Claire's repeated claim that "I don't know what I want, but I know I don't want this" is evidence that she sees problems in the conventional scripts of femininity and is bent on discovering ways to interrupt those scripts (see McCabe 2004).

## FROM GIRLHOOD TO GIRLHOODS: WHERE DOES ALL THIS TAKE US?

In this chapter, we can see how the growth of both academic and public interest in girls has produced an extensive range of discourses that lay claims to the truth of girlhood. For the large part, the representations we have seen in this chapter, taken from popular culture, construct a negative vision of girlhood. Where feminists might see justifiable anger and nascent political sensibilities, viewers of commercial media will see stridency, over-entitlement, teen angst, or simply bad behavior. Feminist academic researchers studying girl cultures in school have reported that many adult teachers (often women) see assertive girls as "bordering on rude," "real bitches," and a "bad influence," whereas boys displaying similarly disruptive classroom behavior are regarded as "loveable rogues" (Reay 2001: 161; Jackson 2006: 350, 355). Because discourse structures "the possibilities for thinking and talking," it offers a conceptual framework and classificatory models for mapping the world around us (Yon 2000: 3). In other words, the various discourses circulating in popular culture mediate public thought about girls: we start to judge girls, to think about them, to talk about them, and to categorize them in relation to the kinds of representations described in this chapter. The power of the various popular, academic, and professional texts we analyze in this chapter lies in their ability to cohere as social knowledge, to gel together as a narrative that is seen as symptomatic of girlhood itself.

As Stuart Hall (in Grossberg 1996: 143) notes, a discursive formation is produced when enough talk, text, and representation on a particular subject creates a distinctly new body of knowledge, one that appears natural and inevitable—as if it has always been there, staring us in the face. As Foucault (1972: chapter 2) explains, a discursive formation gives cohesion and definition to contradictions that are held together by their proximity in language and representation. Discourse thus offers the language by which we discuss girls and a framework for what makes "sense," what feels "right," and what has value as "truth" within our society. When such a formation takes hold in the public's imagination, it becomes a convincing reality rather than being recognized as a socially constructed "extended collection of instances" (Smith 1988: 37). While we are not likewise suggesting that the discourses described in this chapter can stand in for embodied girls, we do suggest that these narratives about out-of-control girlhoods, at one level, make the "normal" girl imaginable. In other words, the cultural presence of the girl who is not only "not normal" but also undesirable helps define the boundaries of normalcy for everyday girls. We cannot help but wonder how much the girlhoods described in this chapter derive this power from their postfeminist context (see Karlyn 2006).

In this chapter we have discerned a number of distinct discourses of "girlhood" and girl power currently in circulation. More often than not, they seem less to be in competition than to be shading into each other without apparent contradiction. In framing a story about a group of five misbehaving high school cheerleaders, for example, the online version of *Newsweek* provided alternate headlines: "'Mean Girls': Boozing, Bikinis and Bullying" and "Scandal: Cheerleaders Run Amok in Texas." Based on such mainstream media coverage, it only made sense for the editors of a popular blog to dub the story "Mean Girls Gone Wild!" And we have already remarked upon how discourses about girls' meanness and those about overachieving girls discuss "alpha girls," albeit to signal bullying and leadership, respectively.

We have noted other similarities among the discourses in this chapter, as well. Girls who diverge from the norm by virtue of their race, class, sexuality, body type, and ability are largely invisible within popularized discourses of girl power, with the exception that "wild girls" are coded as working class and racialized, and there is some presence of queer girls in discourses about girls' rebellion. In addition, the discourses we identified share a number of taken-for-granted assumptions, such as certain behaviors as "natural"—as "what girls do"—and postfeminism as girls' field of action. Across the various forms of popular media, one can sometimes detect a mild critique of consumer culture aimed at girls, but a deeper analysis of larger power structures is consistently absent. Heteronormativity, compulsory heterosexuality, patriarchy, and oppressive constructions of gender, race, and class go unnamed and unchallenged. Feminism, if it is identified at all, is at best equated with individual choice or a call for more women at the top of various institutional hierarchies. At worst, feminism is reduced to a joke or a set of anachronistic, arcane, and rigid rules that misguidedly straightjacket real girls faced with the complexities of today's world. Real feminists (versus the stereotype) who enter the discursive fray often find themselves speaking with less authority; they are said to have "an agenda," and their conceptual tools get dismissed as passé, irrelevant, and inaccessible.

We take all these observations as evidence that prevailing representations do not open girlhood to the kind of critical analysis that could harness girl power to movements for social justice. Instead, these popular discourses together construct a troubling message about girls' agency: empowered by feminism and favored by a restructured economy, girls are beyond societal—read: parental—control. As persistent and discouraging as this message may be, feminists, particularly young feminists trying to reach a girl audience, are not backing down. The twenty-eight-year-old founder of the online blog Feministing.com, Jessica Valenti, has written a book she wishes she had read in high school: *Full Frontal Feminism: A Young Woman's Guide to Why Feminism Matters* (2007). Valenti argues that antifeminists have had some success in scaring women away from calling themselves feminists, even though many younger women actually espouse feminist values or do feminist work. "What's the best way to keep young women away from something? To tell them it's ugly and uncool, and that boys won't like them if they do it," explained Valenti (interviewed in Barcella 2007: para. 9). Valenti's counterstrategy is to make feminism cool again (through a playful, ironic style, pop culture sensibility, a progressive vision, and incisive analysis of issues that matter to girls) and reframe antifeminism as "someone trying to pull the wool over young women's eyes, or get one over on them" (para. 9).

In this chapter, we have surveyed the arena of popular media, because the images and discourses that these media make available give girls easy access to representational systems and offer resources girls can use to negotiate their identities. At the same time, they are the backdrop against which their identity practices will be read as a source of public "concern." As we have seen, popular media—particularly commercialized culture—often work to reinscribe dominant discourses of girlhood and girl power, but also sometimes offer possibilities for alternative identities and transformative discourses. It is precisely these possibilities that interest us. As noted in Chapter One, however, we cannot simply read the social world off cultural texts about girlhood. The social power of discourse can only be found in the everyday practices that give life to "girlhood." In the remainder of *"Girl Power"*, we explore a number of questions that are raised by popular debate over what it means "to be a girl today." How do girls themselves participate in the struggle to define "girlhood"? What does "girl power" mean to "ordinary" girls in everyday settings? Has it opened new futures for girls in the way that many commentators claim? Which girls? Are girls today in control of "who they are" and "who they might become"? In order to answer these kinds of questions, we turn to interviews with actual girls. What might girls themselves contribute to public debate on the state of girlhood?

NOTES

1   Moreover, treating adult women as children justified arguments to exclude them from voting; women were seen to be "ignorant" of their political interests.

2   Walkerdine (1997) brings out class dimensions by noting, historically, how middle-class girls have been seen as in need of protection but working-class girls as a threat.

3   The widespread assumption that girls today are without politics is a corollary to the proposition that youth today are apathetic. Declining voting rates by youth are usually the evidence for this concern (for a discussion in the Canadian context, see Cook and Westheimer (2006: 354), citing research by Ottilia Chareka and Alan Sears). Youth cultural studies scholars, however, have stressed the importance of seeing youth participation in nontraditional ways (e.g., Harris 2001a and b). Although it is crucial to notice how youth are excluded and marginalized, it is also important to examine new or emerging forms of civic engagement. "Skate parks and related skateboarding activities serve as an important example of the way in which teenagers actively contribute to shaping their communities, whether this is seen positively or negatively" (Weller 2006: 567).

4   As shown in the remainder of *"Girl Power"*, this is not to say that these discourses in any way *determine* girls' understandings. On the contrary, we are interested in how girls actively resist or rewrite dominant discourses of girlhood; as in the case of conformity, these actions take meaning from available representations.

5   In her *New York Times* piece on Mean Girls, Margaret Talbot hung out with Rosalind Wiseman, author of *Queen Bees and Wannabes*, as she conducted her Empower Program sessions in various schools. Talbot began to worry that "maybe this [adult] attention to the details [of girls' friendships] can backfire, giving children the impression that the transient social anxieties and allegiances of middle

school are weightier and more immutable than they really are" (2002: para. 68). Ironically, this concern about casting the Mean Girl phenomenon in stone amounts to a single paragraph in an in-depth feature article for the *New York Times Magazine*, with the title "Girls Just Want to Be Mean."

6    This view obscures the rather obvious fact that all the school shootings in Canada and the USA to date have been carried out by boys.

7    A number of feminist academics have analyzed why and how poor, working-class, and racialized women have been positioned—against dominant ideals of white, bourgeois femininity—as sexually promiscuous. See, for example, Skeggs (1997), Walkerdine (1997), Kelly (2000: 44–45), and Jackson (2006).

8    Academics and journalists have been pointing with some concern to the over-programming of the children—boys and girls—of today's elites for a while now. In a piece for *The Atlantic*, writer David Brooks described "The Organization Kid," a group of elite college students growing up "in a world in which the counterculture and the mainstream culture have merged with, and co-opted, each other" (2001: 49). See also Alissa Quartz's book, *Hothouse Kids* (2006).

# 3

# DOING "GIRL POWER"

In Chapter Two, "girl" acts as a sign. Like other concepts in our study, "girlhood" is a discursive means of grasping a certain dynamic within processes that construct a social order (see Connell and Messerschmidt 2005). In other words, it is not meant to invoke a specific set of physical characteristics that in themselves define who is or is not "a girl." The result, as Aapola, Gonick, and Harris (2005: 3) have pointed out, is the challenge of how to write "about girls and girlhood when we are also trying to use an analysis which understands them as identities and cultural constructions which are not coherent, stable, and unchanging." Like Aapola and colleagues, "We struggle with how to talk about girls' lives when doing so creates the very exclusions we are attempting to redress." Thus, reference to "doing" girlhood and our use of performativity are reminders that "girl" is an embodied practice and that, once brought into existence, the sign "girl" functions as self-evident proof of girlhood's prior existence. The purpose of *"Girl Power"* is to explore how this comes about.

In Chapter Two, we have seen how popular culture signifies girlhood in increasingly complex ways. We purposefully highlighted how academics have participated—intentionally or otherwise—in normalizing girls' lives. This chapter reflects our awareness that this book, while written primarily for our colleagues and students of Girls' Studies, in all likelihood will contribute to public debate on the meaning of girl-hood and thus to the growing scrutiny of girls' private lives. Rather than become paralyzed by this recognition, we want to make our study accountable to our readers[1] by recounting not simply why, but how, we undertook *"Girl Power"*. Why should our account of girls' agency, for example, carry more weight than accounts that we criticize?

Recent years have seen a proliferation of academic books that allow us to "listen in" on the inner lives of girls.[2] Taking the form of autobi-ographical writing, academic surveys, and ethnographic interviews, much of this work emerged in response to research on the "silencing" of girls by what Pipher (1994) called a girl-poisoning culture (also see Gilligan 1982). By connecting this silencing to a drop in girls' self-esteem as they navigate puberty,[3] attempts to recover an "authentic voice" often enact feminist longing to recapture the innocence of girl-hood. This occurs when speaking "Selfhood" is mistaken for an "au-thentic" girlhood, illustrating the Foucauldian notion that regulation can take the form of not only repression but also an impulse to "tell" (Brumberg 2000). Recognizing this problem, a number of more recent scholars draw on poststructuralism to understand how girls are dis-cursively positioned to speak "as girls" (see Driscoll 2002; Cook and Kaiser 2004).

We have been inspired by this latter approach. We share Clegg's (2006) concern, however, that while poststructuralism has usefully drawn attention to discursively constituted possibilities for new sub-jectivities, it cannot account for the emergence of these possibilities. One result can be a "recipe" for political inertia (page 318) because there is no way of connecting discursively constructed subjectivities, hence agency, to the extra-discursive conditions of girls' existence. In challenging this tendency for cultural analysis to depoliticize femi-nism, Clegg (2006) employs a post-positivist "critical realism" (which we share).[4] At the ontological level critical realism maintains that the social world cannot be reduced to the conscious experience of the speaking Subject (page 316). While we may begin investigation from "inside" her experience, critical realism treats subjectivity (revealed to the researcher as "discourse") as a form of practical consciousness; "practical" in the Marxian sense that consciousness arises through the everyday activities of reconstituting the social world. Much of this ev-eryday activity is directed by processes beneath the level of ordinary consciousness. However immediately imperceptible, our everyday "mundane" activities are coordinated by interests that lie beyond each of us as individuals (also see Smith 1987). For example, we have already drawn attention to the commercialized interests driving much of girl power culture. While this culture may imply that power is "everywhere," we do not thus conclude that it is "nowhere." One goal of our work is to bring the operation of power into debates over the meaning of "girlhood" today.

One way that we do so is by treating discourse as a vehicle of power that mediates social interaction by facilitating embodied action. We accomplish such a task by considering not simply how discourses invite specific subjectivites, but also how they coordinate identity practices among girls as social actors. Such an approach directs attention away from individual Speakers to the context of their speaking; it enables us to think about agency as a collective as well as an individual process. While we do not claim to have resolved all the challenges that such an investigation necessarily faces, we do hope to inspire further research into the ways that power operates through discourses of Selfhood. In this spirit, we make our work accountable for the life it gives to a category that we at the same time find problematic: girlhood.

Our work has been inspired by Dorothy Smith's injunction[5] to begin inquiry from "where people are" in order to organize our inquiry around "what people do" rather than around established categories that mystify or distort our understanding of the social world. She contrasts this way of proceeding to conventional sociology, which she characterizes as "ideological." By "ideological," Smith (1980, 1999) does not refer simply to the way sociology has been written from the perspective of the powerful to serve the interests of those in power. Rather, it is a matter of how conventional discourse in sociology organizes the researcher's consciousness; people as agents of history disappear as the analyst looks for and sees "norms," "systems," "roles" and so forth. The analyst transforms the actualities of people's lives into a conceptual mode of ruling that:

*[margin annotation:* read Smith (text I have writing the social)*]*

> … involves a continual transcription of the local and particular activities of our lives into abstracted and generalized forms... The practice of ruling involves the ongoing representation of the local actualities of our worlds in the standardized and general forms of knowledge that enter them into the relations of ruling (1987: 3).

Similar to Smith, we begin inquiry from "where girls are" and "what girls do" as a social group whose lives are coordinated by conceptual practices of power. These practices employ frames of "intelligibility" (Hall 1973) such as those described in Chapter Two that construct "girl-hood" in specific ways while rendering vast areas of girls' lives unknowable. But to include girls' lives in sociology is not a matter of simply documenting girls' practices; to do so would reduce the researcher to a recorder. Rather, the goal of the analyst is to explicate the processes through which cultural understandings of girlhood work to shape girls' lives, but also how girls' lives are transformed into public "knowledge" about girlhood. This means that although our research begins in the local, immediate world of girls' lives in and around school in order to give girls a presence as actors and knowers, we do not remain in the local. Our task is to explicate not what girls do or know, but how their doing and knowing reconstitutes, at the same time that it is constituted by, social relations that operate prior to (and during) inquiry. These relations exist in the everyday "doing" that brings the gendered world into existence through the activities of embodied individuals.

 Following Smith (1999), we view the discourses that sustain girls' activities as an entry point into what she calls "relations of ruling": a complex of organized practices, including discourses, that interpenetrate multiple sites where power operates. For us, sites of operation include the school as a social institution. The reconstitution of social life through this site is never perfectly achieved, however. Attempts to formally classify and sort pupils according to an institutional mandate, for example, can incite struggle and resistance at the same time that it supports reconstitution of the social order. The same can be said for the reconstitution of gender.

In the final analysis, Smith's sociology inspired us because it helps us see how power operates through everyday rather than extraordinary practices. It draws attention to how venues, such as the public school but also the university, are implicated in the conceptual practices of ruling. Moreover, Smith encourages us to see how feminist researchers and girl advocates together might realize the promise of a sociology *for* women and girls rather than *about* women and girls. Such a sociology will show how the gendered world is an ongoing accomplishment sustained by the subordination of women. In doing so, it reappropriates the power of discourse in the service of feminism.

## THE RESEARCH DESIGN: RETHINKING OUR THINKING

*"Girl Power"* has roots in previous work by Dawn (Currie 1997, 1999, 2000) and Deirdre (Kelly 1993, 1997, 2000) on the social construction of girlhood. As educators, they were encouraged by the increased visibility of girls in both popular and academic discourse during the 1990s. They were troubled, however, by the way that feminism was taken up by much of this discourse. As noted in Chapter One, girl power culture began in feminist-inspired Riot Grrrl music as part of a broader movement of "consciousness raising." This movement inspired the production *by* girls of a politically subversive culture *for* girls (see Riordan 2001). Appropriated by commercial interests, however, girl power was extended to a range of products produced for—rather than by—girls. One result has been the expansion of what Goldmann (1992) calls "commodity feminism" through T-shirts with "girl power" slogans, for example (see Attwood 2007). In an effort to challenge this depoliticizing impulse, *"Girl Power"* came into being as a study intending to honor the voices of girls while troubling the regulatory impulse of various public interests—often fostered by academic writing—in girlhood. One point of intervention was debate concerning girls' "empowerment." Specifically, we questioned whether the empowerment of girls as celebrated in popular culture signals positive change in the everyday life of "regular" girls.[6]

In order to explore this kind of question, Dawn and Deirdre proposed a study that reflects the language and assumptions common in the academic discourse surrounding girlhood throughout the 1990s. The stated objective was to:

> ... contribute to our understanding of...socio-cultural processes which empower girls in their decision making ... In *"Girl Power"* "empowerment" refers to an experience of autonomy accompanied by sense of purpose. Empowerment is studied through analysis of respondents' narratives of decision making in areas that they identify as relevant. Ideally, empowerment contributes to self-esteem and good problem-solving skills, although the process of decision making rather than the outcome of decision making is the research problematic. Conversely, "disempowerment" refers to experiences of decision making characterized by a sense of loss of control. It contributes to difficulties in identifying and setting goals or solving everyday problems. Although focused upon individual decision making, the purpose of this study is to identify the socio-cultural rather than cognitive/affective aspects of decision making that surround the transition from puberty to womanhood. Thus the theoretical objective of *"Girl Power"* is a sociological understanding of agency, experienced through the construction of "Self" as a social project (1999; original proposal).

In retrospect, this initial thinking was heavily influenced by the kind of sociology that, in Smith's words, participates in the conceptual practices of power (see Smith 1990a). One obvious way in which this is evident is through identification with adult-oriented discourse about "the problems of girlhood." To be sure, this thinking was also influenced by conceptions of potential adjudicators and what the publicly funded granting council would deem as worthy of research. Given that Dawn and Deirdre never intended to contribute to the notion that adult feminists should or can "save" girls from girlhood, one of the most important early decisions was to rethink the general premises of the study[7] once it was funded.

Reshaping the study's objectives began through a series of exploratory focus group discussions[8] with young university women who shared retrospective accounts of their lives in secondary school. Their most vivid recollections concerned the dynamics that regulated their social lives at school, the meaning of membership in various social groups that characterized the school culture, and the impact that membership had on participants' sense of themselves as they struggled to understand: "Who am I? What can I do? And not do? How do I want to be seen by others? And who might I become?" These kinds of questions directed us to the kinds of "decisions" that typically escape adult attention so that the research was refocused toward informal systems of meaning making supported by school-based youth cultures. We refer to these cultures as "peer cultures." For the large part, they are formed around same-aged classmates. We view these cultures as *semiautonomous*: while youth creatively construct the meanings that they give to their social worlds, their meaning making is mediated by the belief systems, values and knowledge of extra-local culture expressed in adult talk, commercial culture, and scientific "wisdom" about adolescence.

This rethinking rendered the study much more exploratory and open ended. As described below, research proceeded through a series of stages. Focus group discussions were followed by exploratory interviews with girls twelve to sixteen years of age[9] that aimed to enhance our understanding of how everyday girls "do girlhood" at school.[10] These interviews helped us see how competing discourses of adolescent femininity play out as everyday "drama." The early interviews fleshed out the ways in which power operates through discourses that engage girls in actively constructing competitive hierarchies based on girls' subordination to boys. Given our interest in the ways that girls can creatively renegotiate meanings of "girlhood" and potentially resist femininities that reconstitute girls' subordination, we then intentionally recruited girls who talked about what we call "alternative" ways of doing girlhood.

By "alternative," we refer to femininities that do not follow the tenets of what Connell (1987) calls "emphasized femininity": an appearance-based femininity based on girls' preoccupation with gaining boys' approval and sexual interest. We found these alternative femininities in interviews with girls who consciously "went against" the competitive dynamics described in Chapter Four and some of the popularized images of girlhood discussed in Chapter Two. We also found them in interviews with girls who took up subject positions not historically available to girls; here we refer to girls who, despite resistance on the part of boys, encroached on male-dominated space by taking up skateboarding. These girls, whom we dubbed "Skater girls," interested us because they did not resignify girlhood simply as an identity category but also as a specific "embodiment" of femininity. Against a display-oriented femininity that requires girls to (appear to) be athletically inept, Skater girls transgressed normative definitions of not only what girls should look like but also what girls can do. They knowingly made "unfeminine" spectacles out of themselves as they straddled their skateboards, spread-eagle for balance. They braved ridicule and rejection by peers as well as the physical pain that accompanied learning to skate. Given the way that gendered definitions require specific forms of embodiment in order to "make sense" and to be accepted, we were also attracted to girls who used their "computer savvy" to "play" with their gendered identities online.

Reflecting the way that recruitment thus targeted specific groups of girls, our seventy-one participants resulted in three thematic clusters of interviews, each discussed in the following chapters. Shauna, a doctoral student in Educational Studies at the time of the fieldwork, was hired as our primary research "assistant."[11] Given her interest in girlhood/girl culture and her youthful demeanor, Shauna was ideal for the project; it soon became apparent that she would be integral to the entire research process, including data analysis and write-up.

Below we describe how Shauna recruited girls and carried out interviews. We follow a discussion of "fieldwork"[12] with an extended discussion of how we "worked over" transcripts. Like Gonick (2003:

9), we are interested in girls' articulation of the discursive structures that make "girlhood" viable as a lived social category. Thus we begin from the premise that girls' talk has the potential to give us access to the world as experienced by girls. The operative word here is "potential," however (see Hey 1997). In our work, we draw attention to the difference between "listening" to girls—as the fieldwork practice of interviewing—and subsequent claims about what we "heard" as presented in research write-up.[13] The transformation of "what girls say" into "what researchers claim they said" is a mediated process that too often remains unexamined. As Phillips and Jorgensen (2002: 153) remind us, while interviewing is the co-construction of meaning, write-up (usually) entails a one-sided reconstruction of meaning in research reports. The nature of our study did not allow us to collaborate with study participants on either data generation or analysis. In an attempt to make our findings accountable to readers, below we discuss in detail how our interviews, as "data," were reconstructed into "research findings."

## GENERATING DATA: LISTENING TO GIRLS

Between August 2001 and February 2003, Shauna recruited and interviewed most of the girls in *"Girl Power"*. During one phase of the project, another research assistant, Lori Macintosh, also conducted four interviews for the computer girl sample. Recruitment took place across the city of Vancouver as well as in outlying suburban areas.[14] Shauna began locating girls who were interested in participating in our study by attending community center activities such as "block parties" and dances. She set up booths at these events where girls could sign up to be interviewed about "what it is like to be a girl today." In exchange for their time, girls were offered movie passes to local cinemas. Community centers and smaller "neighborhood houses" across the city became central locations for meeting girls. Here Shauna approached youth workers first, who put her in touch with interested girls.

As the project progressed, Shauna worked to broaden the scope of recruitment in order to ensure that girls from middle-class, working-class, and working poor households were represented, as well as girls from a variety of races and ethnicities. As themes emerged from the data that furthered our interest in girls' agency, she worked to locate girls who were specifically "into" skateboarding and computers. She began to "hang out" at skate parks in the downtown area and posted flyers in coffee shops and Internet cafes. She also spoke to girls and their parents at malls and the Pacific National Exhibition (PNE). She asked teachers if they knew any girls who might want to be interviewed. Occasionally, Shauna saw girls walking down the street with skateboards and offered them *"Girl Power"* flyers to take home to discuss with their parents. On other occasions, she would meet parents of teenage girls while shopping or being out in the city and ask them if their daughters might be interested in being interviewed. Through these formal, informal, and ad hoc methods, the sample eventually grew to seventy-one girls.[15]

It was imperative that girls and their parents felt comfortable with the interview process, so girls were asked to choose a location for their interview. Most girls preferred rooms in community centers and neighborhood houses, or an empty classroom after school. Many girls invited Shauna to their homes, where she conducted interviews in living rooms, in kitchens, and on bedroom floors. Occasionally, she interviewed girls in coffee shops and mall food courts or outside at picnic tables. More often than not, girlfriends were interviewed in pairs, and on occasion as a trio. While some girls expressed nervousness before or during the interview, many noted after the fact that they enjoyed the experience of the interview. Several also commented that they had "learned" things about themselves in the process.

Shauna was thirty-one when she began interviewing girls for *"Girl Power"*, but she had a demeanor that caused others to see her as someone in her early to mid-twenties. As well, her keen interest in girls' culture and girls' style meant that she had easy rapport with most girls, who did not see Shauna as a disconnected adult who knew nothing about their interests. Often, her enthusiasm took discussion on tangents during interviews, adding to the spontaneity of girls' talk. After interviews, girls sometimes engaged her in discussions about her own style and familiarity with popular culture, particularly music and television. At the time, Shauna was an avid follower of *Buffy the Vampire Slayer* and *Gilmore Girls*, two shows that most of the girls watched to some degree. She also followed pop music and was familiar with Madonna, Avril Lavigne, Britney Spears, Christina Aguilera, Gwen Stefani, Lauryn Hill, and a number of pop-punk and rock bands that many girls mentioned.

But Shauna's youthful demeanor and love of girls' culture did not always make her job in the field easy. For example, Tori, a hardcore working-class skater, was skeptical of Shauna's interest in skater girls and agreed to do the interview only because her best friend, Priscilla, had asked her to. Tori let Shauna know right from the start that she was "unsure" about the interview process and wondered why Shauna wanted "to know these things" about girls. After the interview, Tori told Shauna that she needed to "see" her first, before she could decide if she wanted to do the interview. She admitted that Shauna did not "look like" what she had expected. Despite this "advantage," Shauna was careful to remind girls that she was a researcher from a university in order to avoid being seen as "one of them." As Stacey (1988) suggests, when researchers are too friendly or comfortable with research participants, it is easy to forget that the "tape recorder is always on." Shauna ensured that girls did not see the interview as "just a chat between friends" (see Cotterill 1992; Kirsch 1999).

Tori's skepticism helped Shauna to reflect on what it means to interview girls. While she enjoyed the rapport generated as a "girlie" looking adult, she was continuously confronted by her power as a researcher. Her questions to girls on occasion opened up sensitive issues that caused them to feel pain, sadness, or anger. These emotions were most often generated when discussing popularity, drawing attention to the way that some girls felt isolated or shunned at school. Her questions also opened up discussion around racism and how Chinese Canadian girls sometimes wanted to "act white" or how aboriginal girls were seen to be on the lowest rung on the social ladder in their school. Girls sometimes spoke of how boys treated them, harassed them, and made them feel inferior. Girls also sometimes spoke about their strained relationships to their parents. But these difficult conversations did not overshadow the fun girls had with their friends or the joy they experienced when flying down the street on a skateboard. Conversations were never dominated by any one thing, but instead roamed through aspects of girls' lives that they deemed to be important and meaningful to them. Shauna's power as interviewer was also not absolute, as girls challenged her to reframe questions and to clarify what she meant, for example by "feminism." Girls also brought up oblique references to sexuality as a topic that Dawn and Deirdre—for ethical reasons—had instructed Shauna to not initiate. Specifically, girls often referred to classmates as "sluts" and justified this labeling through graphic discussion of their purported sexual behavior. They also introduced terms not employed by adults, such as CBC (Canadian-Born Chinese), Banana (white on the inside, yellow on the outside), and FOB (Fresh off the Boat). Although "Shauna the adult" asked the questions, girls were treated as "experts" on their lives and on girl culture.

Shauna experienced both successes and failures in the field. When girls wanted to talk, interviews flew by at a rapid pace. Sometimes girls would offer much more than she had imagined, taking questions to their limit and pushing discussions to greater depths. Other times, when girls did not want to talk or became quiet as a result of some difficult topic or memory, the interviews were harder, and girls needed time to recover or regroup. At other times still, questions simply fell flat as a girl shrugged her shoulders with an "I dunno" and a sigh that indicated that Shauna needed to rethink what she was doing. But rather than treating these moments as "imperfect" interview experiences, Shauna used them to reflexively revise her approach. Questions thus shifted over the course of data generation. No matter what occurred during the interviews or what mistakes Shauna felt she had made, overall, girls astonished us with their profound insights, keen observations, and ability to articulate the complex realities of living life as a girl.

## RECONSTRUCTING DATA: ACCOUNTING FOR WHAT WE HEARD

As outlined in Chapter One, the task we set for ourselves is to understand girls' talk as a way to accomplish their social presence in particular contexts of interaction (including the context of our interviews; see Phillips and Jorgensen 2002). As we began to listen to our participants, new questions emerged: Why are specific girlhoods valued more than other ways of being girls among youth? How are these girlhoods different from, or similar to, those given value in adult-oriented culture? Why does "playing" with gender—as a potentially subversive activity celebrated by postmodern writers—risk social marginalization? These new questions are important because they moved research beyond description, from what girls said and what girls did to an exploration of how their actions work to reconstitute a social order. Here we found Gee's (2002) approach to discourse useful. He distinguishes between social languages employing referents that are recognized beyond the immediate context of their use and language-in-use or stretches of language that make up conversations or stories in a local context (page 17). While the latter can employ discourses that gain meaning within the broader social context, they do not necessarily do so. In keeping with our view of youth cultures as semiautonomous spheres of cultural production, our investigation interrogates the relationship between discourses generated by girls as they construct particular, local meaning in the context of everyday life and those generated through what Smith (1987) calls the extra-local relations of ruling. Thus our study of discourse helped us see how youth cultures are sites of creative production mediated by dominant culture.

In working specifically with discursive expressions of Selfhood, we faced two specific challenges. The first concerns the way that self-expression is mediated by available language. As noted by Smith (1990b), established languages and frames of reference that orchestrate everyday life have been authored by those allied with dominant institutions; when drawing on these languages and frames of reference, speakers outside the relations of ruling lack the symbolic forms, images, and concepts that capture their experiences of exclusion (1987: 58). Reflecting girls' marginal status as cultural producers, the language available for participants to speak with Shauna "as girls" often limited their ability to express what they were thinking and feeling. The second challenge arises from the first and concerns the unstable and contradictory nature of many of our participants' self-expressions. As noted by Scheurich (1995: 243), meaning is a "shifting carnival of ambiguous complexity, a moving feast of differences interrupting differences." This "wild profusion" leads him to conclude that:

> In an interview, there is no stable "reality" or "meaning" that can be represented. The indeterminant totality of the interview always exceeds or transgresses our attempts to capture and categorize. When we think we "interpret" what the meaning or meanings of an interview are, through various data reduction techniques, we are overlaying indeterminacy with determinacies of our meaning-making, replacing ambiguities with findings or constructions. ... we are misportraying what has occurred. (page 249)

While Scheurich does not then reject the value of interviewing for social research, he admonishes us, among other things, to foreground the open indeterminancy of the interview interaction itself in our write-up. Such foregrounding signals the analyst's recognition that "interview data" are the co-construction of unstable and context-specific meanings.

We agree with Scheurich that meaning always exceeds what has been recorded in any interview because, in principle, an infinite number of ways of understanding the same text are available[16] (see Gee 2002: 30-34). Statements that are produced within any specific domain tend to be similar and repetitive, however, due to the social character of discourse as communication. Along these lines we are interested in the rules (what Foucault calls "regimes") that determine what can be said as meaningful to other participants in that discourse. These rules work to delimit meaning. In understanding how discourse works in this way, we can understand, in part, how power works through discourse.

In short, when working with interviews as "discourse" rather than representational "data" that can be sorted and classified through conventional ways of working as sociologists, we are faced with the paradox that language limits what can be spoken, but at the same time opens what was said to the indeterminancy of meaning. This paradox does not lead us to reject the belief that interview data can tell us something "factual"[17] about the lives of our participants. We recognize that girls' claims about "what happened" at school or reports of what they said or did or felt are mediated descriptions of their experiences, but we treat them as more or less accurate. Treating them as fictional — whether in the sense of nonfactual or of being socially constructed as "real" — would silence girls by implying that only academics can make sense of the world (see Alvesson and Skoldberg 2000; also Hames-Garcia 2000; Moya 2001). Thus we take girls' representations of their lives at school at face value. These representations directed us to the puzzles we need to solve in order to understand how power works through language and discourse. The real challenge lies in recognition that our research has the potential to "normalize" girls' experiences by "trapping" their experiences within the categories and meanings of academic discourse that wants to "fix" meaning. Because we do not want to exhaust the possibilities for girlhood in this way, we treat our own text as we do our interview texts — for what *"Girl Power"* accomplishes in our understanding rather than as offering an "authentic" representation of girlhood. In other words, we do not want the reader to look for — and find — a girlhood that was waiting to be "discovered" by our research.

Although aware of the complexity and instability of meaning, we are wary of a position that argues for the necessary failure of representation.[18] However theoretically troublesome, this book is made possible by treating subjectivity and agency as "something" that can be recognized and analyzed by researcher(s) and their readers. Within this context our goal is not to attribute these constructs to an authentic Subject who exists "beyond" our text, but rather to draw attention to what our manner of thinking and speaking about girlhood opens to interrogation. In this spirit, the remainder of this chapter describes how we worked over our transcripts as the basis for claims about what we "heard" in girls' talk.

## THINGS THAT CANNOT BE SAID: THE LIMITS OF LANGUAGE

While a number of writers have drawn attention to the gendered nature of language as limiting women's talk (Spender 1980), in our work the language and discourses available to girls are not framed by the subjectivities of only male speakers, but also of adults. Despite the fact that Grover (girls selected their own pseudonyms), for example, was among the more articulate girls in our study, she complained that "Sometimes there is something that you just can't describe." She tried to explain this feeling to Shauna:

Grover: It's even like a noise. Like there is just certain—you know, when you have a color. Like a really soft kind of purple or something and you know, you can't really describe it all the time. So you just use the [tapping sound] 'cause like that kind of, just kind of, you know—

Shauna: You use noises to describe something?

Grover: Well just that one noise describes that color, that certain shade. It's just kind of like—

Shauna: ... Why not just use words available to you?

Grover: Because they don't seem to suit it right.

Grover was not alone in her struggle to find words that could adequately capture how she felt. Near the end of her interview, Pete explained: "I notice it's been very hard to like describe all that I'm feeling about this stuff. And it just seems to be like another answer is how I feel. But it's—I don't know. In our heads we are thinking it and we're like 'It doesn't make sense' and then we say it, and we're like 'Oh!' [surprised at our answers]."

Despite the limits of language, as Cimitele (2002: 278) points out, to be without a language does not mean to be without a voice. Rather, it means that the analyst must learn to hear what cannot be said. Engaged in this kind of learning in her research with adult women, DeVault (1999) found that women who wanted to talk about their lives very often had to "translate" their words, "saying things that are not quite right, or working at using language in nonstandard ways." By drawing attention to this problem, her work reminds us that features of girls' manner of talking should not be seen as deficiencies in linguistic skill, but rather "as adaptive responses to constraints on their speech" (page 61).

Within this context it is less surprising that the girls we designated as "empowered" often struggled with the difficulty, if not impossibility, of representing their feelings. We needed a method for listening "beyond and around" girls' words, paying particular attention to confusing rather than "obvious" meanings in interview transcripts. Like DeVault, we heard girls' expressions of self-doubt as signals of feeling and thinking in ways that fall outside available modes of expression. When Sara, for example, declared "I don't know if I'm saying that right," we did not hear her as expressing a desire to "please" Shauna, as conventional interview textbooks might advise.[19] Rather, we heard Sara's expression of self-doubt as a lack of faith in available systems of representation. It became important, therefore, to listen to girls' hesitations, gaps and contradictions in order to hear what they might tell us about girls' lives "outside" established ways of adult talking. However "awkward," preserving the "presence" of girls' subjectivities requires us to attempt to make visible what they found difficult to articulate.[20] For this reason, we are attracted to postmodern deconstruction because it draws attention to what makes girls' speaking possible, rather than to claim "authentic" meaning for their words.

"Deconstructive listening" encourages us to hear the unspoken discourses that make certain ways of thinking and speaking available, and other ways more difficult, if not impossible. It therefore helps us to hear the regulatory function of discourse. Let us take a closer look at the uncertainty expressed by Sara. It came during a point in the interview when Shauna asked her if there are any "expectations" associated with being a girl:

> It has a lot to do with how you act, and how you dress, and how you look. And guys have expectations and girls have expectations. And, you know, cracking up to what they want you to be, it's tough. Because guys expect you to look gorgeous, look the way they want, and act the way—act the way they want you to act. And girls want you to act the way they want you to act. I don't know if I'm saying that right.

On the surface, it may appear that Sara was struggling to please Shauna, by constructing the "right" picture for the "university research-er"—"I don't know if I'm saying that right." What we heard, however, is Sara's struggle to express her experience of how femininity is policed by girls as well as boys. Sara had little difficulty expressing the opinion that guys "expect you to look gorgeous, look the way they want, and act the way they want you to act" because it is "common knowledge" that femininity is a display for male visual pleasure. In contrast to the clarity in which she is able to describe boys' sense of entitlement to femininity as male-centered, Sara makes the somewhat ambiguous statement that girls "want you to act the way they want you to act." Because Sara lacks a frame of reference linking boys' sense of entitlement to the heteronormativity of patriarchy, she lacks the language to understand the role that girls often play in sustaining male privilege. Sara recognizes the double standard governing femininity, but is uncertain how to express it. Her statement thus illustrates how hidden but active processes can monitor girls' talk, giving them access to some meanings while denying or limiting access to other possibilities. In Chapter Four we see the consequences of this "policing."

## THE CONTRADICTORY NATURE OF GIRLS' TALK

A central task of our data analysis was to identify the discourses through which girls accomplished a specific social action, that of constructing a Selfhood. While this initially struck us as a straightforward task, it was much more complicated when we encountered contradictions in girls' constructions of themselves and their place in the social world (for a fuller discussion see Currie, Kelly and Pomerantz 2007). The challenge is illustrated in the following exchange with GG and Vikki. Within the context of their interview, Shauna (deliberately) positioned the two girls as "powerful" in order to hear how the girls would take up this positioning:

| | |
|---|---|
| Shauna: | Speaking of "girl power," how do you get power at school? |
| GG: | As girls? |
| Shauna: | Yeah. What is it like? |
| GG: | With the guys, you just have to show that you are tough and not the little sissy that they think you are. A lot of guys, like they think you are like this little innocent girl. They're wrapped around you, like "I will protect you." All macho man. ... But that's not what we're all about. I mean, we can defend ourselves! |
| Vicki: | You have to be like one of those outgoing controlling people who like, knows what to do in every situation. |
| GG: | Or everyone is going to treat you like some sissy who needs to be defended all the time, which is not so true. Girls can defend themselves. |

So far in this exchange, GG and Vikki have constructed two mutually exclusive Subject positions for girls: the "little innocent girl" who needs male protection versus the girl who can "defend herself" and who can control any situation. At first GG ridicules the innocent girl by describing her as a "*little* girl" and by calling her a "sissy." GG and Vikki reject this identity category and affiliate themselves instead with "girls who can defend themselves." It therefore is interesting to listen to the continuation of this exchange:

| | |
|---|---|
| Shauna: | And we're talking not physical, we're talking— |
| GG: | Oh no. Even verbally or mentally or emotionally. Like we can defend ourselves in all of those categories. We don't need some macho man to stand up for us. I mean, it's so cool when a guy does, but ... I like it when a guy—I think it's so cool when a guy is like "Don't mess with my girl" sort of thing. ... You know that the guy cares for you, obviously. Right? And when he stands up to one of his buddies and says "Hey. Don't mess with my girl" like that's pretty good. Like he is actually going against one of his really good friends for you and that's gotta mean a lot. |

Neither GG nor Vikki saw this subsequent positioning as perhaps contradictory to one where girls are "in control" and "can defend themselves." In order to understand the basis for their reasoning, Shauna asked GG whether or not it has ever happened to her, that a guy "stood up" for her. At this point GG confessed, "No. Only in the movies." What her response tells us is that even though GG and Vikki consciously positioned themselves in a feminist-oriented identity of girls who can defend themselves and who do not need boys to protect them, the ambivalence resulting from attraction to the notion of romantic love undermined this affiliation. The specter of a boy protecting "his" girl does not simply undermine GG's construction of herself as a girl who can "defend herself"; it engages GG in a discourse that historically has offered cultural support for male violence.

This kind of "reasoning" was not limited to GG and Vikki; we heard it in other interviews. Contradiction draws attention to the way that girls must navigate between competing discourses, each offering a unique "way of being" and yet together limiting girls' self-expression. Thus, contradiction is not treated as ambiguity or confusion on the part of the speaker. Because it testifies to the open-endedness of meaning making, it opened our interview transcripts to the study of girls' discursive agency. As noted by Foucault (1990), competing discourses within any field form a system of stabilizing strategies and disorienting elements that can produce variant effects:

> To be precise, we must not imagine a world of discourse divided between the dominant discourse and the dominated one; but as a multiplicity of discursive elements that can come into play in various strategies. ... Discourses are not once and for all subservient to power or raised up against it, any more than silences are. We must make allowance for the complex and unstable process whereby discourse can be both an instrument and an effect of power, but also a hindrance, a stumbling-block, a point of resistance and a starting point for an opposing strategy. (page 100)

Because a speaker seldom positions herself simply "inside" or "against" any available discourse, Foucault referred to the "tactical polyvalence" of discourse:

> Discourses are tactical elements or blocks operating in the field of force relations; there can exist different and even contradictory discourses within the same strategy; they can, on the contrary, circulate without changing their form from one strategy to another, opposing strategy. (page 102)

The point is that we cannot know in advance how any specific speaker will take up available discourses and what the effect of her positioning may be.

It interested us that the theoretical indeterminacy of meaning does not result in an "undoing" of the Subject (see Currie 1999); despite the complexity of working through available systems of meaning-making, as speakers the girls in our study sustained coherent and unique Selfhoods (see our "List of Participants"). This coherence required the "work" of assembling discursive elements according to context-specific logic. This logic is provided, in part, by what we dubbed "trump discourses." A trump discourse is the overriding discourse that imparts context-specific coherence to a speaker's statements, no matter how contradictory her statements may seem to the researcher. In the context of contradictory meanings, a trump discourse operates to anchor meaning. Because it operates as "common sense" to the speaker, it is more often than not "latent" in girls' talk; that is, it remains unspoken. One goal of our analysis is to bring these foundational discourses into view. In the following chapters we will see that a trump discourse often draws meaning from adult cultural practices; these discourses thus testify to the mediated nature of youth culture. At the same time, young people often talk in ways that adults may not understand,[21] indicating how trump discourses can "come from below." Identifying these discourses helps us to see how power works, as both a "negative" and "positive" force in girls' constructions of Selfhood. By positive we refer to opportunities for girls to refashion girlhood. Importantly, trump discourses cannot be identified as a theoretical exercise because they are context-specific; they reveal themselves in the talk and everyday, "mundane" activities of actual girls.

The analytical significance of trump discourses is illustrated in Shauna's interview with Jordan, a member of the "popular" clique[22] at her large middle-class school. In describing her group, Jordan claimed "if you're nice to us, if you respect us, we'll respect you":

Jordan:   We [friends] treat like other people like as if, like how we would want to be treated. Like we don't go around, like being—like pushing people like down—
Shauna:   Right.
Jordan:   No we don't.
Shauna:   OK.
Jordan:   We've done that a couple of times but—
Shauna:   You've pushed people down?
Jordan:   Yeah, just like Grade 9 girls.

As we will see in the next chapter, "popular" kids are the most powerful peers at school and have reputations for being "mean." In her interview Jordan distanced herself from this identity of being mean, justifying her action—pushing other kids around, something she had already labeled as "not nice"—by telling Shauna that the Grade 9 girls were sleeping with their boyfriends. Jordan smoothed over the contradictory description of her group as "nice" because "they don't push other kids around," by positioning the girls whom they had pushed as "sluts."

Although meanness violates the socially valued "nice girl," we will see in Chapter Four how "slut" is used as a regulatory label: powerful girls employed this label to position girls they did not like. This use of "slut" enabled socially powerful girls—labeled by their peers as "popular"—to claim agency but to "denounce it" in others (see Fine 1988; Tolman and Higgins 1994; Kitzinger 1995; Tanenbaum 1999/2000; White 2002). In the above example, a discourse condemning girls' sexual agency acts as a "trump" discourse, allowing Jordan to claim the tenets of middle-class "niceness"—they "treat other people like how we would want to be treated"—by erasing evidence to the contrary—as "sluts," Grade 9 girls do not fall into the category of people who deserve to be treated in that way. Jordan can make contradictory claims without consciously "lying" to Shauna, because the discourse she draws on to arrive at this claim operates to her as "common sense." Her contradictory statements thus tell us something, but not about the speaker as much as the social context of her everyday life "as a girl." The contradiction in this interview excerpt is a "symptom" of something analytically significant beyond the immediacy of Jordan's talk (see Currie 1999: 110–11). In the following chapter we will see how Jordan's description of the Grade 8 and 9 girls—whether "truthful" or not—is organized by discourses we identified in Chapter Two.

In summary, contradiction draws attention to the way that "becoming" results from struggle with various available and competing ways of being (Brown 1998: 106). It acknowledges the doubleness of discourse as a process that arranges us in particular ways, but also enables us to arrange ourselves. Rather than smooth over inconsistencies, contradictions, or gaps in girls' stories in order to tell a coherent story, moments of rupture are read as symptoms of unspoken but socially powerful discourses that shape girls' understandings of girlhood. Our goal is to hear the trump discourses that enabled our participants to negotiate competing and contradictory discourses of girlhood in order to talk coherently "as girls." Hearing these discourses is not to say that girls simply "parrot" available discourse (see Brown 1998: 105).[23] On the contrary, it is to recognize the complexity of the language work through which girls (often) struggle to control their sense of "who they are" and, following from this, their place in the social order.

## "GIRL POWER", OUR BOOK

As noted in Chapter Two, "girlhood" is not an "innocent" state of being that comes into existence "naturally," as female children grow to womanhood. Rather, girlhood is a historically- and culturally-specific identity, therefore burdened with societal expectations that shape how a girl may think of both herself and her female peers (see Scott 1991). These expectations take many forms, implicit in competing discourses about girlhood. In the chapters that follow we lay out the various ways that girls in our study took up, refused, or transformed these available discourses of girlhood. This is not to imply that these discourses "determined" girls' performances; rather, it is to recognize that no matter how personal gendered identities may feel—because they convey "who we are"—girlhood is accomplished through social interaction with others.

Our first data chapter, Chapter Four, explores the dynamics of normative girlhood through what Connell (1987) calls an "emphasized femininity." Within school-based peer cultures, such a femininity positioned girls according to their looks and their ability to attract boys' attention. Here we see how "popular" girls gained and exercised power through performances of heterosexuality that drew on—without naming—the sexual double standard. We follow this chapter with a discussion of girls who consciously rejected this way of doing girlhood through skateboarding. As a way of doing girlhood, skateboarding challenged not only the tenets of femininity, but also those of masculinity. It shows how girlhood cannot be separated from girls' sexed bodies. We therefore follow this chapter with an exploration of interviews with girls who used their computers to "do gender" in the disembodied context of cyberspace. This exploration is based on interviews with girls who played with their gendered identity online.

While these data chapters are organized around distinct ways of doing girlhood, our analytical interest concerns the kinds of discourses that sustained our participants' doing and what these discourses tell us about the gendered operation of power. Chapter Seven discusses girls who demonstrated relationships to the identity categories of girlhood that were much more complex than the first three data chapters may imply. Specifically, we explore how some girls were able to consciously position themselves "in-between" peer groups, taking advantage of fissures and contradictions in and among various discourses. From inter-views with these girls, we see the way that power can operate "from below." In other words, we do not see resistant forms of girlhood as, simply, adoption of alternative "lifestyles" or cultural practices, but as actively challenging dominant constructions from the everyday contexts where girls are. Given our interest in facilitating girls' abil-ity to do girlhood in this way, we explore girls' relation to feminism as a discourse that has the potential to challenge girls' subordination by enlarging available meaning making for girls. Chapter Eight brings analytical conclusions of *"Girl Power"* together, contrasting personal power that enables individual transgression to social transformation through collective action. In keeping with our commitment—as femi-nists and as teachers—to scholarship that matters, Chapter Nine con-siders the implications of our study for future research and for teaching girls as agents of their destinies. However coherent we have been able to make the following story from our data, we recognize that research is always partial, always ongoing. We thus would never claim to offer a (new) "truth" of girlhood; rather what we hope to offer is a new way of thinking about girls' subjectivities, agency and empowerment.

NOTES

1   Hoping that many of these readers will be young women who participated in our study.

2   For voice books on adolescent girls see, for example, *We're Here, Listen: A Survey of Young Women*, by Canadian Advisory Council on the Status of Women; *Raising their Voices: The Politics of Girls' Anger*, by Brown; *Giving Youth a Voice: A Basis for Rethinking Adolescent Violence*, by Barron; *Voices of a New Generation: A Feminist Anthology*, by Weir and Faulkner; *Turbo Chicks: Talking Young Feminisms* by Mitchell, Bryn Rundle and Karaian. We acknowledge the importance of voice books for politicizing, among other things, racism and able-ism within the women's movement.

3   Kling, Hyde, Showers and Buswell (1999) report that the largest gender differences in self-esteem are found in late adolescence, or high school; these authors claim that these differences are not enough to suggest that problems of self-esteem are rooted in gender.

4   Clegg (2006: 316) does not suggest "that poststructuralism and critical realism are compatible at a philosophical level." Rather, she "does put to rest the myth that there is no alternative to poststructuralism except a reversion to a crude version of the unified rational subject, which poststructuralism has so ably deconstructed."

5   Following Karl Marx.

6   We use the term "regular" to counteract the tendency for researchers to focus on girls who are more likely to gain media attention—White girls acting in ways that violate middle-class expectations, working-class girls "in conflict" with social service workers, racialized girls from immigrant families, pregnant schoolgirls and so on.

7   It is perhaps significant that the original proposal, which adopts conventional social scientific thinking, was funded.

8    Three focus group discussions were carried out with six university women aged 18 and 19. Three of these participants were White European Canadian, one was Chinese Canadian, one Iranian Canadian and one was Indo Canadian. While the first session took the form of "mediated" discussion based on a painstakingly prepared schedule of topics, two subsequent sessions moved into a more open, participatory mode of discussion stimulated by video clips of popular television shows portraying the social life of high school students and by small group work. While focus group discussions helped us prepare for fieldwork, it took only three sessions to recognize that retrospective accounts would not be as fruitful as we had anticipated. Of course, we also recognized that women attending university are significantly different from the girls we hoped to recruit into the study.

9    A number of commentators question the meaningfulness of age as a social marker (see Wallace and Kovacheva 1995 and Wyn and White 1997). For us, the salience of age comes from recognition that dominant institutions, including those associated with medicine, law and education, are sites of age-specific discourses that stipulate what is "normal," what is "allowed" and what is "appropriate" for individuals of specific ages.

10   As the focus of the study became the everyday dramas that dominate girls' lives at school, the educational activities of the school and the girls' relationships with teachers are (simply) a "backdrop" for the research (see Ortner 2002). Of course, we recognize that the school, as an institutional context of girls' everyday lives, places restrictions on the identities that youth can perform, through dress codes for example. We consider the importance of the school as a regulatory institution in more detail in Chapter Nine.

11   Here we point out that the institutional context of the research placed restrictions on how the research might be carried out (for example, a participatory ethnography by Dawn and Deirdre would not be possible) and what kinds of topics might be discussed (for example, Dawn and Deirdre would not expect student assistants to competently and ethically negotiate sensitive topics concerning

sexuality, for example). We also thank our other student assistants, especially: Aftab Erfan, Lori MacIntosh, Abby Wener Herlin and Caroline White.

12    We use this term even though we reject the way that it implies a social world "out there," inhabited by people who become "curiosities" for the researcher.

13    We are reversing the everyday sense that "hearing" is the passive act of registering sounds, while "listening" is the active process of attending to meaning. For researchers, interviewing typically entails listening to participants and later "working over" transcripts in order to represent what participants "really" had to say, what the researcher "heard." We do not mean to imply that listening by researchers is always passive—see DeVault (1999) Chapter Four, for example.

14    Vancouver is a coastal city and major seaport located in the Lower Mainland of southwestern British Columbia, Canada. According to the 2006 census, the greater metropolitan area of Vancouver had a population of 2,116,581, while the city itself had a population of 578,041. In the city proper, 16% of families were lone-parent families (most of those, 81.5%, were female lone-parent families) (Statistics Canada 2007). While regularly voted one of the world's most livable cities, Vancouver is also home to Canada's poorest neighborhood, the Downtown Eastside, which in the past decade has had the highest HIV infection rate among injection drug users in the Western world. Poverty and addiction levels are particularly high among Aboriginal people, who face discrimination as well as cultural challenges transitioning to urban life. Vancouver is one of North America's most expensive cities, with an extremely tight rental market. The challenge young people face finding affordable housing is the subject of much media and political discussion.

The economy of the surrounding province is still largely resource-based (mining, forestry, oil and gas, and fishing); Vancouver, however, acts as an executive city for those industries. It also is a center for film production, new media (e.g., video game development), and tourism. Simon Fraser University professor Paul

Delany describes Vancouver as a prime example of the postmodern city, "a place where different semiotic systems are juxtaposed, instead of a place where culture unfolds or accumulates through time" (Delany 1994).

In 2006, half of the population had a mother tongue other than English or French; 8% did not have knowledge of either or both official languages (English and French). About one-third (32%) spoke a language other than English or French most often at home. Just over half (51.2%) of Vancouver's population was Canadian citizens by birth; the rest were immigrants to Canada or non-permanent residents. The city is racially diverse: 51.0% of the population was categorized as "visible minorities" (which the *Employment Equity Act* defines as "persons, other than Aboriginal peoples, who are non-Caucasian in race or nonwhite in colour")—what we prefer to describe as "racialized" persons. Of racialized persons, 58% were Chinese, 11% South Asian, 10% Filipino, 5% Southeast Asian, 3% Japanese, 3% Korean, 2.8% Latin American, 2.5% "multiple visible minority," 1.8% West Asian (e.g., Iranian), 1.8% Black, 0.6% Arab, and 0.3% "visible minority not included elsewhere" (Statistics Canada 2007).

15   Participants ranged in age from 12 to 16 years. At the time of their first interview, four girls were 12 years of age, 16 were aged 13, 28 were aged 14, 18 were aged 15, and 5 were aged 16. Based on information the girls provided about their parents' occupations and educational backgrounds, 7 girls came from upper-middle-class families, 36 from middle-class families, and 28 from working-class families. The sample was racially diverse, reflecting the demographics of the Vancouver area: 41 were White (European ancestry), 18 Asian-Canadian (with ancestry primarily from China, but also the Philippines, Korea and Bangladesh), 5 were of mixed racialized identities, 4 were Aboriginal (including 3 Metis, that is, of Aboriginal and European ancestry), 2 were from Iran, and 1 participant was Latina. Seven of the girls were born outside Canada, 12 had parents born outside Canada, and 11 spoke English as an additional language. Three girls identified as bisexual, and the rest implied or stated that they were heterosexual. Sixty-nine of the girls had never left school, while 2 girls had been out

of school for one year and were one grade "behind" as a result. Collectively, they attended 20 different secondary schools and 3 elementary schools (23 girls were in schools located in upper-middle class neighborhoods, 16 in schools located in middle-class or mixed neighborhoods, 23 in schools in working-class neighborhoods, 7 girls attended a private girls' school, and two attended a Catholic school.) Fifty-five girls lived in Vancouver, and 16 lived in small towns, cities, or suburban areas outside of Vancouver.

16  The problem goes beyond the limits of language and discourse co-constructed during interviews. There is also the problem that a transcript is not a neutral, straightforward rendition of words on a tape. See Potter (1996).

17  By "factual" we refer to claims about "what happened" and reports about what any participant did.

18  We are not able to fully articulate our critique of this kind of thinking; suffice it to say that while we treat language-in-use as constitutive of the social world, we do not treat it as determinative. One problem with the rejection of a reasoning, knowing Subject is that this rejection defies the everyday practices of the academic (Alvesson and Skoldberg 2000).

19  This is not to say that we cannot claim that this did not arise in interviews with Shauna.

20  We recognize that this way of working allows us to insert ourselves into the text.

21  On this point we also note that slang often comes from pop culture, especially commercialized culture aimed at young people. Producers of this culture knowingly include antiestablishment or antiauthoritarian messages (including the so-called 'cool hunters'). Here it is important to note that youthful opposition to adult authority has often been coded as masculine (for example, the underachieving Bart Simpson) and conformity (such as to school) as feminine (for example, Bart's overachieving sister, Lisa).

22   In Chapter Four we elaborate our use of the term "popular"; it does not always refer to kids who are well-liked by their peers.

23   Drawing on Bakhtin, Brown (1998: 105) maintains that girls learn to ventriloquate, a process "whereby one voice speaks through another voice or voice type."

# 4

# "THE POWER TO SQUASH PEOPLE"

### POPULAR GIRLS[1]

Falling between the institutional contexts of school and family life, youth culture is what Bettis and Adams (2005: 6) call a "liminal" space: the "betwixt and between" place, out of constant adult surveillance, where adolescents carry out important identity work. These places include the school lunchrooms, hallways, parks and malls where young people "hang out." Within the "freedom" offered by this space, young people creatively negotiate among themselves "who they are" and "where" they fit into the social world.[2] Their self-expressions of identity, however, cannot be read as freely chosen ways of being. Whether amusing, puzzling, or worrisome to adults, the identity labels that characterize youth culture have consequences for participants and are therefore important to study if we are to understand the identity practices of young people.

While identity labels are employed to signal Selfhood, they also regulate peer groupings (see Ortner 2002; Milner 2004). This organizing property of identity labels is important, because, in the words of Emily, "most people don't define us for who we are, but for who we hang out with." Girls typically treated the categories that thus defined them as "common sense":

> Everyone has their own clique. Uhm, it seems to be that a lot of the Caucasian people are in their own group and normally, all the—uhm, different races would be in their own group. Such as all the Japanese [sit] together, all the Chinese together, all the Koreans together. Basically, it has always been that way (Mia).

By "common sense," we refer to the way that Mia—herself half white and half Chinese—went on to explain that kids are simply "more comfortable" when they speak "their own" language. It also helped construct a status hierarchy based on command of English. One expression of this hierarchy was the way in which non-Caucasian kids distanced themselves from new immigrants as "Hongers" (recent immigrants from Hong Kong) or FOBs (immigrants "fresh off the boat"—see Pyke and Dang 2003).

These kinds of dynamics enabled white students like Amanda to deflect racialized segregation back onto marginalized groups: "[the ESL kids] don't really talk much, and they have their own little group. They like don't speak English and stuff, so then they can't of course communicate with other groups. So then they just stick with their own kind." What we hear in this kind of talk is the way that language, when taken for granted as the context of everyday life, can render socially and culturally determined constructions a "natural" feature of everyday life. In the above examples, it operates to mask racialized segregation of the informal spaces of the school. In this chapter, we explore how the language employed by girls during their interviews works to naturalize the gendered dynamics of peer interaction.

Our entry point into girls' social worlds was a seemingly "innocent" label that was prominent in girls' talk: "popularity." Being identified as a member of the popular crowd was desirable to many girls because, according to Vikki, the popular crowd consists of "cool kids." As explained by GG, if you're not popular, "You're just one of those *other* people." Given the significance of these dynamics for girls' social lives at school, our initial attention was directed to the ways that "popular" girls perform girlhood. While historically boys have been expected to perform masculinity through competitive activities such as athletics (see Askew and Ross 1988; Eder and Kinney 1995; Gilbert and Gilbert 1998), femininity has been associated with competence in social relationships. Feminists have contended that girls tend to avoid the kind of conflict that might arise in competitive contexts and behave in ways that preserve relationships (see Gilligan, Ward, and Taylor 1988; Gilligan, Lyons, and Hanmer 1990; Brown and Gilligan 1992). It would be reasonable to assume, therefore, that being popular plays an important role in the social lives of girls.

The high status of students designated as "popular" by their peers is a consistent finding in adolescent research (see Eder 1995; Merten 1997; Simmons 2002; White 2002; Milner 2004) and in our study cut across racialized groups. As in this previous research, girls in our study distinguished between two meanings of *popular*. For example, Vikki explained, "There's the sort of popular people, but they're not—they're not like *not* popular, but they're not *popular*. And then there's the popular people who like go out, and they *do* stuff." Erin differentiated between "good popularity"—being liked by classmates based on getting along with others—and "bad popularity." She defined the latter by referring to girls who manipulated others: "Like, 'If you're not nice to me...' or '[If] You don't do this for me, then,' you know, 'I will do this.' 'I'm going to crush you like a bug.'" As seen here, the two meanings of "popularity" are actually at odds. On the one hand, girls employed popularity to signal being well liked by peers, similar to how adults might use the term to denote middle-class "niceness." On the other hand, popularity also designated kids who are not necessarily liked by their peers but are considered "cool" because they "go out and *do* stuff" (see Duncan 2004).

In this chapter, we explore the latter category, signaled in our narrative by capitalizing the "p" of "Popular."[3] Because Popular girls were described as the "girls with power," it seemed to us that understanding their power among peers would help us locate girls' agency in its sociocultural context. As we shall see, Popular girls embodied the tenets of idealized femininity and, as a consequence, they symbolize a way of doing girlhood that is socially rewarded by (adult) teachers as well as peers (see Bettis, Jordan, and Montgomery 2005: 71). Subsequent chapters show that whether aspiring to be Popular or "something else," the idealized femininity embodied by Popular girls was a point of reference for girls' gendered performances. In this sense, discourses that sustain Popularity for girls are "productive" because they not only shape the way many girls "do gender," but also how the gendered performances of all girls are read by others. Their power lies in the way that they make seemingly innocent categories of girls' talk actionable.

As already hinted at above, the power of Popular girls did not always operate as a positive force. Like many other participants, Beverly,
of Chinese-Canadian heritage, complained that Popular girls initiated
much of the teasing at her school. This teasing was directed toward
"unpopular" kids:[4]

> But, you know, the Popular kids, they're *popular* and all that. So they like to
> make fun of unpopular people because they dress weird or they can't talk, you
> know. If you're from Hong Kong. Somewhere like that. You have an accent.[5]

Despite the racism that we heard in this excerpt, conflict surrounding
Popularity was given more significance by our participants. For example, while Jordan—a middle-class white girl who was among the Populars at her large urban school—described racialized dynamics among
the boys at her school, she discounted these dynamics among girls.
"The girls—it's more like—It's not really race. The groups, it's more like
popularity. Like the Popular girls are in a group and then there's like
'the others.'" The girls drew Shauna's attention to subtle differences
between various Popular cliques, which seemed to hinge on what was
accepted as appropriate display of skin:

> The typical white group I see at school would have their pants all the way
> down to almost where you could see their underwear or lower. They like to
> wear the furry hooded jackets, tight light blue jeans and also, I'm guessing they
> are called skater shoes. That is fairly different from the Asian group because
> the Asian group does not like to show their belly that much. They also wear the
> hooded jackets with fur, but their shoes are different. The Asians would go for
> the Nike Shocks instead of skater shoes (Xiu cited in Pomerantz 2008: 94).

As shown here, it is not a matter of simply *what* to wear, but of *how* to wear
the right clothes. Pomerantz (2008) explores the meanings of these kinds
of differences among peer-based school groups. Reflecting the importance of exactly how much sexualized display is appropriate, in her study,
white girls were viewed by some Asian girls as "trashy" for wearing their
pants "all the way *down!*" while Asian girls were viewed by some white
girls as "hoochies" who wore their pants too "tight" (pages 94–95).

Christine and Kate tried to explain to Shauna why girls designated as "cool Populars" were not necessarily liked by their classmates:
"There's so much gossiping and like backstabbing, whatever. You
know, people don't like people. Then those people who aren't liked
don't even know it... They [Popular kids] look down on them as if

they're not worthy of walking past them, or whatever. It's just like 'Eew.'" Vikki accused them of being "backstabbers":

> I don't like the way they lead you on. You know what I mean—like a boy does. Sometimes you think that they like you, and then in the end they don't like you and stuff. So they lead you on in the friendship. You think they want to be your friends, but once you start getting close to them, they turn away.

Although most girls did not like this kind of behavior, many simply accepted the dynamics of Popularity. While Riva exclaimed, "I don't even know why they're Popular," she seemed resigned to accept "that's the way it is." Brooke, a member of the Popular clique at her large middle-class school, dismissed these dynamics as, simply, "high schoolism."

The purpose of this chapter is to understand why high-status girls, who are not necessarily well liked, are designated by classmates as "Popular." Why are behaviors that generate conflict among peers socially rewarded? In other words, how does "Popularity," in the sense used here, operate as power? What does Popularity tell us about the sociocultural context of girls' agency? We answer these kinds of questions from analysis of interviews with thirty-two girls. These interviews were conducted in the initial stages of fieldwork when we wanted to understand life at school "as a girl." Interviews were organized around open-ended topics such as whether participants liked their school, membership in peer groups, the activities which this membership endorses, what they enjoyed the most about school, and so on. Reflecting our interest in whether equality-seeking discourses, such as those of feminism, influenced these girls' sense of themselves and who they could be, near the end of interviews Shauna asked girls what they knew and thought about "girl power" and feminism.[6]

Most of the interviews in this chapter were conducted with pairs (and on occasion trios) of girlfriends to encourage free-flowing dialogue. The sample for this chapter consists of twenty-two white Euro-Canadian girls, three Asian-Canadian girls, and seven girls of other racial or ethnic identities. Nine girls came from working-class families, while we classified twenty-one girls as coming from middle-class families and two from upper middle-class families. The schools attended by these girls also varied, although most were located in middle-class neighborhoods. Of the thirty-two girls included in this chapter, eleven were "Popular girls" or past members of a Popular clique.

## POPULARITY AS "THE POWER TO SQUASH PEOPLE"

Although the girls in our study attended a range of schools, their descriptions of Popular girls were consistent across interviews and resonated with popularized representations described in Chapter Two.[7] Virtually every description echoed Mia's explanation: "They're tall, skinny. Yeah, they tend to wear a lot of like low-slung jeans, tank tops that bare their belly a lot... Not all of them are blond, but [they] all have long hair." In addition to looks, Popular girls had to display the "cool" attitude: "It's hard to say what 'cool' is, but you have to like wear the right clothes and talk the right way" (Liv). For most participants, the "right clothes" included brand names such as Mystic Steed jeans and Aritzia tops. According to Jordan, kids wearing "knock-offs" would be considered "scrubs."[8] The "right" clothes are expensive—for example, Jordan claimed that the jeans in question are "$200 each for like a pair."

However careful a girl's choice of dress, to be Popular, her choice must convey interest in boys. Twelve-year-olds Sally and Marie emphasized that "If they [girls] don't go out with anybody or something, or they don't *want* to go out with guys yet, then they're not considered 'cool.'" Brooke confirmed this claim, telling Shauna that "basically, the more guys you know, the more like popular you are." When asked how to maintain Popularity, she replied, "Date a certain guy. Not date certain guys. You know. Just hang out with the *right* people, basically." Thus being Popular meant that "You have to hang out with the right crowd every day, even though you want to hang out, I don't know, with somebody else" (Anna).

Across interviews, girls claimed that having attention from boys is a source of power (see Duncan 2004). Jordan, a member of Brooke's crowd, bragged that "guys think we are hot." This meant that Popular girls like Brooke and Jordan had to "keep up" their reputations because, "If you do even one little thing wrong, it gets talked about everywhere" (Anna and Vera). Gaining attention from boys "the wrong way" could earn even Popular girls bad reputations, the most common one being a "slut." When asked what she meant by "slut," Amelia described one of her classmates: "She goes out with guys, and the way she dresses. She usually wears like these really, really short denim dresses with a denim tank top on and stuff like that, right? She wears lots of makeup and stuff. She tries to make herself pretty." Shauna asked Amelia about trying to "look pretty," since it was a common activity among the girls:

Like me, right? I'll probably put like a little bit of eye shadow on and stuff like that. Like just a little bit, you can barely see. She puts on this really whole bunch of blue, and she'll put like this weird color lipstick on, and lots of black mascara and stuff like that, right? She just looks like a slut by the way she dresses.

As seen in Amelia's explanation, the line between everyday practices of femininity and those earning the label "slut" is very fine (see Nilan 1992).

Despite the dire consequences of their labeling, girls' distinctions between "good" and "bad" displays of femininity were very ill defined: "Like, low-cut tops and uhm. I don't know… I think that low-cut tops are bad, but I don't see anything wrong with showing your stomach. There's nothing revealing about it" (Liv). To us, distinctions seemed to rest on girls' sexualized agency:

Amelia:  She thinks she's pretty and stuff like that, right? And she'll walk past a couple of Grade 10 guys, and then she'll look back and I'll see them glancing at her and stuff like that… A whole bunch of guys will be just staring at her, right? It's disgusting.
Shauna:  Which part is disgusting?
Amelia:  Just *her*. The way she dresses.

As suggested by Amelia, our participants were more likely to blame girls than boys for the dynamics[9] that positioned girls as sexualized objects of boys' attention. In the above example, the girl in question violated unspoken "rules" about just how much agency girls can express in their pursuit of Popularity. While girls can attract boys—through their embodiment and dress—they should not be seen as pursuing boys. Girls who actively used their sexuality to attract boys were likely to be severely sanctioned. Brooke called this kind of attempt at upward social mobility, "getting in the back door." She claimed that "with girls, you can't—like you can't really get *rejected* from a guy. I mean, like… You know. Like if you're not Popular, and if you're not like pretty or whatever, then uhm. Then you can… Like you can get with someone and become "easy," kind of. It's a way you get, uhm, kind of *known*. It's a way, a back door into getting into certain groups of people. Because then, if you hang out with like a Popular guy, then you'll hang out with all the guy's girlfriends."

Getting "in the back door" was not as easy as it sounded, however. For starters, boys could take advantage of especially younger girls who attempted to gain Popularity in this way. Among girls, it could result in conflict, because membership in the Popular crowd was highly guarded:

> Like the Popular girls walking down the hall, they don't look at anyone. They don't smile at anyone. They don't say "Hi" to anyone, for some stupid reason… I see someone saying "Hi" to a Popular girl and they just kind of like "Hi" and roll their eyes at them and walk away. That's mean (Riva).

As well as making girls like Riva feel "like they're less of a good person," Vikki claimed that some kids are afraid of Popular girls. In fact, she reasoned that being mean could enhance one's Popularity: "She doesn't seem like a bully, but what I've heard, there are some things that she's done that are really nasty. So a lot of people are scared of her. So she kind of finds she's like on top of the Popular people." Liv, a white working-class girl who was also a member of the Popular clique at her school, did not try to hide her unkind treatment of other girls. She bragged, "We're kind of at the top, like the most popular, most known people. But like that doesn't mean that we get along with everybody. Like I know a lot of people that don't like me. And I know a lot of people I don't like… Basically, if someone bugs me, I do something about it. And sometimes I hurt them."

While Liv's comment implies the use of physical aggression, a more potent—and more commonly mentioned—tactic to keep a girl "in line" was to ruin her reputation.[10] Popular girls were often blamed for starting rumors:[11]

> I find that she can be pretty annoying, or like sneaky sort of. If she wants to like start rumors. Stuff like that. Like I've gone through—I was actually pretty far off with Lynda at the beginning of the year, and I had a big problem with her 'cause like I heard some things she would say about me. And so I would confront her. And she would lie about it, or whatever (Vikki).

This kind of behavior made girls claim that Popular girls act "superior than you sometimes because they sort of have that power. They feel that they can do whatever they want, and say whatever they want" (Vanessa). As a consequence, Popular girls could make girls like Vanessa feel insecure: "Like you want to be part of the conversation, but you don't want to let yourself out totally in case you do something stupid, or say something stupid. You know, embarrass yourself."

Given so many negative descriptions of Popular girls, we were curious about how they maintained the high status that gave them social power. Part of the answer lies in the fact that Popular girls were not often challenged. On the contrary, being associated with Popular girls could reap "benefits" among one's peers. Even Riva, who openly criticized Popular girls to Shauna, also confessed that she "didn't know why," but "when like one of my Popular friends is paying me a lot of attention in front of a lot of people, you feel important." As a result, many girls aspired to be among the Populars. Onyx and Grover referred to these girls as "wannabes." However, whether a "wannabe" Popular or not, many girls simply did not want to become enemies of Popular girls. While Riva claimed that she didn't "feel intimidated by them or anything," she also indicated "I don't really want to make enemies with them. That's like a big thing 'cause if they make up something, it goes all around. Like everyone knows."

The association of meanness with Popularity was so strong that twelve-year-old Eve claimed that "you have to put people down to make yourself really Popular" (see Merten 1997; Duncan 2004). It led Vikki to reason that boys are attracted to "mean" girls:

> They can be bitchy. They can be "all that." That's why they are those kind of people. And so guys like that 'cause they think that those girls are "all that stuff" and [that] they are really cool and we like them. And they're all sexy and whatever… Like sometimes you know, you see in the movies when girls are all like bitching at the guys. You'll be like "blah, blah, blah" and the guy will just go into the kiss sort of thing 'cause he gets turned on by the girl getting like so—all in his space. She's just sort of "there."

Despite our personal feelings about the dynamics of Popularity, in the final analysis we found it understandable that many girls admitted to "going along" with Popular girls even though they might disapprove of their behavior. As already suggested by Riva, many girls lived in fear of "being next":

> …they have the power to do more things because they can afford to. They have the power to set trends because they can afford it. They have power to squash people because they have support… I do not like being around [those] people because I don't like the attitude, but I'll be friendly up front. You know, be civil. I just won't hang out with them (Kate).

Kate's fear was well founded. Jordan, for example, claimed: "I hate being cruel to people. Unless they ask for it. If they ask for it, I go ape shit."

What girls described to us as "meanness" has been called relational or social aggression by adult professionals (see Simmons 2002; Underwood 2003). Both the participants in our study and previous researchers describe this aggression as a specifically female behavior. In fact, several girls claimed that one of the best things about being a girl is that girls can be "bitchy."[12] Jordan described "cat fights"—which she also called "bitch fights"—among girls with glee: "It's like, 'Did you hear that she got with somebody?' 'What? Who are you to be saying this?' 'It's not like you were there. How do you know what happened?'" She gave Shauna an example of such a fight:

> Like my friend Sheila walks by this girl Terri and goes "slut." And then walks to her class. And then Terri's friend Marlene comes up to me and goes "So your friend Sheila called my friend Terri a slut." And I was like "What am I supposed to do about it? Why are you telling me this?" She's like—she doesn't even know Terri. And I go like "Why don't you just tell her this? Why do you have to go through me?" And then people are like, start circling around. And I'm just like "Whatever." And then I walk away.

Like many other girls, Riva denied that boys acted in similar ways: "Maybe they [boys] talk behind people's backs, but they don't show it as much or they're not—they don't—I don't know. If you say "Hi" to them, they say "Hi." But girls can be really cruel."[13] It also interested us that, with very few exceptions, racism was not included in girls' descriptions of "meanness." Even when Kate was singled out because of her "color," she did not see this treatment as mean:

> They're like, "Oh. You're brown but not…"—but they're not mean about it. They're never really mean people… It's like "Oh you have brown skin." You know, "You're this" or "You're that" just because they're being dumb at the time. Or they're just mad at you. But nothing like "Oh, because you're brown you're bad or you're unacceptable to be with." Nothing like that.

While racialized segregation characterized larger school cultures, most of the friendship cliques interviewed in our study contained a racial and ethnic "mix" of members.[14] Here we do not claim that racialization is unimportant in dynamics among girls (see Jiwani, Janovicek, and Cameron 2001; Pantin 2001; Jiwani 2006). It interests us that while there were

Popular girls among various ethnic groups, the standards for Popular femininity applied across these groups: regardless of their racialized identities, Popular girls must be pretty, thin, and dress according to what is "in." Within this context, the dynamics that enforced rules of femininity were identified by girls as more salient than those regulating membership in racialized groupings. We thus take up the question of why "meanness" was reserved for girls' behavior in particular and why it was such a recurring theme in our interviews. Like Riva and Kate, we see this behavior as an exercise of power. Rather than dismiss it simply as what Brooke called "high schoolism," we locate meanness within the sociocultural processes that positioned our participants "as girls."

We have already seen that to be Popular, girls had to look "perfect," "...like all the movie stars and stuff like that. You know, they're all like 'Oh, I'm so fat' and they diet and stuff like that. And then they just get more skinny" (Vanessa). Given this imperative to look perfect, it is not surprising that meanness among girls included a lot of ridicule and sarcasm about girls' physical appearance:

> Well, Kathy has this really bad problem—she thinks she's fat but she isn't. And her own boyfriend keeps saying that. And they're always bugging her about it. And then Melissa, she thinks she's really ugly, but she isn't—she gets bugged about that a lot. And I don't know. With me they don't really have anything to bug me about, so they make something up (Liv).

As Liv suggested, being called "fat" was a common form of name-calling. Girls often teased each other about their weight if they wanted to be hurtful. GG took delight in the fact that her classmates would soon enter puberty:

> Like they're both really skinny [now]. And like I'm waiting for the day when— it sounds mean—but when she starts putting on pounds like she does. Like I'm more chunky than her. I'm like—so she says it as a joke but it still gets to you. Like 'cause a lot of people tease her about being flat [chested] and I'm always there to support her, but she sometimes calls me "a cow" and stuff and I'm like, "Where did that come from?"... Like, you know, if they want to make you feel bad, that is something you can say—I could totally bring down someone [by talking about her weight].

As evident in GG's glee, girls tended to monitor each other's weights. Jordan, an outgoing Popular girl, told Shauna "I'm like self-conscious. Like weight-wise." She compared herself to other girls in her clique:

> Well, Sabina and Katherine are like really skinny—they could be models. And they're like really gorgeous and everything. And then my friend Lynda—uhm. She's in shape and everything. I'm not in shape. Just, like I don't compare to them.

Jordan's preoccupation with not only their weight, but also the physique of her girlfriends, reflects her knowledge that boys prefer girls who are skinny. Brooke, for example, reported that:

> I hear them [Popular boys in her crowd] a lot, pointing out some of my friends' weights. They'll just be like, "I need a girlfriend." I'll be like "Go out with Cindy." And they're like "No way!" And I'll go like "Why?" "It's just too—she's too big for me." Kind of like that. You can just tell that someone skinny over someone not as skinny, the skinny one would get the guy.

In Jordan' case, a boy used references to her weight to "get back at her":[15]

> I didn't wanna like "do something" with a guy and so he called me "fat." And I'm like, my self-confidence like went way down when he called me fat because then I was like, "If you think that, I wonder like how all the other guys think."

At first Jordan "cried" over this insult. Then she sent him "a nasty e-mail." In the end, the boy in question apologized and Jordan concluded that his behavior was "understandable." "Like it was just him protecting himself. I think it was like his insecurity. Like, 'Oh, she didn't want to get with me'—like, 'I've got to do something about it…' He felt so bad, he didn't deserve it."[16]

While a girl's weight could be a sensitive point, a perhaps more severe—and common—form of ridicule was sexual name-calling: "Like they [other girls] call us 'lesbians' or 'sluts' and 'bitches'" (Marianna). Even though she disapproved of these tactics, Marianna confessed using these tactics in retaliation. When called a "flat [chested] bitch," "I went up to her and I used the term 'dyke…' I don't feel that was very nice, but [it was] something to get back at her, even though it's really hard to believe I would say [that] stuff." As testament to the severity of this label, Marianna felt it necessary to emphasize to Shauna, "I'm not attracted to girls. And I don't, I'm not, I'm not a—I'm *not* a lesbian."[17]

More often than not, sexualized insults accompanied fights over boys:

Lydia:    We were going out, seeing each other, but it was kind of secret. And
          then this girl found out that I went out with the guy I liked before.
          And then she was talking to my brother in the cafeteria. And she
          goes "Oh my god, your sister is such a slut." And then my brother
          told me. And I was like "I can't believe she said that." Like, you don't
          say that to someone older than you, right? Because—You don't say
          that even if—but she thinks she is all hot and stuff and whatever.
          And we just like—
Jordan:   She's ugly.
Lydia:    Yeah. She's been gone around. She's—
Forsyth:  She is the high school bicycle.
Jordan:   She is a walking STD... Ever since then we've been like, "Oh my
          god I smell herpes" when she walks by. And we would like stare her
          down.

A lot is at stake in this kind of name-calling. As Brooke told us, "If word of mouth spreads, people think you're something that you're not." Jessica emphasized that girls "work hard to get certain reputations and they work hard to keep it. One girl left our school because she couldn't stand her reputation... She was always getting rude jokes thrown at her over the Internet and all that stuff. And she just couldn't take it anymore and so she left" (see Bright 2005). As seen by this story, while name-calling could start as conflict between individual girls, meanness is amplified through group participation.

In summary, in our study "meanness" refers to acts of ridicule, name-calling, backstabbing, gossip and social exclusion. It interests us that such offensive behavior was frequently attributed to Popular girls. Popular girls like Jordan might relish this reputation. Jordan claimed that being "Popular" gave her group an advantage at school because they had the power to "scare the crap out of them [other kids]." Rather than view this kind of attitude as a problem of individual girls, we are interested in the "meaning of meanness" as a social construct (Merton 1997). What does meanness, attributed specifically to girls, tell us about the gendered operation of power? Are girls now the over-empowered beneficiaries of a girl power "movement," as some antifeminists claim? (see Agrell 2005).

## AGENCY AND POWER: POPULAR GIRLHOOD REVISITED

What we hear in girls' talk about Popularity is the performance of what Connell (1987: 183) calls "emphasized femininity": the practice of heterosexual femininity that is "oriented to accommodating the interests and desires of men" and thus to reconstituting women's subordination. As a dominant way to do girlhood, the value given to emphasized femininity could make school stressful for many girls because, in the words of Vikki, "Nobody likes you if you're ugly and fat." At this point, GG elaborated: "Guys don't like you if you don't have big boobs and a big ass, 'cause when you wear tight jeans or something, they want to see your shape. They want to see those big, like boobs." However, as also noted by GG, it was not simply acceptance by boys that made school stressful: "You have to worry about girls' opinions too. Like they'll be like, 'Eew! *What* are you wearing?' Like, 'What's your brand of clothes?' sort of thing. It's like you totally have to be 'up there.'"

As used by the girls in our study, "Popular" signals membership in the prized—and well-guarded—clique of an idealized girlhood that meets the standards of "emphasized femininity." Across different school contexts, only girls who were pretty, not fat, attractive, and attracted to boys could hope to ever gain membership in the Popular clique. As a "universalized" standard, it cut across class and racialized divisions.[18] Even though local cliques created ways to distinguish themselves as "unique," the general parameters of Popularity were very similar. In the final analysis, however, the rules of idealized femininity are the most "punitive" for girls who do not meet the prevailing norms of school-based cultures; that is, girls who are not "pretty," who are "overweight," and who will never win boys' approval, especially because they are, or are perceived to be, lesbian (see Duncan 2004).

Given that the attributes of emphasized femininity must be confirmed by the reactions of others, even Popular girls could feel insecure about their status. In a moment of candid reflection, Brooke claimed that being Popular was "creepy." Her insecurity was heightened by the way that girls' bodies and demeanor are under constant public assessment (by adults as well as peers). Girls themselves engaged in this surveillance in order to identify the latest trends, compare their weight and physical development to classmates, determine which girls to associate with (or avoid), and monitor the reactions of boys to their sexualized self-presentations. Mimicking classmates, twelve-year-olds Sally and Marie referred to this policing as "peer pressure":

Sally:   Why are you doing this? Why don't you have that?
Marie:   Clothes, acting—
Marie:   You're so dorky!
Marie:   You don't go out for lunch—that kind of thing.
Sally:   You don't have a lot of money.

Listening to Sally and Marie talk this way draws attention to the complexity of the contexts in which adolescents "make themselves" as self-conscious projects. One problem with invoking "peer pressure" to describe this complexity is that it locates the dynamics described above solely in youth culture itself. Our goal is to understand how the dynamics of girls' interactions are also mediated by adult culture. We are drawn to the notion that the liminal space of youth cultures operates as local "communities of shared practice" (see Eckert and McConnell-Ginet 1999; Paechter 2003a, 2003b).

A community of practice describes the formation and perpetuation of:

> An aggregate of people who, united by a common enterprise, develop and share ways of doing things, ways of talking, beliefs, and values—in short, practices... Once launched, it has its own life and trajectory. The development of shared practices emerges as the participants make meaning of their joint enterprise, and of themselves in relation to this enterprise. Individuals make sense of themselves and others through their forms of participation in and contributions to this community. The community as a whole makes joint sense of itself through the relation between its practices and those of other communities (Eckert and McConnell-Ginet 1999: 186).

Paechter (2003a) describes the performances of masculinities and femininities by youth in terms of localized communities of shared practice. Because style is central to these performances, membership in any community requires mastery of the behaviors and activities that define that community's practice (page 70). Mastery is not about simply reenacting rules formulated by a leader, however, as much as it comes from participation in the production of a shared meaning that demarcates group boundaries through a shared identity (Lave and Wenger 1991).

Paechter (2003a) points out that the cultural naturalization of gender difference gives these communities added significance in the lives of young people because it results in an imperative for young people to get their gender performance "right" (also see Davies 1989, 1993). Among youth,[19] localized communities of masculine and feminine practice emerge through groupings that sustain shared repertoires of performances. As in our study, repertoires cohere around what is important, what to pay attention to and what to ignore, who to talk to, what to talk about, and what to leave unsaid (2003a: 72). By locating girls' performances within a local community of practice, we are reminded that while gendered identities, in theory, can (perhaps) be infinitely malleable, embodied practices are always situated.[20] Situating girls' identity practices within a local "community" enables us to hear *social* subjectivities in our interviews.

Throughout this chapter, we have seen that girls had no trouble reciting to Shauna the standards to be met in order to gain the status of Popular when femininity is practiced. Despite local nuances, Popular girls were described in surprisingly similar terms: as noted above, they were pretty, they wore the right clothes, and they were the subjects of boys' interest. As members of the Popular crowd, they hung out with the "cool" kids and, in Vikki's words, they "did stuff." These standards comprise what Chambers, Tinknell, and Van Loon (2004) characterize as a morality that shapes how both girls and boys perceive and evaluate the feminine subject positions available in school-based cultures. Whether any specific girl herself subscribed to these standards, her identity practices took meaning from these conventions.

These standards remind us that, whether conscious or not, heterosexuality makes normative femininity "intelligible" (Renold 2006: 493). This compulsory nature of heterosexuality for girls is made visible in the talk of twelve-year-olds Missy and Eve, who recalled using sexualized "put downs" for classmates as part of their everyday vocabulary, even before they actually understood their meaning:

Shauna: A "ho." [Repeating what Eve called a "bad word" that she had used in a conflict with a classmate.] What does "ho" mean to you—just so that we get it straight?

Eve: I'm not too sure because—

Missy: I know what it means! ... It means "whore."

Eve: Isn't a whore like a prostitute?

Missy: Yup! ... A "whore" in our class was kind of a popular word. Like "Ho ho."

Eve: And we were in Grade Six and we didn't know what it meant [even though they used it to label other girls].

However "naive" this exchange may seem to adult readers, it illustrates the way in which the regulation of female sexuality becomes
a "normalized" aspect of growing up as "a girl."[21] It shows how the
labels employed by girls to keep each other "in line" are symptoms of
hidden discourses that account for the performativity of gender. Regardless of the specific conventions of any local community of practice, the use of sexualized labels to regulate girls' gender performances
was ubiquitous; more often than not, "slut" was applied on the basis of
a girl's appearance and demeanor rather than actual sexual behavior.
In our research, "slut" is a "symptom" of unspoken but potent discourses that sexualize gender, operating beneath the everyday level of
ordinary consciousness.

While these kinds of processes contribute to the acceptance of heterosexuality as "natural," Skeggs (2004) reminds us that the moral
imperative that links heterosexuality to femininity is a historical accomplishment. Given the importance of self-restraint and self-discipline as
virtues of nineteenth-century bourgeois life, "proper" femininity became a marker that distinguished the "upper" from "lower" classes.
The (purported) sexual excesses of the lower orders, in particular, stood
in contrast to bourgeois femininity and were visually coded through
the prostitute's body. The sexual "excess" of the prostitute became a
cultural signifier for lack of constraint, coded in a way that women's appearance became a signifier of conduct. The classed and racialized body
of the prostitute epitomized public disorder: during the nineteenth
century, "whore" was not used to label women selling sex but was applied to women who broke middle-class rules of propriety, exceeding
the bounds of respectability by not behaving like "a lady" (page 38).
The prostitute reminded (white) middle-class women of the "dangers"
of femininity "gone wrong" (page 167). More generally, women's bodies became a site where class and racialized struggles are played out,
because the female body came to symbolize moderation, restraint, and
self-discipline (see Hesse-Biber 1996).[22] As a result, while all girls can
be targeted with the label "slut," it is harder for some girls—those not
conforming to white bourgeois standards of girlhood—to escape its
damaging effects.

As a signifier of public morality, heterosexuality is gendered through
a double standard of sexual conduct that authorizes male agency. By
fashioning the female body into a sexual object for male viewing plea-

sure, girls are denied expression of sexual desire, even while it can appear that they exercise power. As Fine (1988) notes, while it may indeed be girls themselves who police the boundaries of femininity through assessment of each other's appearance and sexual agency, they do so from the standpoint of male desire. Such a standpoint shapes female desire in specific ways. Without really being able to articulate "why," Susie, Dephy, and Tina (all Popular) agreed that, even though they recognize that guys will "BS" girls when "they just want ass," "you fall for it":

| | |
|---|---|
| Tina: | They'll [boys] be really, really nice. |
| Susie: | Yeah. He tries to be totally sweet. And he tells you— |
| Dephy: | They say a lot of BS... |
| Susie: | Like you know that you're falling for it, but you do it anyways. |
| Tina: | Yeah. It's like smoking. People take up smoking like to relieve stress and everything. But they know it's bad for them. So when a guy's nice to you— |
| Susie: | You know it's bad for you, but you like it anyway. |
| Dephy: | Yeah. |

Within this context it should not be surprising that researchers find higher self-esteem among girls who have male (romantic or otherwise) friends than among girls who do not have boyfriends (see Thomas and Daubman 2001.

Despite the increasingly explicit sexualized nature of popular culture, as Kitzinger (1995: 194) points out, there is little public discussion that explores the operation of power within heterosexual relationships in ways that "neither ignore social structures nor dismiss women's choices and agency." Without a discourse that enables girls to understand the contradictory dynamics that sexualize their practices of femininity, it should not be surprising that girls take up the language of everyday heterosexism. Kitzinger (1995: 194) concludes: "When women [read: girls] talk about 'slags' and 'reputation,' they could be talking, instead, about power and powerlessness, freedom and exploitation, self-determination and oppression." Instead, the heterosexism of mainstream culture shapes their talk toward girls' responsibility for boys' desire. Like other participants, Jordan attributed the difficulty for girls to maintain "their reputations" to other girls, despite the fact that she herself pointed blame in another direction: "Like guys tell their friends [if they 'got with' a girl]. And then their friends tell their friends, and then my friend Carla, where she works... it's like the gossip place." Despite

her recognition that boys often control public knowledge of a girl's behavior, Jordan turned rumor making back onto girls. She claimed that
while boys' behavior might be "noticed," "rumor-wise they're like completely ignored... Girls like to talk about girls more than guys—guys
are boring. No good rumors come out of them."[23]

While we do not deny girls' propensity for rumor-mongering and
backstabbing, what we hear is the way in which a double-standard
masks the ways in which boys are in control of the sexual reputations
of girls. As Thorne (1993) notes, the homophobia shaping boys' peer
culture promotes heterosexual rivalry among boys, encouraging them
to make insincere advances to girls as "one-upmanship" or to sexually
exploit young girls. Despite these dynamics, it interested us that many
girls in our study maintained that girls and boys are equally powerful.
They based this claim on the way that girls' have the (apparent) ability
to sexually manipulate boys:

> Susie:    Because the guys, if they want anything [stated earlier as "a little
>           ass"] from the girls, they have to be nice.
> Dephy:   Yeah.
> Susie:    Even in the movies and stuff. The girl in the relationship always has
>           like more power or whatever. So I don't know.
> Shauna: Dephy—what's your opinion?
> Dephy:   Uhm. I don't know. I'm thinking of something, but it's not quite
>           coming out yet—it's right there.

One consequence of this ability for girls to cultivate male sexual interest could be the equation of girls' power with female sexuality. Earlier in this chapter, Brooke claimed that girls have an advantage over
boys in terms of gaining Popularity. Like Susie, Brooke was referring to
the way that girls can "use" their sexuality to get what they want. This
kind of thinking led Erin to claim that one of the best things about being a girl is "getting free stuff." When asked how, she explained: "Well,
they have these things at the video stores—it's 'two-for-one' Tuesdays.
But I mean, if you look really cute and really whiny for a bit, like on a
Sunday, and be like 'Can it please be Tuesday for five minutes?' Then
they'll give you the two-for-one stuff." She continued with a further
example: "Girls like can flirt with the bouncer of a club and get in, as
opposed to guys." When Shauna asked her whether she had ever done
that, however, fourteen-year-old Erin replied: "Like flirted at a club?
No. I'm not old enough." And yet she maintained a clear distinction be-

tween the "right" and "wrong" way for girls to use sexuality: "There's some advantages to that [flirting to get what you want]. I think that if you did it like *mildly*, it would be OK. But if you did it to some really horrible extremes, then it would be kind of taking advantage more." Sara, on the other hand, described how "mild flirting" helped her and a friend gain entry to a concert:

> We went to Gold Finger and Reel Big Fish. And there was no tickets left, and so we'd be waiting in line for like three hours. And then they started letting people in, like after about an hour after the concert started, if you like paid for your ticket then. And they were just about to close the gate right, as we were approaching. And then we started flirting with the bodyguard and we got in... Yeah. It's not like we were flashing him or anything. We weren't—[we] just like looked at his name, and we're like it was like joking [deep voice] "How you doing?" You know?

Given their association of female sexuality with girls' power, it is not surprising that girls made "contradictory" statements about "dressing up" as both the "best" and the "worst" aspect of being a girl. On the one hand, Rose maintained that the best thing about being a girl "would be being able to dress up... if you're a guy and you like told some of your friends, "Oh yeah. I thought I would wear this today because *I really, really* like it, I really like these pants," they'd probably be going—[breaks into laughter] but if you're a girl they'd be just like, 'Oh. Cool.'" But this "freedom" was double edged: while a number of participants agreed with Rose, they simultaneously maintained that the mandate for girls to dress in certain ways was the most difficult thing about "being a girl." They concluded that school was easier for boys: "Yeah. They just roll in, put on the clothes that they want, wander to school. As long as they've got a wallet that's fine. Because girls, they have to get up early and do all of the prep work with hair, and makeup, and make sure that their outfit looks OK" (Erin). In the final analysis, the perceived advantages or disadvantages came down to the role that girls' appearance plays in gaining Popularity:

> Riley:     Well, most girls want to be Popular. Like most girls, they really want to be Popular and want everyone to know their name and stuff and everyone to say "hi!" to them in hallways...
>
> Tiffany:  Most girls expect other girls to be just like everybody else. They want you to be skinny and really pretty and just like, have everything going for you... It's kind of harder to be a girl than it is to be a

guy—There's more competition with the other girls. The guys, they
punch each other out and they'll be best friends again. A girl can't
do that. It's harder. You have to put makeup on in the morning, do
your hair, make sure you look good to leave the house.

As shown above, however consciously critical girls may be of the
mandate to be attractive to boys, they are also well aware that "good
looks" are vital for women (see Weitz 2001; Hesse-Biber 1996). While
girls may be told "they can be anything they want to be," their everyday
life testifies to the importance of being pretty. A further complication
arises because, just as girls learn that female heterosexuality is social
capital, their sexual self-expressions are publicly problematized. Despite the overtly sexualized nature of the stardom enjoyed by girls' pop
idols, sexually-forward behavior by schoolgirls is heavily sanctioned
by parents and teachers. Because male sexuality, on the other hand, is
culturally defined as natural, urgent, and difficult to control, as shown
by Amelia's censure of her classmate, girls are given responsibility for
the effect of their sexualized body on boys (see Allen 2004; Chambers,
Tincknell, and Van Loon 2004). The result is that girls must navigate
between "two worlds":[24]

Tina:     I can't think of how to word it. It's kind of like you have to—well, for
          a guy's respect, in a way you have to be kind of like sexy and stuff.
          But then, in a way to get a girl's respect you have to be non-sexy and
          that. And so, I don't know—
Dephy:    You have to juggle. You have to watch what you say.
Tina:     But you can't be a hypocrite at the same time, so—
Dephy:    It takes a lot of self-confidence, if you're going to flirt with a guy,
          then you're going to get—
Susie:    Slack for it later
Dephy:    Yup.
Tina:     From a girl. You have to be okay with who you are. Like, you have
          to know like, yeah—like you have to be self-confident. You have to
          know who you are so you won't care when people say stuff about
          you, because a lot of people are going to say stuff.

In the face of this uncertainty, the disapproval of peers, especially of
high-status members of one's community of practice, gains power.
Meanness among girls, as the discursive positioning of each other
within this community, is an exercise of the power. Power is exercised
not simply through display of the status markers that gain currency
in a celebrity-oriented consumer culture—being pretty, being "skinny"

and being what the girls called "hyper"—but also through distancing oneself from the obverse of these markers. While the discursive nature of this positioning may encourage adults to dismiss girls' "rivalry" as trivial, it has "real," material effects in the lives of girls.

While our participants expressed awareness of the negative meanings accompanying the sexual labels used to position girls, a surprising number of girls who used them freely puzzled over the basis for their existence. For example, Jordan reasoned: "I don't understand why guys never get in trouble for that kind of stuff [behavior that earns girls the label 'slut']. Like not really in trouble. Say like a guy is going out with somebody and uhm … If a guy is going out with this girl, and then he cheats on her, usually the girl attacks the other girl, rather than getting mad at the guy. I don't understand that." Jordan's talk signals the limitations of not only the language surrounding sexuality, but also of the prevalence of male-centered discourses through which girls are encouraged to understand themselves and their place in the gendered order. When girls define themselves through this language and discourse, their identity practices "naturalize" not only a sexual double standard but also the discursive "othering" that girls experience as meanness. Although Brooke, who benefited from prevailing rules of Popularity, easily recognized that boys enforced the standards of idealized femininity, she concluded: "You can't really change it, but … I think like, 'What could I do?' I can't change someone else's opinion on someone, kind of. I like—and I just kind of—I'm good at blocking things out. I just kind of block it out. I'm just kind of like—[that's] how we're supposed to be. Because I think, 'Well, it doesn't really matter. In three more years…'" When adult commentators likewise treat girls' heterosexual competition and meanness as an "inevitable" part of "growing up," they also promote a discourse that naturalizes these dynamics.

## CONCLUSION

While participants associated meanness with the power of Popular girls, we are not claiming that only Popular girls engage in the competitive behaviors described in this chapter. Our goal is to draw attention to the dynamics of all-girl cultures rather than to individual actors. We have tried to show how an unspoken double standard gives rise to a moral order that shapes youth cultures as situated communities where gender is practiced. The high status enjoyed by Popular girls is authorized by "rules" that sustain a heteronormative order that is marked by the female body. Meeting unspoken but demanding standards of normative femininity makes "appearance" a socially important preoccupation for most girls. Popular girls who "valorize" these standards can, in turn, enforce these standards in their community of practice; they (attempt) to regulate group membership by robbing a specific—often rival—girl of the ability to define for herself "who she is" and "what she is all about." This behavior, in effect, replays the patriarchal "othering" of women by men, indicating how few avenues there are for the "legitimate" exercise of power by girls. Thus, what girls (and many adults) might attribute to Popular girls as "personal power" lies in "rules" that authorize their "performativity" of a specific way of doing girlhood. In our work, agency refers to the conscious, self-directed actions of girls—to what girls say and do to accomplish girlhood. *Power*, on the other hand, refers to what makes girls' saying and doing possible. In this chapter, we have seen how girls' power is shaped by double standards that work to male advantage. These standards do not regulate "simply" girls' relationships with boys; they also regulate all-girl communities in which gender is practiced (see J. Holland et al. 1991; Hey 1997). Whether consciously deployed by girls, these standards normalize heterosexual competition and inequalities.

As discussed in Chapter One, Pipher (1994) popularized the view that the contradictory messages surrounding socially accepted ways of doing girlhood silence girls, because they require that girls must put their authentic selves aside in order to become what our culture values in women. As shown by our research, however, empowering individual girls to simply "find their voice" may not be liberatory in the ways Pipher implies; in fact, if personal empowerment does not "trouble" the socially constructed nature of gender itself, girls can be rewarded for speaking themselves into existence through available, conventional scripts. What her approach neglects are the sociocultural conditions under which girls become speaking Subjects. It fails to distinguish between the performance of gender through self-directed action and the performative aspects of gender that shape girls' behavior; in other words, this approach conflates agency and power.

Although we do not disagree that individual girls might benefit from projects that give them the confidence to speak about their lives "as girls," we set as our task an understanding of how speaking "as girls" is possible. Interpreting girls' competitive and socially aggressive behavior as an indication that girls are over-empowered or becoming "too much" like their male counterparts is misleading. On the contrary, girls are "correct" in their implicit recognition of the cultural significance of the female body as signifier of the moral order. Given the association of "youthfulness" with the desirable (but not desiring) female body, we should not be surprised that girls will organize their aspirations, hence attention, around their sexed bodies (Francis 1999). Within this context, encouraging girls to adopt middle-class imperatives as corrective can reinforce rather than challenge the moral order that sustains this preoccupation. The complexity of girls' empowerment lies in the fact that girls' agency comes through a socially constructed girlhood whose formation is embedded in precisely what projects of empowerment must encourage girls to challenge: hidden standards—racialized, ableist, class-based and heterosexist—that are constitutive of Selfhood for girls. This is not to say, however, that girls never challenge these standards.

Despite the focus we have given Popular girls in this chapter, a number of participants consciously positioned themselves against the "girlie girl" symbols of an emphasized femininity that gave Popular girls currency in their local school cultures. For example, Sandy complained that Popular girls "all act like 'Aaahhh.' Ditzy like." Pete was annoyed over "the way they live their lives through an image that kind of pisses me off. The whole 'girl thing'—being skinny, thin, pretty, makeup. Uhmm. Lots of money … Kind of living their life for a guy." In the following three chapters, we explore interviews with girls who positioned themselves against conventional femininity and refused to let boys "call the shots." In telling their stories we do not mean to imply that there is a subversive girlhood (a "good" femininity) that can replace a "bad" (conventional) femininity. Rather, we are interested in how the practices of girls like Sandy and Pete create a space within peer culture for alternative and resistant expressions of girlhood.

NOTES

1   An earlier version of this chapter appears as: Dawn H. Currie, Deirdre M. Kelly and Shauna Pomerantz (2007). "'The geeks shall inherit the earth': Girls' Agency, Subjectivity and Empowerment" *Journal of Youth Studies* 9(4): 419–436.

2   In this sense, school is the site of the production rather than re-production of identities, as socialization theory emphasizes (see Levinson and Holland 1996).

3   Other names used by girls to refer to what we call Popular girlhood include preppies, poppies, valley girls, and Bun girls (because at one time they all wore their hair in buns). Unlike the preppies in Bettis, Jordan, and Montgomery's (2005) study, Populars are not described by their peers as "nice"; on the contrary.

4   Here we understand "unpopular" to refer to kids who are not part of the Popular clique rather than to kids who are not liked.

5   Evident here and later, the dynamics surrounding racism and talk about racialized identities were often couched by participants in terms of "language differences." As discussed in footnote 14 and elsewhere below, this "framing" masks racism and also contributes to internalized racism. For example, Asian Populars needed to speak "good English" and, like Pete, differentiated themselves from FOBs—"fresh off the boat"—who tended to speak Chinese (Mandarin or Cantonese) with their peers. Mia (half Chinese Canadian and half Euro-Canadian) talked about Asians born and raised in Canada (including herself) as being "white-washed." When asked to explain, she said, "If you're not fully white, you act and think completely white... So it's like you're being washed... It's just that you have all the white values and the way they think or act." Pyke and Dang (2003) analyze this set of attitudes as "internalized racism." We see these racialized terms as another example of the power of informal discourses employed by youth and as signaling how these discourses are mediated by dominant culture that is racist as well as sexist.

6    Given the exploratory nature of interviews, Shauna followed a semistructured interview guide but asked a lot of open-ended questions; while a similar range of topics was covered in many interviews, the results cannot be "tallied" for comparison.

7    However heterogeneous gender practices can be "in theory," some ways of doing girlhood are more socially valued, hence consciously emulated, than others. Thus Pete claimed that Popular girls can "be any race," but "they are usually like—quite often they are blonde." To this claim, Zoe, her interview partner, added: "They are like the ditzy girls. Yeah, the whole popular thing. They just [focus on] dress and stuff."

8    This derisory and classist label concerned more than the right styles, however. Jordan elaborated: "They [scrubs] wear like imitation jeans to try to be like that. And then their hair is gross. Like they don't know how to style their hair... Like there's also the kids that are like have these big coke bottle glasses." We see here—and discuss below—the way that "right" implies a moral imperative.

9    Here we recall how Jordan was able to arrive at the conclusion that the girls her group called "sluts" "ask for it... They live up to the name."

10   We are not denying girls' use of physical aggression. Although it did not emerge in our study as a common occurrence, during the timeframe of our research considerable media attention was drawn to the trial surrounding the 1997 murder of Reena Virk, a fourteen-year-old Indo-Canadian girl, by mainly white classmates in the "peaceful suburbs" of the provincial capital. Significantly, the local media used this example of girl-on-girl aggression as evidence that girls are "over-empowered" and unable to cope with the gains we accredit to feminism. Moreover, the media described Reena as a "troubled girl," a "misfit" who had stolen another girl's boyfriend and spread rumors, ignoring the racialized nature of the murder (See Jiwani 1999 and 2000).

11 Jordan pointed out however that because Popular girls are in the limelight and thus well known, they are the subject of gossip around the school. It is interesting to remember that she also claimed that boys' behaviors were not "interesting enough" to be the subject of gossip.

12 We acknowledge that girls standing up for themselves in ways that feminists encourage can result in being labeled as a "bitch." For example, Brooke described a time when her girlfriend came home crying because a guy had "grabbed her ass." While Brooke told Shauna that she herself would have challenged the guy (something her friend did not do), she elaborated: "They're (guys) not used to someone standing up to them and so right away, if you know—it's not so much about being a bitch but it's just like standing your ground. Being like 'You're not going to use me. You're not gonna.'" When Shauna opined that it's not bitchy to stand up for yourself, Brooke replied "Yeah! But people do. The guy does. The guys immediately, it's like 'Whoa!'" Within this context, it is significant that she later said "We need feminists."

13 Contrary to girls' claims, Thorne (1993) explores how sexual rivalry among boys fosters their use of competitive insulting that includes derogatory comments over each others' girlfriends' appearance and behavior (also see Bamberg 2004). We also heard examples of boys' "meanness" in our interviews. Erin, for example, recounted a time when her friend was targeted by a guy: "Arnie asked her out and—this happens quite a bit—and she said 'No' because she didn't want to ruin their friendship and she was interested in someone else and stuff. And instead of taking it like a guy, he got all—like feeling rejected. And then he waged war against her. Like he always made fun of her. He calls her like stuff. Just all sorts of stuff. Like he'll make fun of everything that she wears. Her hair or whatever she does. And I think it hurts her a bit." We found it interesting that Erin could "forgive" her friend Arnie. When Shauna asked Erin what her friend did about this teasing, she replied: "Nothing really… It's just really an attitude. Like I can see there is a better person inside of him. And so I can appreciate that. And I think it's just—one day, he'll grow into the other person."

14  In our study, both Anglophone and ESL girls claimed that racialized dynamics were a result of language differences. Although further research is needed, our study suggests that language differences act to mask racism by "naturalizing" racial segregation.

15  While the boy who was rebuffed by Jordan retaliated by calling her "fat," in Liston and Moore's (2005) study, girls who refused to have sex were frequently labeled "sluts" by boys (page 220; also see Bamberg 2004).

16  As we discuss much later, this kind of reasoning reflects the way that gendered dynamics can be "naturalized" in girls' thinking.

17  Duncan (2004: 146) found that being "a lesbian" was a descriptor least likely to be associated with being a Popular girl.

18  This is not to say that this standard is not marked by class and race. White middle-class girls are "advantaged," as are fair-skinned, petite, nonwhite girls from middle-class families. Because Chinese-Canadian girls tended to be "petite" and fair skinned, they had an advantage over African-Canadian girls in terms of prevailing beauty standards. Scott (2002) found that in the context of US schools, Black girls' interest in boys was likely to be seen as a symptom of their "hypersexuality." It is also important to note that Jordan herself was not "thin" but rather embodied what might be called a "stubby" physique; her Popularity was sustained by an ability to support the power plays of dominant girls in putting targeted girls "in their place."

19  Researchers have reported the importance of gendered repertories among children as young as four years of age (see Connolly 2006).

20  It is this socially regulated character that distinguishes communities of practice from friendship networks. Thus we distinguish our approach from those who have analyzed girls' relational aggression within the context of, or in terms of, the dynamics of girls' friendships (see, for example, Gilligan et al. 1990; Walkerdine 1990; Hey 1997).

21  Chambers, Tincknell, and Van Loon (2004) draw attention to the
    subtle ways in which this mandate can be reinforced through the
    "sex education" that is typical of public schools in the UK. Al-
    though this curriculum may be designed by concerned adults with
    the intent to empower young women, they found that girls are ac-
    tually being encouraged to collude with sexual scripts that operate
    to subordinate women to men's sexual desires.

22  The designation of erotic representations as "pornography" dur-
    ing this timeframe signals the role that sexuality played in this
    emergent morality (see Weeks 2003).

23   It is significant to note that Mia commented on the way that ru-
    mors and gossip reflected the racialized segregation of groups. She
    claimed that: "It seems like if you're Asian you'll be more talked
    about in the Asian society than the Caucasian society."

24  See Hudson (1984: 31); the girls in her study also complained
    "Whatever we do, it's always wrong."

# 5

# BREAKING THE RULES

---

## SKATER GIRLS

In Chapter Four, we explored how girls' agency can be directed toward preoccupation with the public presentation of their gendered bodies in ways that win boys' attention. In order to explain rather than simply describe how this agency becomes expressed as "meanness" among girls, we drew attention to the double standard that authorizes boys' heterosexual agency while "punishing" girls who display female desire (see Kitzinger 1995). As we have seen, even the suggestion—taking the form of a rumor—that a girl has been "forward" with boys could be used to "keep her in line." Given the power of this standard, we characterized it as constructing a morality through which both girls and boys assessed the acceptability of their peers' behavior. Most of the girls called it unfair, even while—like many adults—they nevertheless accepted it. In fact, some girls took pleasure in boys' insincere advances; as Susie told Shauna, even though you know that these insincere advances are "bad for you," "you like it any way."

More than one girl who openly criticized the reality that girls but not boys get "reputations" as sexual agents also indicated that she "did not know why." Like Brooke, who called girls' meanness "high schoolism," these girls concluded: "You can't really change it." In the closing chapters, we discuss the "naturalization" of a social order that reconstitutes girls' subordination in this way. In this chapter, we focus on girls who did not resign themselves to boys' privilege, exploring interviews with girls who consciously rejected the display-oriented girlhood that made some of their classmates Popular.

While the dynamics described in Chapter Four were found (in varying degrees) across the different schools in our study, competition for Popularity is only part of the story. Despite considerable inducement, not all girls accepted the rules enforced by their socially dominant peers. We were encouraged when Pete and Zoe criticized what bothered many other girls:

Pete:     When girls sleep with a guy, it's heard [gossiped about].
          And I still think it's kind of slutty for the guy to be
          sleeping with a girl at this age, or something.
Zoe:      Yeah. It's gross.
Pete:     It is both glutty and slutty, guy slut and girl slut.
Shauna:   I've never heard that word [glutty] before!
Pete:     Oh! We made it up. We make up a lot of words. Yeah,
          "glutty"—guy slut.

As we discussed in Chapter Three, the language and discourses available to girls can delimit their understanding of the social world. It is significant both that Pete and Zoe had to make up a word that allowed them to express their criticism of the sexual double standard that monitored their behavior and that, without an available language, they were still able to do so.

Understanding why these girls were able to name, and thus to criticize, what we characterize as a "hidden" discourse is a complex task; we do not claim to have a total answer. In this chapter, we provide part of the answer by connecting Pete and Zoe's rejection of idealized femininity to their participation in skateboarding, an activity that, until very recently, was not open to girls. What interests us is the way in which the identity practices of "skaters" not only positioned girls against the emphasized femininity described in Chapter Four but also required these girls to challenge the sexism of skater culture. In our study, we refer to these girls as "Skater girls" and characterize them as performing an "alternative" girlhood, discussed further in Chapter Seven.

We use the term "alternative" to capture a range of ways that girls consciously positioned themselves against what they perceived as the "mainstream" in youth culture, in general, and conventional femininity in particular. We do not intend to construct a dichotomy between "conforming" and "rebellious" girls; rather, "alternative" signals gendered performances that challenged conventions that heterosexualize femininity. This is not to say that Skater girls rejected heterosexuality; on the contrary.[1] Rather, their gender practices did not enact what Skater girls saw as a "passive bid" for boys' attention. As we will see, alternative girlhoods that embody conscious resistance to emphasized femininity still derive meaning from these conventions. One result is that girls who engage in athletic activities that traditionally have been a venue for enacting masculinity risk having their sexuality called into question. For example, Jordan—one of the Popular girls in Chapter Four—was teased for being "butch" when she won events at a school track meet.[2]

Girls' involvement in skater culture put them into conflict with more than gendered norms. Skateboarding is organized around a distinct culture (see Beal 1996, Borden 2001). Most of the Skater girls in our study identified with alternative rock, punk, or metal music—music that is loud, edgy, irreverent, and often rebellious or anticorporate. As Jessica noted, while the music favored by Popular girls is mainly about "love and relationships," alternative music has songs that emphasize the importance of being oneself amidst pressures to conform. Jessica maintained that these themes are more "meaningful" and are "worth hearing." The lyrics are "about them growing up or having trouble with friends, not liking school or dropping out." Two Skater girls—Tori and Grenn—had been in, or were planning to form, punk rock groups named in ways that signal their criticisms of mainstream culture: "Gadfly" and "Normal" (so named because "we're all the opposite of normal").

As noted in Chapter One, the historical absence of girls in youth studies[3] reflects the way in which girls have not been authorized as legitimate occupants of public space. We thus find it interesting that, at the time of our research, little academic interest had been shown in girls' skateboarding as a "disruption" of the gendered "ordering" of public space. This lack of academic interest stands in direct contrast to a growing commercial interest, evident in magazines, web pages, and fashion targeting girl skaters. In this chapter, we hope to inspire further research into girls' involvement in skateboarding by exploring interviews with girl skaters who, initially by chance, were recruited into our study. Drawing on their experiences of being skaters, we consider what their identity practices tell us about the gendered nature of power, the transformation of girlhood, and the possibility for new, "emergent" forms of feminism. We draw on interviews with twenty girls who ranged from thirteen to sixteen years of age. Eleven of these girls were white Euro-Canadian, four were Chinese Canadian, three were multi-racial, and two were aboriginal. Based on information the girls provided about their parents' occupations and educational backgrounds and their current living arrangements, we classified one as coming from an upper middle-class family, fourteen from middle-class, and five from working-class family backgrounds. Eight girls attended public school in an upper-middle-class neighborhood, six attended public school in working-class neighborhoods, four attended public school in class-divided suburbs, one attended a private girls' school, and one attended a Catholic school. Eighteen of the girls had never left school, while two girls had each been out of school for a total of one year and were one grade behind as a result. One identified as bisexual, and the other nineteen implied or stated that they were heterosexual.

While the identity practices of Skater girls seemed to signal a feminist subjectivity, many of these participants invoked the postfeminist discourse discussed in Chapters One and Two. Emily, for example, claimed "it's pretty much even with guys now." Despite her struggle to be accepted by skater boys as a legitimate participant in skater culture, Emily reasoned that feminists were not trying to make things equal, but rather they were trying to raise women above men. She described feminism as a form of reverse discrimination: "It's constantly, like, a fight, instead of just being equal. They [feminists] just want to be better than men." This kind of reasoning, discussed further in Chapter Seven, underlies the claim by Pete (also a skater) that feminism is "brought a bit too far." These postfeminist sentiments stood in stark contrast to the girls' accounts of trying to skateboard in a male-dominated context.

We begin this chapter by describing skater girlhood, and then recount how a particular group of Skater girls—the Park Gang—responded to the male domination of skateboarding. These girls encouraged and supported one another in their transgression of conventional practices of girlhood. In other words, skateboarding "as a girl" could only be sustained through the formation of a new community of practice. We consider the possibility that, despite their disavowal of feminism, the politics of this emergent community exemplifies both a discursive and an embodied re-signification of not only girlhood, but potentially also of feminism. Thinking about this possibility is more complicated than we at first imagined, however; in Chapter Seven we (re)consider the Park Gang's transgression for what it tells us about girl power and girls' empowerment.

## RESIGNIFYING GIRLHOOD

Although skateboarding entails a range of activities and varying degrees of engagement in skateboarding culture, we discerned three distinct ways that girls from a range of backgrounds participate in what we call skater girlhood. "Hardcore" or "serious skaters," among them Tori from a working-class background, referred to themselves as skaters. They frequented skate parks, had mastered a number of tricks, and knew how to assemble their own boards. Those we designated, more simply, as "skaters" included Priscilla, an aboriginal girl from a middle-class background. Like other Skater girls, she enjoyed the "lifestyle" but skated less frequently than the "hardcore" Skater girls and had mastered only the basics, although she did know a few tricks. Finally, our category Skater girl includes "skater affiliates" like Gracie, Sandy, and Amanda—all middle-class but of different ethnic backgrounds. They were identified or known as "skaters" among their peers, based on their friendship with other skaters, an affinity for skater culture, or both. These diverse positionings within skater culture reflect the way that any of the girlhoods discussed in this book are snapshots of ongoing projects of "becoming"; girlhood is always in the process of formation and is never really fully formed. What the Skater girls in this chapter shared, and what initially brought them to our attention as performing an "alternative" girlhood, was the way that they consciously distanced themselves from conventional girlhood.

No matter which degree of involvement girls maintained in skateboarding, they described Popular girls as trendy, boy crazy, and clueless. Epitomized by the Popular girls described in Chapter Four, these girls were seen to waste their energy by worrying about clothes, looks, and boyfriends. Their tight low-cut tank tops and low-riding jeans from expensive, brand name stores were a particular point of derision for Skater girls. While some of the skater boys were attracted to the Popular girls' display of sexuality, Skater girls generally tried to resist enacting this kind of "feminine" power, seeing it as "fake" and as based on a passive bid for attention from the boys. Gracie complained that Popular girls often played at being seen as "dumb" and "tough," while Sandy described their performance as "a façade."

Reflecting these complaints, Skater girls actively resisted the emphasized femininity performed by Popular girlhood. They described themselves as individuals with unique personalities who took pride in being different, fun, and alternative. They could go to great lengths to differentiate themselves from the Bun girls[4]:

> Yeah, because, you know, the whole thing, like, where a lot of girls want to be sexy? That is totally the opposite of us. We don't. We don't and we kind of don't really like those kind of girls that do, because it's for popularity and stuff like that (Zoe).

Through skater style, these girls wanted to "be their own person," "to stand out" (for example, by wearing safety pins as earrings), or be "funky" (for example, by dying their hair blue or wearing an "explosive shirt"). They shopped and dressed to make a statement about their individuality and difference from mainstream kids. As described by Sara, "mainstream" kids were into "like Roxy shoes, Mavi jeans. Like blond hair, baby blue visors, poofy white vests—stuff like that. I'm just describing how they look 'cause that's how you would identify them." In a seeming protest against the corporate consumerism embodied by this style, a number of Skater girls made a point of telling Shauna that they shopped at Value Village and other second-hand clothing stores, while Tori designed her own clothes as a "hobby." Grenn and Lexi (both from working-class homes) insisted that they were following "no fashion trend at all" and that, as a result, their preppy classmates designated them as "weird." Whatever image they intended to convey, skateboarding required these girls to wear comfortable clothing that enabled them to move with ease on their boards. Zoe explained: "Like other stuff—you know, that really tight stuff, those can get annoying after awhile. And you can't do anything on a board in it."

Given their conscious rejection of commodified expressions of Selfhood, the increasing popularity of skater style among non-skating peers complicated the otherwise mundane act of adopting casual or alternative clothing. Madeline pointed out that some girls at her school bought expensive skater paraphernalia that they did not use, or even need, for skateboarding. These kids were called "posers." A poser wears the right clothing, such as wide sneakers with fat laces, brand name pants and hoodies and, of course, carries a skateboard. But posers do not really skate. Although boys can be posers, too, girls who attempt access to the label "skater" in this way are singled out for this derogatory title. It is assumed that poser girls hang around the skate park as a way to meet skater boys and to flirt. Posers were targets of derision among "real" Skater girls who themselves were often accused, especially by boys, of being posers.

The tendency for "rich" kids to encroach on skater culture because of their ability to sport skateboard "props" annoyed working-class girls like Tori perhaps the most:

> It bugs me 'cause you see all these preppy little kids and they are going and buying skate shoes and skate clothing, which makes the price go up for people like us who depend on that. Like my shoes have the biggest ollie[5] hole in them, like you have no idea!

Tori went on to explain that she used to be able to replace her shoes for $30, but now the "cheapest shoe" cost her $120. Pointing to her skate shoe, she explained:

> This piece in here gets thrashed the most because when you ollie, it rubs up against your board. So you want nice plastic in here and you want the lips to be up high, and in order to get that, you have to pay [a lot].

As a consequence of this kind of problem, the commodification of skater culture sharpened some of the girls' awareness of class relations. At first it seemed a bit odd to us that, despite her skating ability, Grenn was eager to point out that she was "not athletic." When asked if she was "into other sports," Grenn insisted, "No, I *hate* sports! Skateboarding is not a sport!" Although there is no doubt that skateboarding requires physical strength, balance, and agility, to call it a "sport" seemed to associate it in Grenn's mind with the much-hated preppies, who traditionally have used sports (and cheerleading) as a route to social status within school-based culture (see Eder 1995).

Like Grenn and Lexi, Tori's roots were solidly working class, and she spent her early teenage years in a high school of predominantly white students located in a town divided down the middle by social class. In Grenn's case, "There's this side [where we are], and then there's this side over there. *Those* are the rich people." Her school was ruled by "snobby preps" who had "blonde hair," wore "lots of makeup," and were "very slim," almost "anorexic." Preps were described as "rich," they followed "the trends" and wore "good clothes." In Grenn's school, skaters were far from popular, and, in fact, some were labeled "losers" by their peers, reflecting the fact that a small group of skaters were either "into drugs," had left school, or both. Relations between the preps and non-preps, including the skaters, were antagonistic. Explained Grenn:

> They [the preps] don't agree with the way I look. They don't agree with the way I act. They just don't agree with my music. They don't agree with like anything about me, right?

When asked why the preps gave her such a hard time, Lexi explained, "Because I don't dress like *they* do [in tight clothes]." In a passionate statement in support of the "underground culture" of skating and against the "preppy culture" that characterized the dynamics described in Chapter Four, Tori evinced at least a partial class consciousness:

> I don't want to be a part of that [preppy culture], because you see the way people treat each other. You see the way things are stacked up. Like, it's all about what you have and what you don't have [by way of material goods] that makes you who you are.

By contrast, she pointed out that skaters "don't expect anything from you—except *you*."[6]

The commodification of youth culture has been interpreted by some commentators as a signal that young people are "duped" by capitalist interests and "self-absorbed" about their appearance. Here we see that the commodification of "alternative" style, such as that adopted by Skater girls, not only increases class antagonisms among youth but can render the sociocultural processes through which they struggle to claim oppositional Selfhoods at least a bit more apparent. Thus, while consumerism supports an individualistic discourse of "identity choices," it also carries the potential to undermine assumptions that our identities are freely fashioned and that "alternative" style expresses an "authentic" Selfhood. It carries the potential for a "critical consciousness" about the everyday politics of doing gender.

This critical reflexivity, which we view as potentially feminist, was sharpened by the gendered conflicts that made it difficult for Skater girls to position themselves in skater culture. Captured by the label "poser" and underlying Tori's complaints, one problem for Skater girls was how non-skating girls were often passive "watchers" who used their inability to skate as a way to meet skater boys: "Like, they get on the board and ask for guys to hold their hand and pull them. And they start screaming, you know, acting weird… We just roll our eyes and walk away" (Zoe). Creating a distance between girls who embody this kind of femininity and themselves as "alternative" was as important to Skater girls as was gaining the respect of skater boys. By purposefully juxtaposing themselves to Popular girls in particular, Skater girls demonstrated an embodied resistance to a form of femininity that they saw as detrimental to girlhood itself. In order to differentiate their gender practices from conventional femininity, as well as to skate comfortably, Skater girls dressed casually, avoided wearing makeup, and did not engage in sexualized display through style. They also spoke their minds and did not pretend to be "ditzy." Most importantly, they did not feign the need for skater boy assistance.

The most notable distinction between Skater girl femininity and that of posers or Popular girls was not simply "discursive." It was found in the difference between "watching" and "doing" at the skate park. As "doers," or girls who actually skated, Skater girls engaged in the embodied resignification of girlhood through distinctly "unfeminine" bodily comportment. Skateboarding is an activity that demands physicality and bravery. To skate is to know how to fall and how to execute complicated and risky tricks. Even the most basic trick, the ollie (where a skater jumps in the air with her board attached to her feet and then lands smoothly on it again) runs the risk of injury. Ollies, kickflips, grinding, and carving are all maneuvers that must be performed fearlessly and with the full knowledge that falling is likely, especially for a novice. This kind of physical audacity is not usually associated with being a girl.

As Harris (1999: 116–117) notes, girls are encouraged to relate to their bodies as objects that exist for the aesthetic pleasure of others and, as we argued in Chapter Four, their bodies symbolize a bourgeois moral order. Young (1989) characterizes conventional femininity as based on a particular bodily comportment that is restrictive of big movement and risk-taking because girls must learn to "manage" their "unruly" bodies. The motility and spatiality for "proper" girlhood is timid, uncertain, and hesitant, as girls are not brought up to "claim" public

*Betty and Veronica as boy watchers at the skate park*

space. One result is that girls are not supported to develop the same confidence and freedom in their movements as boys. Against this convention, skateboarding engages girls in transgressive bodily comportment: girls must be willing to straddle their boards with a wide stance, dangle their arms freely by their sides, and spread-eagle for balance. By thus violating what their classmates often viewed as "proper" femininity, Skater girls courted the surveillance of both skater boys and Popular girls.

Typically, girls are not often seen by either themselves or others as capable of achieving physical acts that require strength or of handling the pain that such physical acts can incur. Emily, for example, told Shauna that she would like to skate, but that it "looks hard." Boys alone are ascribed the confidence and craziness needed to carry skater tricks through to completion. When asked why girls did not skate as much as boys, Onyx noted that girls are likely to see skateboarding as "a guy thing to do. It is our thing to sit around and chit chat and gossip and stuff and watch them skateboard." Grover added, "Yeah, and some girls are kind of, like, scared." Indeed, some of the less serious Skater girls confirmed Emily's claim that girls "don't want to continuously fall." In contrast, "guys, they fall and they keep falling, but it's amazing, but they always get back up and, like, try the same thing again. It's quite amazing." Overall, boys were claimed to be more "risk taking" than girls. "They don't care if they, like, get bruises and stuff. They'll be, like, 'Yeah! Cuts!' And then girls will be, like, 'Oh no!'" (Amanda). In short, "doing" skater girlhood challenges the discursive limits of what girls and boys are able to "naturally" accomplish. We were thus curious to know why not all girls were so intimidated.

Onyx retorted that she and her friends "did not think like that. We wanted to try it." Trying gave girls first-hand experience of the risks that boys were seen to "naturally" embrace. Kate did a "face plant" during her first attempt to skateboard:

> She [her friend and interview partner, Christine] lives on a really, really steep hill. And I decided I was going to go down it [laughs]. And it was really steep and [had] bumpy spots and everything, and I didn't make it very far, and I jumped off the board, and I like slid on my hip and my eye and I got like a black eye and everything.

Rather than get "freaked out," Kate maintained with pride, "I'm back on there, still doing like weird stuff." Despite socially and self-imposed sanctions, girls like Kate willingly accepted the risks involved in skateboarding as a way of setting themselves apart from the emphasized femininity that made other girls Popular. Not only did girl skaters challenge the skater boys at the park, they also challenged forms of femininity with which they disagreed. Their purposeful self-positioning as "skaters" worked to push girlhood in new directions.

Pushing the boundaries was not as "simple" as the above account may imply, however. This is because skater girlhood entails the kinds of activities that have not only been designated as "unlady-like" in the past, they brought Skater girls directly into a social space dominated by boys. While we have seen in Chapter Four how girls police the boundaries of idealized femininity, boys—especially skater boys—policed the boundaries of skaterhood as a community of masculine practice. Paetcher (2003b: 548) maintains that "communities of practice of masculinity remain relatively powerful compared to those of femininity." How were the Skater girls in our study able to sustain their transgressive practices in the face of hostility and resistance on the part of boys who "owned" the identity label "skater"?[7]

Until recently, girls' presence in public spaces—especially the streets—has been seen to invite sexual harassment or to signal engagement in prostitution. Girls, like adult women, have been physically as well as discursively "confined"[8] to the sphere of family life. One result is that girl culture, when acknowledged, has been characterized as "bedroom culture," a culture reconstituting the private sphere as predominantly "feminine" space (see Harris 2001b; also Kearney 2007).[9] One challenge for Skater girls, therefore, was claiming a presence in the public places where skateboarding is performed. While Vancouver has several good places for skateboarding, most are burdened with a reputation for drugs and vandalism. The largest skate park in the city was recently shut down due to its high level of drug trafficking and the defacement of property. Underground skaters, who detest anything remotely mainstream, avoid the parks, confining their practice to the streets, the parking lots of local establishments, and the (now monitored by security) area surrounding the art gallery downtown. For those skaters who do not mind mainstream skateboarding, skateboard parks are the best place to practice, learn tricks, and participate in skate culture. But no matter which location, at the time of our fieldwork, there were very few girl skateboarders.

Sandy, a self-proclaimed skateboarding "coach" for her friends, announced in no uncertain terms, "Like, a lot of girls don't skateboard!" Despite the media frenzy around teen pop singer Avril Lavigne, who was dubbed a "skate punk" in her early career due to her style and loose connections to skateboarding, girls are often relegated to the sidelines while the boys "do their thing." While young women (in their twenties and early thirties) are more visible in skateboarding parks, it is rare to find girls actually using boards in skater parks (see Leventhal 2005). What is more likely to be observed is a bevy of girls hanging off the railing as watchers, fans, and girlfriends of boy skaters, making it much harder for girls than boys to gain legitimate skater status. This context makes the story recounted below significant; as a result of recruiting girls into our study through referrals, Shauna happened upon a group of eight skater girlfriends whom she dubbed "the Park Gang." For our purposes, their experiences illustrate struggles surrounding girls' performance of a consciously alternative girlhood.

## THE PARK GANG

The members of the Park Gang were fourteen and fifteen years old at the time of their interviews—born in the decade defined by a backlash against second-wave feminism (Faludi 1992). They all lived in an area of Vancouver known for its family orientation, professional demographics, and urban chic. Four were Canadian-born Chinese girls, two were white, one was a Canadian-born Latina, and one was half First Nations, half white. With the exception of one girl, who attended a Catholic school, the girls all attended a large urban high school known for its Asian population and academic achievement. Skateboarding was a passion for four of the girls; two of the girls called themselves "coaches" in the sense that they skated but preferred to "just help"; and two of the girls were what we called skater affiliates—they were involved in skate culture, music, and style as were all of the Park Gang, but without the desire to actually skate. Together, the Park Gang hung out at a skate park that would be considered amateurish compared to the larger and more daunting parks downtown. This particular park was connected to a community center in an affluent neighborhood. Unlike other skating venues, this park was relatively clean and safe. Perhaps as a consequence, it was a hangout for different youth, many of whom did not skate but instead congregated on the benches, picnic tables, and steps that surrounded the concrete area designated for skaters. This was a place where girls and boys gathered to socialize.

Members of the Park Gang were relatively new skaters when Shauna met them. Grover started because a friend did not want to learn alone:

> ...there are not too many girl skateboarders, so it is kind of better—she felt more comfortable if there was, like, you know, another person that could be with her. And so she asked if I wanted to try it, so I said sure, and, um, her brothers started teaching us and I found it was something that, it was a lot of fun, so I just stayed with it, so I'm still learning.

When more of the Park Gang decided to try skateboarding, they ventured into the skate park with their boards for the first time, hoping to gain acceptance and to practice. To their disappointment, the park proved to be "owned" by skater boys, who put the girls under surveillance. Skater boys constantly asked members of the Park Gang to show them what they could do. Zoe found this questioning of their abilities off-putting. She admitted that, "sometimes we don't want to skate around them [boys] 'cause, like, they do really good stuff and we're just kind of learning."

The Park Gang quickly realized that being the only girl skaters at the park singled them out for harassment. To the skater boys who dominated the park and acted as its gatekeepers, the park was "their" space—a space that left very little room for girls unless they took up the traditionally feminine positions of watcher, fan, or girlfriend. Gracie theorized that girls skate less than boys due to this kind of territorial attitude: "Some [girls] are kind of, like, scared, because, um, of what people might think of them." When asked what she meant, Gracie responded that the lack of girls who skated at the park might make the boys question girls' right to belong. Onyx added that the skater boys viewed the Park Gang as "invading their space." Grover felt that the Park Gang threatened the skater boys "just because, you know, girls are doing *their* sport." She went on to explain the attitudes of some of the boys at the park:

Sometimes, they'll be kind of, like, rude, like, I don't know if it's on purpose, but they just, you know, have this kind of attitude… I guess they think they're so good and one of them or two of them—I'm not sure if all of them are, like, sponsored by skateboarding companies—so they always feel, like, you know, they're kind of superior and so, you know, we're only a year younger, so it's kind of, like, we're obviously not as good as them, but they kind of forget that they had to start somewhere too, so, and it would be harder for us because we're girls.

Predictably, the gendered politics of the park soon rendered it a contested space. Grover, Gracie, and Onyx understood that the boys were threatened by their presence but wished the boys could appreciate how hard it was for girls to get started. They wanted the boys to see them as equals who deserved the same kind of camaraderie that the boys gave each other. Instead, the boys saw the Park Gang as interlopers with little legitimate claim to the space. Some of the boys accused some of the Park Gang of being posers. This accusation required immediate action to prove the skater boys wrong, as recounted by Zoe:

… there's this one time where a couple of the guys thought we were just—they said it [that we were posers] out loud, that we're just there for the guys and we're like, "No!" And they're like, "But you're here all the time, like almost every day, skateboarding, and so are we." So we did this whole thing where we didn't come there for quite a while just to show. And then we came back and they stopped bugging us about it.

The girls involved in the park boycott practiced at an elementary school for two weeks and went to the park only when they knew the boys would not be around. When asked what they had gained by boycotting the park, Zoe responded, "That we're not there just for the guys and we're not there to watch them and be around them." Upon returning to the park, the girls suddenly received more respect and experienced less harassment from the skater boys. Zoe noted a distinct change in their attitude. "I guess to some level, they treated us like an equal to them, kind of." Instead of placing the girls under surveillance, the skater boys watched the Park Gang in order to assess "how they were doing." They took an interest in the girls' progress. When asked if she thought they had successfully changed the opinions of the skater boys, Zoe enthusiastically replied, "Well, yes!"

In essence, the girls involved in the boycott retreated to a safe space where they were not being monitored. When they reemerged, the Park Gang was ready to fully occupy the subject position of "skater." In so doing, the girls resignified who a "skater" could be by challenging the skater boys' power to name who had a legitimate claim to the park. By monitoring the subject position of "skater," the boys not only guarded the "purity" of the masculinity that characterized their community of practice, they retained some control over the girls' sense of who they were. Recognizing how unfair boys' privilege is, the girls responded by retreating to a space where they were free to think and behave as "skaters." When they returned to the park, they were armed with both a sense of confidence about their skating abilities and a sense of entitlement to the "skater" label. They took authorizing power away from the boys and legitimated themselves.

Before the boycott, skater girls were thought of in a very specific way: as posers, flirts, or interlopers. Working together the girls altered how the boys thought of them and, more significantly, how they thought of themselves. The Park Gang recognized how they were being subordinated at the park and successfully challenged the process of belonging. They did so in part by positioning themselves against the common label used to position girls in skater culture: that of "poser." Changing their positioning within skater discourse and skater culture required the girls to challenge not only the male domination of skater culture, but also the tenets of "proper" feminine decorum. In this way, the Park Gang legitimated the subject position of "skater" for girls at the park and expanded the possibilities for subjectivity within girlhood. As Pete pointed out:

> Lots of girls have actually started [skating] because my group started and then they kind of feel in power. I think they kind of feel empowered that they can start now, that it's okay for girls to skate.

Clearly, the Park Gang's resignification of girlhood enacted a politics that worked to reshape gender categories in a male-dominated locale. As Grover and Onyx explained to Shauna, some girls "are scared" to challenge boys' domination of public space. Grover maintained that while some girls might like to try skateboarding, they are "kind of like scared because of what people might think of them. They might think that the guys are kind of—you know. Like 'What are you doing?'" As a result of purposefully positioning themselves as skaters, the Park Gang worked toward an embodied resignification of girlhood that challenged the male domination of public space. In order to do so, they had to challenge not only skater boys, but also the emphasized femininity that earns girls "rewards" in male-dominated culture.

## GIRLHOOD IN THE REMAKING?

In summary, Skater girls consciously positioned themselves against "posers"—girls who attended the park to attract the romantic interest of skater boys. Poser girls were well-coifed and polished in their self-presentation. Their demeanor suggested that they were physically "inept." The girls in this chapter rejected such a feminine performance, which they derided as a ploy for boys' attention. Skater girls were clear that their primary purpose in life was not to earn boys' interest as sexual objects. Instead, they strove to be accepted as boys' equals through demonstration of their competence in skateboarding, an activity historically associated with alternative masculinity (Beal 1995, 1996). In order to do so, members of the Park Gang found it necessary to come together to share their knowledge and encourage one another. This sharing demonstrates how the mutual recognition made possible through a supportive community can further girls' capacity to transgress gendered conventions. Intentional or not, their performance of an alternative girlhood represents a collaborative challenge to gender inequality, the kind of collaboration that we usually associate with feminism. This challenge is not an inevitable consequence of taking up what has been historically male-dominated space, however. Grover and Onyx, for example, expressed a preference for boys' culture and distanced themselves from girls because "if you hang out with girls you won't know as much ... it [girls' culture] gets repetitive."

Tori spoke about "skater culture" with a more oppositional, working-class inflection than most participants. Perhaps in solidarity with male skaters, Tori resisted her friend Priscilla's attempts to generalize about, and criticize, boys' behavior. For example, in response to Priscilla's complaint about being propositioned by older men and being "gawked at," Tori retorted, "Chicks are as bad as guys for sitting there and turning people into meat [sexual objects]." At one level, Tori can be heard as rejecting a gender essentialism espoused by other girls in our study. Yet, at another level she can be seen as blocking an exploration of gender and enforced heterosexuality as shaping girls' behavior. Drawing on a fierce individualism evident in skater culture more generally, Tori argued that guy skaters "don't mean to discriminate" against girls, but there are just not many girls willing to endure the physical pain involved in learning how to skateboard. She did not report feeling "intimidated" by boys, the way other girl Skaters did. We do not think it a coincidence that Tori was the lone girl in the Skater sample to refer to herself (without irony) as a "skater chick." Our impression is that the more hardcore Skater girls like Tori identify with skater culture, the less likely they are to see sexism operating at anything but an individual level. We also suggest that all-girl communities of practice are much more likely than mixed communities to encourage a dialogue and critique of sexism.

That is not to say that the girls who skated in all-girl groups identified with feminist critiques of male privilege. Madeline described herself as a feminist but quickly added "although not full-fledged." Her feminism was about standing up for herself "as a girl," especially when ridiculed by boys as a skater. Gracie and Sandy likewise saw feminism as needed to "make sure that there is always that equal power." They opined that even Bun girls would stand up for themselves in the face of sexism. At the same time, while Gracie declared, "I am a feminist," her interview partner Sandy's identification was "qualified": "I wouldn't say I was a feminist. I mean, I am for it." Other Skater girls expressed opinions that ranged from ambivalence to antifeminism. Gauge claimed: "I always thought being a feminist was kind of silly."[10] As we have seen, Emily found value for feminism "in the past" when "guys were more like 'in charge,'" but argued that today it is excessive because feminists are "trying to boost the women above the men." As a consequence, she reasoned "It's constantly like a fight instead of just being equal. They just want to be better than men." In the final analysis, few of the Skater girls in our study unequivocally claimed an identity as feminist. Nevertheless, their actions were no small challenge to the gender expectations of both female and male classmates.

Skateboarding "as a girl" entailed both physical and social risks. According to Tori, "you've got to be fearless as shit" in order to skate because "24/7... you're riding along cement. When you fall, it *hurts*. It doesn't hurt just a little bit—it hurts a lot." Unlike the case for boys, getting hurt was seen as a deterrent for girls, leading Amanda to claim while boys "don't care if they, like, get bruises and stuff," girls would be, "Oh no!" The glee with which Zoe described the first time that she "wiped out" is therefore impressive: "I fell really hard. I was just, like, 'Aahh!' kind of." Despite this "initiation," "then I just wanted to do it again, because it was like 'Wow!'"

Skating entailed more than physical risks. Zoe reported that the Park Gang endured gossip by the Populars at school: "I've heard people talking. One of my friends said 'Oh. They think you're weird.' [It's] because we're not so ditzy and we make up these words. And we're always like energetic people and we're really our own group kind of like." She went on to explain that being "energetic" meant that they were getting more attention than the "ditzy" girls who "don't really like [it] so you're kind of, not on their good list if you're getting all the attention." Social conflict with Popular girls was about more than "stealing their show," however. Reflecting its origins in California surf culture, skateboarding positions girls against the moral order described in Chapter Four. In mainstream culture, skateboarding is associated with nonconformity, specifically to middle-class mores supporting respect for private property, the work ethic, and capitalist consumer culture. At many of the schools skaters had reputations for "partying" and being "into" marijuana, earning them the label "slacker" among mainstream classmates.

At Grenn and Lexi's school, skaters were considered "losers" by their peers. Both girls had been challenged to physical fights by Populars who did not like "how they looked." Here we remind the reader that Grenn and Lexi described themselves as coming from the "wrong" side of a town divided down the middle by class. Their case shows how clique membership, while not entirely determined by class, displays a polarization of attitudes toward class characteristics. In the case of Skater girls, embodiment of working-class characteristics was a moral stigma. As Eckert (1989: 4, 5) notes, the categories used to organize school-based peer cultures—in her study, jocks and preps on the one hand and "burnouts" on the other hand—can be seen as "adolescent embodiments of the middle and working class, respectively." Grenn and Lexi's anger at Popular girls can thus be heard as a displacement of class antagonisms (see Bettie 2003). Skater girlhood can be seen as their rejection of the school's role in privileging certain (i.e., middle-class) students. In Tori's case, we have seen how it led to at least a partial class consciousness. Thus, working-class girls like Tori took up skater girlhood discourse in a more oppositional way than the middle-class girls in our Skater girl sample. By contrast, the middle-class girls appeared to be attracted to skater culture as a way to distance themselves from the sexism of mainstream school-based culture and, if academically high achievers, to be seen as fun (see Kelly, Pomerantz, and Currie 2005).

Whatever their conscious motivations, skateboarding aligns girls with values and styles of self-presentation that, historically, have signified masculinity rather than femininity. Skater girls took pleasure in the mastery of the physical competence required to skateboard. This mastery put their identity practices into direct conflict with the mandate for girls to act like "proper ladies" by exercising bodily constraint and avoiding physical risk-taking. As a result, Skater girls disrupt the heterosexual matrix that Butler (1990: 151, note 6) identifies as the "prop" of gender inequality. This matrix refers to a "grid of cultural intelligibility through which bodies, genders, and desires are naturalized." It forms "a hegemonic discursive/epistemic model of gender intelligibility that assumes that for bodies to cohere and make sense there must be a stable sex expressed through a stable gender": masculinity is read to express male bodies, femininity female bodies. This matrix thus accounts for the performativity of conventional gender identities because it provides a taken-for-granted framework for normative relationships through our identities as "girls" and "boys," "women" and "men."

Reflecting the power of this matrix, the baggy and "comfortable" clothes preferred by Skater girls (hoodies, T-shirts, baggy pants, and sneakers), coupled with their physical deportment, gave their performances an ambiguous status in the heterosexual hierarchy that characterizes school-based peer cultures. Spunk and Gauge were deemed "weird" because, as they explained, "we dress so differently." Dressing "weird" did not distance Skater girls simply from female classmates who policed conformity to emphasized femininity. Their appearance carried the possibility of not being perceived as "dateable" by boys, many of whom tended to prefer girls who dressed in overtly sexual styles. Grover liked a certain skater boy, for example, but noticed that his current girlfriend dressed in a conventionally feminine way. Despite her disappointment, Grover maintained matter-of-factly that "I wouldn't try to become a Bun girl just to satisfy him." In this sense, Skater girls do not simply avoid the need to navigate the "two worlds" described by Dephy, Susie, and Tina in Chapter Four; their gender practices located them in a "third," contested space. By "third" we argue that the Skater girls disrupt the binaries that sustain the cultural intelligibility of gender. It is not that these girls adopt practices associated with masculinity: although Skater girls do take up a more active, "in control" Subject position, this positioning is differently read and evaluated than when performed by boys. Their identity practices signify something altogether different. In other words, we do not view Skater girls as "tomboys." While "tomboy" is generally used to imply the rejection of anything associated with girlhood, and the temporary loyalty to masculine practices, Skater girls did not disavow girlhood but rather celebrated it. Even though they complained about girl culture, Grover told Shauna that the worst thing is "guys who think they're better than girls, and girls who think guys are better than girls." Thus we do not see Skater girls as realigning themselves into the more powerful, masculine position but challenging the gendered order in ways that tomboys do not.

In summary, girls' conscious positioning of themselves as "skateboarders" necessitated the embodied resignification of girlhood as well as the category "skater." Bringing Skater girlhood into existence reauthorized the Subject of skateboarding discourse, undermining the power of boys to grant membership in skater culture as a community of gendered practice. As optimistically claimed by Pete, "Lots of girls have actually started" skateboarding because "they [now] feel in power." Through their performances as "skaters," members of the Park Gang challenged rather than reconstituted norms that governed peer culture at their school. For this reason, despite the rejection by many of the Skater girls of feminism as an identity category, we heard a feminist subjectivity at work: the politics enacted by Park Gang girls was based on their awareness of how the rules of conventional femininity (and masculinity) limit girls' sense of "who they are" and "who they can be." In other words, their politics was informed by recognition of how they had been constituted as girls in and through discourses surrounding both "femininity" and skateboarding. Their transgression makes visible the socially constructed—therefore malleable—nature of girlhood. Can we thus claim their practices as an emergent feminism?

## FEMINISM IN THE REMAKING?

The transgressive actions of the Park Gang approximate what Misciagno (1997) calls de facto feminism or "feminism as praxis." Misciagno argues that, in the context of late modernism, feminism is better understood through the individual and small group practices of women rather than looking for the large-scale social action and explicit political agendas that characterized second-wave feminism. While the latter was ostensibly organized around "leaders" who raised consciousness and motivated others into action, de facto feminism arises from the everyday efforts of individual women to grapple with the contradictions in their lives. Thus, de facto feminism embraces the practices of women who do not explicitly identify as feminists but whose everyday actions create greater freedom for women generally. It emphasizes that becoming a feminist is a much more complex and ongoing process than typically acknowledged: one is not positioned simply either "inside" or "outside" feminism by taking up a Subject position in feminist discourse (see Currie, Kelly, and Pomerantz 2007). This is because discourses are not once and for all subservient to power or raised up against it. Rather, they are complex and unstable. They can be both an instrument and an effect of power, a point of resistance and—possibly—a starting point for an opposing strategy (Foucault 1990: 100).

While Skater girls can be credited with resignifying girlhood, in the final analysis, we view their actions as feminist in *effect* rather than *intent*. Like Misciagno, we are open to the idea that feminism is being resignified through the actions of girls and women who struggle to redefine the parameters of girlhood and womanhood; this idea enables us to think about feminism as in a constant state of becoming. In becoming women, girls bear "the permanent possibility of a certain resignifying process" (Butler 1992: 13); in the same way that they resignify what it means "to be a girl or woman," they actively resignify the possibilities of what it means to "be feminist." Just as there is no pregiven girlhood, there are no pregiven "feminists." Here Budgeon's (2001) notion of emergent feminism avoids replaying a dichotomy between "old" and "new" feminisms as a form of generationalism (see Parkins 1999; Firth 2002).

Whether or not the Skater girls in our study will "become" self-identified feminists is a historical and not theoretical question. Theoretically speaking, however, we do not support the view that gender equality will come through individualized transgressions that draw attention to the instability of the cultural markers of femininity. While power works *through* discourse, we do not view discourse *as* power. As noted by Weedon (1987: 112), "to be effective, they [discourses] require activation through the agency of individuals." Because we see experience as a potential "source" of knowledge about how power operates, it seems to us that girls who push the boundaries of girlhood—as do members of the Park Gang—are more likely than those benefiting from conventional girlhood to critically interrogate the confines of girlhood.

Despite complaints by socially powerful Popular girls about the mandate to dress and behave in conventional ways and that school was much "easier" for boys, they nevertheless received benefits from the heteronormativity of school-based culture. These are the girls who were likely to describe "girl power" in terms of female sexuality, drawing on a discourse that reinforces the very conventions they found problematic. As a result of this contradiction, even though many girls complained about the effects of the double standard that regulated their behavior at school, they also expressed confusion about its existence. Among these girls, Riley (a nonskater) told Shauna: "If a guy were to sleep with say fifteen girls, everybody would like reward him for that. But if a girl were to sleep with fifteen guys, she would be called a 'slut' and have the worst reputation. I don't understand that! It doesn't make any sense in the world to me." Riley's puzzlement shows the difficulty many girls had in naming what they experienced as problematic. While we found it interesting that the Park Gang "made up names" in order to criticize the everyday dynamics of youth culture, we found the necessity for them to do so alarming. As Pete explained, making up words was "kind of having a way to express yourself when there's nothing like—there's no word to explain what you're feeling. So you kind of make something up." We have already seen that what they "made up" included words that enabled them to criticize the sexual double standard that denies girls and women agency. The Park Gang coined the term "glutty" in their critique of a standard that favors boys. In like fashion, they used the term "skank monkey" to designate the male equivalent of Bun girls, allowing them to express what they saw as the superficiality of the Popular crowd at their school.[11]

We cannot definitively say whether or not the made-up language of the Park Gang came before (hence enabled) their transgression of established peer-based culture or is a consequence of pushing established boundaries past their limits. Whatever the case, it testifies to the importance of what we have highlighted as their community of practice.[12] Gracie maintained that Park Gang members gained self-confidence from their group because, when among themselves, "We don't really care" [what others think] and "don't laugh at each other [when they try things]... When we're all together, I think it's easier for us to be more, you know, out going and more ourselves... I don't really feel like I'm all myself at school unless I'm with them." In the same way that this community supported what Misciagno might characterize as feminist praxis, it supports the kind of dialogue that enabled girls to invent "names" for what oppressed them. As Lave and Wenger (1991) note, the transformative potential of membership in a community of practice comes from participating in the production of meaning regarding collective activity. For us as teachers, this necessity for girls to invent a language that identifies women's subordination is disturbing, because it testifies to the continued ability for male privilege to define our lives as women (see Lees 1986). Without a language to name this privilege, the knowledge about gendered power shared among the Park Gang will not extend beyond their local community of practice—to classmates and teachers, for example.

In closing, if "girl power" is to empower girls, it must do more than enable them to find their voice; as we have seen in Chapter Four, the nature of discourses that are available to enable girls to speak "as girls" matters. As feminists, what we would give girls is a language and discourses that show them how "girlhood" is a social construction that positions "girls" as subordinate to boys. What makes feminism relevant today is not whether young women take up the identity as "feminist," but whether male privilege continues to shape girls' thinking—and girls' opportunities—for "who they are" and "who they can become." While gaining a voice is a place to start, speaking *about girlhood* is as important as speaking *as girls*. We take up this challenge in Chapter Nine.

NOTES

1    While an extended discussion is beyond the limitations of discussion here, it is important to note that we deliberately did not initiate discussions of sexuality during interviews, despite our recognition of its importance. This decision was based on a number of considerations that include: ethical issues accompanying the employment of graduate students; the institutional requirement for ethical approval of our research; and consideration of parental concerns over recruitment of girls—as described in Chapter Three—by our research assistants.

2    Importantly, Jordan went on to say: "I've only been called butch once, so it doesn't really bother me, but then there's like—uhm, an incident in Grade 9 where like—I didn't want to do something with a guy and so he called me 'fat.'"

3    The exception is the study of juvenile delinquency. Here feminist researchers pointed out that girls' delinquency, unlike boys' agency, took the form of "status offences" that violated the norms of middle-class femininity (see Schlossman and Wallach 1978; Kelly 1993).

4    As noted in Chapter Four, note 2, Bun girls were Popular girls who earned this name because they, at one time, all wore their hair in buns.

5    An ollie, the basis of most other skateboarding tricks, consists of a girl smacking down the end of her board, moving her foot forward to bring the board up in the air, then landing with her feet equally apart in the middle of the board.

6    It interested us that Tina claimed that she preferred skater boys to "all the preppy, like party guys. They want less. They want friendship. They are more into you and not into how much you drink and stuff like that." At this point, her interview partner, Susie, interrupted, adding, "And how much you put out."

7    Here we acknowledge that male relatives (brothers and male cousins) often introduced the girls to skateboarding. As we describe below, in Grover's case, a friend's brother played an important role. It would be interesting to know to what extent the success of Skater girls (like the Park Gang) works to change the attitudes of skater boys—hence the sexism—of skater culture.

8    We recognize this confinement as ideological and class-based because, historically, many women supported their families and dependents in the public sphere of employment.

9    While a number of writers characterize girls' "bedroom culture" as a retreat from the public world where "politics" happens, Kearney (2007: 138) argues that "girls' production and exchange of media texts signals their development of what Nancy Fraser calls subaltern counterpublics, 'parallel discursive arenas where members of subordinated social groups invent and circulate counter-discourses, so as to formulate oppositional interpretations of their identities, interests, and needs' (1993, p. 14). In other words, contemporary female youth are not retreating to private spaces; they are reconfiguring such sites to create new publics that can better serve their needs, interests, and goals." The findings from our study, discussed in Chapter Six, support Kearney's interpretation; as we shall see, some girls in our study "played" with their gendered identities online, challenging conventional representations of both femininity and masculinity.

10   Here we note that Gauge's reasoning was based on her belief that feminism denies girls self-expression by dictating that "you're not allowed" to appear or act "feminine." Thus she argued against feminism on the basis that, "You shouldn't try to be someone you're not based on things that people say." We explore this kind of reasoning in Chapter Seven.

11   They also created the term "snorkumdorks" (used in variation). As Onyx explained to Shauna: "If someone's like uhm, we think someone is really stupid... We don't say stupid, we call them a 'stork' and a 'dork.'" Grover elaborated: "So we will say 'snorkum-

dork' or words like that. Just made-up words that really couldn't hurt anyone." Significantly, they compared this way of describing classmates to the Bun girls who used "swear words." As well, Onyx talked about the Park Gang as also making fun of each other, as a way to playfully contrast themselves with the ultra-feminine Bun girls.

12  We distinguish the Park Gang as an emergent community of practice rather than as "simply" a friendship group. Whether the policing we saw in Chapter Four comes to operate to monitor membership in girl skater culture remains to be seen. During interviews, we have already heard distinctions between "authentic skaters" and "posers," for example.

# 6

# PLAYING WITH GENDER

ONLINE GIRLS[1]

*-Chapter useful*
*for my project*
*site (?) +*
*Harris (Future*
*Girl )*

As previously noted, our focus on girl power directed our attention to interviews with girls who openly challenged the rules
of conventional femininity despite their awareness of the possible negative consequences. Girls who "played" with gender online
were among those participants. Unlike skateboarding, computer use
has attracted much interest among academics, reflecting its increasingly important role in the formal curriculum of most schools and as an
informal pedagogy. Previous research has documented the gendered
nature of technology use, showing that girls are more likely to be surfing the net than to be learning computer programming and design (see
Cooper 2006; Jenson, de Castell, and Bryson 2003; Mercier, Barron, and
O'Connor 2006). In this chapter, we are interested in whether, and how,
identities in cyberspace itself are gendered. We recognized early in our
study that the Internet is often an extension of the dynamics characterizing school-based cultures (see also Clark 2005; Thiel 2005). Marie,
for example, told Shauna that she had been harassed online by a guy
who called her a "gay slut"—"the so-called term for 'stupid.'" Several
other participants mentioned rumors or gossip that had been spread
online, and a few described their own activities of being mean online.
Cherry claimed that instant messaging actually encourages people to
be "a little meaner than they are in real life, because it's not like you're

face to face." Cherry's interview partner, Alana, described how easy it was to exclude a "clingy" classmate she disliked: "She kept trying to talk to me on MSN, and she was just being like really annoying, and so I blocked her."

Without discounting these types of online exchanges,[2] in this chapter, we are interested in the possibility that the Internet can also enable girls to "escape" the gendered dynamics of their local peer culture.[3] So far we have investigated the ways that girls positioned themselves (and others) in various discourses that constructed them as particular "kinds" of girls. We have seen that girls' embodiment plays an important role in how their performances of girlhood were given meaning in relation to their sexed bodies. When girls themselves participated in that assessment, their understanding of themselves and their social world was framed by a gender essentialism that sustains belief in natural differences between girls and boys, women and men. Such a belief places limits on girls' thinking about "who they are" and "who they can become." Might girls' participation in a virtual community of disembodied users challenge this essentialism?

Unfortunately, previous research has found that gender essentialism pervades video games, one of the venues through which young people participate in virtual communities constructed through computer use. This essentialism is evident in: (a) the games' design and marketing (Ray 2004; de Castell and Bryson 1997); (b) the masculinist culture of video gaming (Alloway and Gilbert 1998); (c) the absence of women' and girls' characters, the stereotypical representations of female characters, or both in many games (Deitz 1998, Martin 1999, de Castell 2002); and (d) boys' policing of gaming as belonging to them alone. In the general population, video game playing (whether on computer or console systems) is a comparatively rare activity for girls. "Almost 60% of boys in Grades 3 to 6 play video or computer games almost every day"; that number drops to 38% for boys in Grade 10. For girls, 33% of Grade 3 girls play interactive games every day, but only 6% of Grade 10 girls do (Canadian Teachers' Federation 2003: ii; see also Sanford and Madill 2006). Further, the genre of video game played differs by gender. Boys are more drawn to action and later also to role-playing games that feature fantasy, violence, and strategy, while girls are more attracted to games, like *The Sims* and *Neopets*, that offer both social interaction and story (Canadian Teachers' Federation 2003: iv).

Although almost all of the girls recruited into the computer cluster of our sample played games on computer and console systems regularly, they did not—with a few notable exceptions—identify as "gamers." Collectively, they painted the portrait of a typical gamer as a boy playing by himself in a darkened room for hours on end, who is highly technical, has fast reflexes, enjoys violence, and is perceived as a "geek," "nerd," or "loner." Shale mentioned owning and playing *Tomb Raider*, attracted to its main character, butt-kicking Lara Croft. But she got turned off by Lara Croft's graphic representation: "It just gets so repetitive having this chick with overly large boobs and a really, really huge butt, with a shadow under her butt, [so] that when she climbs up stuff, the shadow gets left behind for a couple of frames." Rose, Shale's friend and interview partner, agreed: "It's just the sexism that gets me. It's really annoying." Alana and Cherry saw their video game playing as a holdover from their days of being "really" serious "tomboys." In a similar vein, Marcia liked to play Internet pool and "killing games" like *James Bond*, a First Person Shooter game, and this, she said, marked her as "like a boy in that sense—a stereotypical version of boyish." Grenn and Lexi loved to play video games, including fighting games like *X-Men Academy*, which they agreed was uncommon for girls. In fact, Grenn was told by a boy she knew that she couldn't "play video games because I'm a girl," a claim she rejected outright.[5] In these ways, the participants in our study whom we dubbed "Online girls" were made aware that boys they knew personally were invested in maintaining video gaming—and any attendant forms of knowledge or social power flowing from that knowledge—as masculine. Like Skater girls, the girls in this chapter challenged practices that sustain the gendered nature of the liminal spaces where femininity is practiced.

Most Online girls in our study were drawn to interactive and storied activities online, including role-play games and fan fiction. In contrast to the video games enjoyed by boys, these activities allow much more player input, hence opportunities to experiment online. In both role play and fan fiction, users are present to each other through self-constructions that take the form of written claims and statements about themselves. Early proponents of the Internet—focusing on available technology of the 1970s—imagined cyberspace might free people to explore different facets of their identity, because (at that time) users lacked a physically present body and other visual cues immediately marking gender.[6] We were curious whether the Online girls in our study enjoyed a freedom to express themselves online in ways not possible at school. Can technology create an alternative space for girls to play with their identities in ways that challenge rather than reinforce the heterosexual matrix that sustains gender inequality?

In Chapter Four, we have seen embodiment is central to the competitive dynamics that characterize established forms of femininity. An individual girl's status in the eyes of her peers depended very much on whether she was "pretty" and "not fat," and how she dressed. Embodiment did not simply delineate differences among girls, however, but differentiated girls from boys. The Skater girls in Chapter Five were required to adopt a style of bodily comportment expected from boys but not girls. One consequence was the social labeling of these girls by their peers as not simply "different," but—in certain moments—as "unfeminine." What might it mean, then, to do girlhood in a community of disembodied participants?

In Chapter Five, we have also seen the importance of mutual encouragement and support among girls who not only pushed the boundaries of girlhood in new directions but, in doing so, challenged the sexism of skateboarding culture. By supporting each other in their efforts to learn and sustain ways of being Skater girls, we saw in the Park Gang the potential for a new community of practice: the Park Gang created a space in skateboarding culture not only for themselves but also for other girls. Thus, Skater girls reconfigured the street as a public space that, historically, has been a domain of masculine practice. In this chapter, communities of practice are also important in girls' identity practices, but here "community" has double meaning: while virtual communities can form through online interactions with strangers, communities also come into play when friends support each other during their online activities. While "going online" can certainly be a solitary activity, in our study, girls often came together to support one another while online, either by being physically present or through private notes using instant messaging (see Walkerdine 2006). Rose referred to her support group as "a little army":

> This one time I was in a chat room and this girl was totally freaking out at me for no reason—I can't remember why. But then I got a whole bunch of people on my side, all yelling back at her, and I'm just sitting there just going "Whew!" I hadn't said a word for half an hour, and there were all these people fighting for me. This is so cool. I had like a little army.

As in the case of the Skater girls, our data suggest that friendship networks can operate as "communities of practice." Below, we direct our attention primarily to girls' participation in the virtual communities that are formed through the use of the Internet.[7] This latter context interests us because in these communities embodied markers of gender, race, and class can be "refashioned." Interviews with girls about "doing gender" in cyberspace gave us an opportunity to further explore the malleability of gendered identities. Online girls blurred or redrew gender boundaries while online; at the same time, we shall see that their experiences draw attention to rules that, as in off-line communities of practice, govern girls' relations to others in cyberspace.

The girls in our study are members of the "first cybergeneration" (Best and Kellner 2003: 85); they were born into, and are growing up in, an everyday culture of computers and online communication. Of 8000 secondary students surveyed by Statistics Canada, 93% had a computer, and 88% had Internet at home (Statistics Canada 2004). Of Canadian teens aged twelve to seventeen, 73% regularly do e-mail, 70% use instant messaging, 29% download music, and 28% play online games with friends (Shaw 2004). The context for these figures includes the sense that, as urban streets are becoming "unsafe" for children, home-based activities are replacing outdoor play. A US Department of Education survey of computer and Internet use by children and youth showed no gender gap in Internet use rates; there were, however, minor gender differences in Internet activities. Girls were more likely to use the Internet for e-mail or instant messaging and completing school assignments, boys for games, shopping, and finding information about news, weather, or sports (DeBell and Chapman 2003: 36). During 2003, lower proportions of lower-income Hispanic and African American households in the United States had personal computers or Internet access (Kearney 2007). Canadian data similarly show a "digital divide" with respect to Internet access, particularly when comparing high-income to low-income households (Sciadis 2002).

Given this documented importance of the Internet in young people's social lives, the paucity of research with actual online participants is perhaps surprising. Much of the existing work on computer-mediated constructions of gendered identities is theoretical in nature (see, for example, Kenway 1997) or text-based (that is, carried out exclusively with disembodied, online participants; see Addison and Comstock

1998; Bassett 1997; Davies 2004; Reid-Walsh and Mitchell 2004). Very little research has been carried out face to face with actual participants of online communities (but see Clark 2005; Holloway, Valentine, and Bingham 2000; Kendall 2002; Thiel 2005; Valentine and Holloway 2002). Given that girls are now being "targeted" by game manufacturers, such research is urgent (see de Castell 2002: 5).

As we became aware of the significance of the Internet in the social life of girls in our study, Shauna and Lori recruited sixteen girls who self-identified as "computer geeks" or "Internet girls." Echoing the types of computer-based activities girls had already discussed, we devised a recruitment brochure[8] that was widely distributed. In this chapter, we refer to these participants as "Online girls." By design (to elicit greater spontaneity in dialogue), almost all of the interviews for this chapter were carried out with pairs of friends. The girls ranged in age from thirteen to sixteen years. Seven were white (Euro-Canadian), seven were Asian-Canadian (primarily Chinese, but also Korean, Filipino, Bangladeshi), and two were "mixed" white and Chinese. Two were born outside of Canada and spoke English as an additional language. Based on information the girls provided about their parents' occupations and educational backgrounds and their current living arrangements, two were from upper-middle class households, ten middle class, and four working class. Two girls identified as bisexual, and the other fourteen implied or stated that they were heterosexual. Collectively, they attended five different high schools (three in upper-middle-class neighborhoods, seven in working-class neighborhoods, and six in a private girls' school).

Girls recruited into the "Online girl" cluster of the larger study were asked about: access to computers and Internet connections; use of computers and the Internet at home, in school, and elsewhere; their history of computer learning and use; favorite types of activities (instant messaging, chat rooms, web pages, surfing, writing, gaming, and so on); competence levels and what it means to be "technical"; influence of online activities on friendships and everyday life; and comparisons of online and offline experiences (for example, meeting people, expressing feelings, forming social groups, being a girl). As in other interviews, in closing Shauna and Lori asked girls what they knew and thought about "girl power" and feminism.

DOING GENDER ONLINE

A number of commentators, in both popular culture and academic writing about the Internet (for discussion, see Yates 1997; Kolko 1999; Valentine and Holloway 2002), claim that gendered boundaries (and by extension possibly those of race, age, ability, and other markers of bodily distinctions) might be erased or transcended in cyberspace. This optimism seemed to be warranted when Mia claimed to be "more comfortable" online because "people don't really know who you are":

> You have really no, like, boundaries online, whereas you do in real life in school, right? Like, you have to act like a girl. If you act like a guy, you can be called something else, right? ... Online you can be like whoever you want to be, or how you feel comfortable, because people don't really know what you're really like if they haven't met you, right?

Reflecting Mia's claim that "you can be whoever you want to be," it interested us that girls could elect to pass as other than girls or as other than "good girls." As seen in both Chapters Four and Five, however, established communities tend to police their boundaries in order to retain the "purity" of their practices (Paechter 2003b: 548). Given that gender boundaries are strongly policed, how easy is it to "be whoever you want to be" online? Are offline boundaries created anew online? Does the practice of being online influence offline identities, especially among one's peers, and vice-versa? And if so, how? To answer these kinds of questions, we focus on excerpts in our interviews where girls talked about feeling powerful or vulnerable online and consider the implications of these experiences in their offline social interactions.

To begin, it is important to note that the Online girls in our study performed diverse femininities. For example, Mia (cited above) described herself as a "night-owl computer person" and "Internet girl." Despite her claim that "you can be whoever you want to be" online, Mia performed a conventional femininity, both on- and offline. At the time of her interview, she was well coiffed and wearing a light-blue, hooded sweatshirt and expensive Miss Sixty jeans. Within the context of the wider study, Mia was among the girls who spent their time shopping for clothing, applying makeup, flirting with boys, wondering how to become or remain Popular, and talking about fashion and popular music. Most of Mia's online time was spent chatting with boys, either on AsianAvenue.com, ICQ.com ["I Seek You"], or MSN. com. Her username on AsianAvenue was *asianbabyface*: *Asian* because she was half Chinese and it started with the letter A, hence guaranteeing her a spot near the top any time someone saved her address to their alphabetically arranged "friends list"; and *baby face* because she was told she had one.

When asked about her favorite websites, Mia said:

> I like to look for lyrics of songs… at lyrics.astroweb.com. There's Hotmail [for instant messaging using MSN]… I also like fashion websites. Like, paulfrank. com's kind of cute… Others like guess.com to see if anything's on sale and things I want to look for when I go to the store… We like seeing online quizzes… stupid things like "What makeup brand are you?"

Mia's mention of the makeup quiz draws attention to the way in which the Internet is implicated in the promotion of conventional gender scripts. However, her description of these quizzes as "stupid" perhaps also suggests ambivalence toward what she had described in an earlier interview as her "really girlie" femininity.

Shale, in contrast, transgressed the conventional femininity and hetero-normative sexuality embraced by Mia. She attended public school in a working-class but gentrifying neighborhood. At the time of her interview, she was wearing a baggy plaid shirt, baggy jeans, and no makeup—a style meant to convey a lack of concern for mainstream fashion. By her own description, Shale was bisexual, a practicing wiccan (paganism, witchcraft), and an enthusiast for Japanese anime, *Buffy the Vampire Slayer*, and the Internet. Shale selected the domain name *shadowchild* for her website, which served as a shrine first to *Gundam Wing* (her favorite anime show), then to *Buffy the Vampire Slayer* and goth (a subcultural style associated with black hair and clothes, horror-style makeup, and symbols of death such as vampires; see Hodkinson 2002).

In a conversation with her friend Rose on the appeal of *Gundam Wing*, both acknowledged that a majority of fans were probably boys. But when Rose suggested that the plot (a guerrilla war against the oppressors of Earth led by five young male pilots from the space colonies known as "Gundams") was the main appeal for her, Shale objected strenuously:

Rose:   I don't think many guys are really in for the war for peace thing [plot]. [Instead] They're like: "Animé! Big machines! Bombs! Explosives!"

Shale:  Hey, hey, hey—*I'm* in it for the bombs, explosives, and the pretty boys. But no, the explosions are really cool, except for they kind of make mistakes, 'cause you can't hear things exploding in space. But I like the explosions.

The Gundams, in typical animé style, are depicted as feminine or sexually ambiguous: wide-eyed, delicate, and slender. In this exchange, Shale identifies with the male fans of the show (she performs as a "boy") but with two twists: she lusts after the "pretty boys" (which positions her as a gay boy), and she displays technical knowledge (associated with a conventional masculinity) by pointing out the inaccuracy of the show's effects.

Shale and her friend Rose used Internet chat rooms to challenge emphasized femininity and perform what we call a "rebellious femininity." They delighted in "annoying" girls with ultra-feminine online names like "Sweet Flower Petal" and dreamed of hacking onto "small websites with the Hello Kitty buttons and saying 'You've been hit by Cookie the Bloody WhaHaHa...' in bright red lettering." They mentioned going into pro-anorexia chat rooms and urging girls to eat. They reported deflating boys' performances of hyper-masculinity in chat rooms by calling into question their claim to heterosexuality:

Rose:   The guys are really fun to piss off.

Shale:  And their names are all like Player 69 [an allusion to their sexual prowess].

Rose:   All you've got to do is poke them on the back of the head [figuratively] and go, "You're gay," and they can go off on this huge tangent. ... It's really funny.

Although few girls in our study were as rebellious as Shale and Rose, other girls shared their experiences of challenging conventional gender rules.

While acknowledging that ways of doing gender online are as complex as those offline, for the remainder of this chapter we attend to interviews with girls who reported "bending" gender and sexuality online or directly challenging conventions of "good girl" femininity; some of these latter Online girls took more initiative in heterosexual relationships than is currently authorized in prevailing rules of romance (we see them as "updating" rather than challenging the rules of romance), while others battled back in cyberspace against sexual harassment. In closing, we return to the types of questions that frame the larger "Girl Power" project: what do online identity practices tell us about the power of discourse, and what do online communities where gender is practiced tell us about girls' agency, subjectivity and empowerment?

## BENDING GENDER

Some of the Online girls in our study described taking on a number of identities online other than their own, although, in keeping with early research into this phenomenon (Roberts and Parks 1999; Schiano 1999), most did not do it often or for long stretches except in the context of role-playing. Seven girls had pretended to be older, although usually just by a year or two; one had switched "race" (Mia, who is part-Chinese, part-White/Jewish, pretended to be blonde and blue-eyed); two had switched sexuality (by becoming "heterophobic" gay men); four had become beings with supernatural powers (two half-vampires, one demon, and one character who could "disappear in a puff of purple smoke"); and five had switched their gender.

Two general observations are in order before turning specifically to an analysis of gender bending and switching. First, the girls who mentioned pretending to be older were those whose primary online activity was instant messaging. These girls were among those most interested in heterosexual romance, and by lying about their age, we sensed that they may have felt they were enhancing their attractiveness to older boys. Second, in all cases of identity switching, the girls took on identities marked as more powerful than their own in the wider society. A partial exception to this might be where Shale (who identified at school as bisexual) and her friend Rose (who identified as heterosexual) took the roles of gay men in an online fan fiction story and yet, tellingly, they did not assume lesbian alter egos.

Based on what the girls in our study told Shauna and Lori, multiplayer role-playing games afforded the most opportunities to do femininity differently online. In keeping with our view of these girls as able to "play" with gender, these games at first appear to afford participants an opportunity to be "what they say." Role-playing usually occurred in text-based chat rooms in real time, where chat rooms—via text and graphics—presented various thematic settings (for example, medieval, fantasy, science fiction). Girls assumed or created the parts of fictional characters. As they interacted with other players, they wrote a collaborative story. The problem, according to Rose, was that "you can get girls who are looking for tragic romance"—the conventional storyline:

> Guys will come up and flirt with them, and they'll be doing the whole, "I've been hurt before, blah, blah, blah…" They say [via a button, which signals action rather than dialogue by turning text into another font], *"Blinks eyes which resemble pools of depthless water*, blah, blah, blah." And I'm just going on, "Come on! This is so annoying!"

Shale concurred: "Lots of the girls, they'll be like, *'Run their hands through their silken golden hair,* blah, blah, blah, blah, blah,' where the rest of the [role-playing] world's kind of going, *'Scratches their head.'*"

In keeping with their rebellious personae, Rose and Shale attempted to rewrite the "tragic romance" storyline. Rose's invented character, Harlequin, was "not good with rules." As she entered a role-playing chat room, "there's this guy going, 'Respect me! Fear me!'" Rose responded by figuratively "poking him." As a result of her rule-breaking, Harlequin "had her neck snapped five times." One of Shale's characters was "this chick named 'Cyn'" (pronounced "sin"), a half-vampire. Another was a "total cool bad girl" who "wears a lot of black" and was "some hunter lady who's going to take out all the vampires of the world." More recently, she had played an "assassin bartender ex-princess type demon chick": "I mean she's quite obviously the sarcastic, scary type; runs around; can be either incredibly melodramatic or incredibly strange, but she's been just about everything." Shale's description of herself as an "ex-princess" ("scary" and "sarcastic") allowed her to communicate simultaneously her familiarity with the passive, storybook subject position—often held out to girls as desirable—and her rejection of it. Although Shale's character was female, she claimed identities often coded as masculine (assassin, bartender, demon). Strikingly (because she did not know Shale), Nina ("very openly bisexual," and "a witch") had created a character very similar to Shale's. "My alter ego is very bitchy, very cynical. She's a dampier—half-vampire." She "is a waitress and a co-owner of this bar that my friend and I created."

Despite the power of their female characters, Nina, Rose, and Shale ran into problems in role-playing chat rooms. Rose often got kicked out by the host for being "disruptive." Shale described entering the "vampire desecrated cathedral" as a "normal girl"; her profile featured the picture of a "cool looking chick" she had found on a website. She discovered the hard way, though, that "if your picture doesn't show some scantily-clad woman, they kick you out":

> I walk into this one place, and nobody talks to me. And I'm like, "Why are you all ignoring me?" … Then you look at like the other pictures, and they're [showing] really, really, really revealing clothing, and you're just like, "Hmm." And then you go and change your picture, and you come back, and they all start talking to you, and you're like, "Wow! You're shallow!"

As shown here, Shale learned that garnering attention online as a girl or woman was bound up with sexual objectification (cf. Rodino 1997: 13-14).

In another instance that Shale described as her most "powerful experience online," she pretended to be her 120-year-old character, Nelly, who became a favorite in a role-play bar: "I'd walk in, and Braden, one of the guys, would go, 'Nelly!' and like give me this huge hug, and then like I'd get free drinks and stuff." Clearly, Shale enjoyed the fact that she had invented a character that many in the bar found fun. A problem arose, however, when a guy began flirting with Shale, deliberately provoking a fight between Shale (as Nelly) and Rose (as Harlequin):

| | |
|---|---|
| Rose: | She [my character Harlequin] had her eyebrow ripped off. |
| Shale: | By the guy who ended up turning me into a goddess, which was really strange. |
| Rose: | I was kind of mad at you for that. I was in the chat room, and I kept raising my eyebrow, and then he ripped it off and he kicks me out, and I was like, "OK." And I went to another room, and then I met up with her [Shale] later. She's like, "Oh, yeah. I'm a goddess. That guy that ripped off your eyebrow made me a goddess." I'm just, "What?!" |

As can happen in offline situations (see Duncan 2004), the girls' anger was turned against each other rather than toward the male character whose flirting had set the girls in competition in the first place.

In other instances, Online girls in our study tried to avoid problems by presenting themselves as men online. Nina's female character (the half-vampire who co-owned a bar) was perceived as too "aggressive," even in the context of online role-playing: "Everyone was saying I was being too aggressive. And I said, 'Okay, I'll save my sweet, loving personality for my female side, and I'll make me a brother' [Nick]. And everyone bought it for awhile, too." When Nina found that her performance of femininity as her female "alter ego" failed to work in online social situations, she had the freedom to play as Nick, whom she described as the more aggressive "male side of her personality." Her performance of masculinity was competent enough for her to pass as a man undetected.

Anna and Beverly also decided to role-play as men. They desired to play games with an already established cast of characters. Anna elected to play her favorite character, Hiei, in the animé show *Yu Yu Hakusho* (Spirit Detective). Hiei is a "tough guy" demon, who assumes the shape of a small young man with spiky hair and a complicated, tragic past. Anna indicated that she chose Hiei because the women characters in the game are "not deep." She explained: "they're like the 'Help me! Help me!' kind of women." Unlike Nina, however, Anna found it difficult at times to competently perform "tough guy" masculinity. "Sometimes I type things that are not manly enough [laughs]. ... The monitor, Athena Zandrite (her username), she just deleted it in the nick of time before people saw it!" Beverly explained that she chose to play a male character in the role-playing game *Warcraft* (via the Battle.net forum), because "if you tell people that you're a girl and stuff, then they would go, 'Oh, don't kill her ... 'cause it's a girl and she's not that strong.'" Unlike Anna and Nina, Beverly found it easy to pass as a man on *Warcraft* because "you don't really say much, because you just like try to kill ... the bad people."

In summary, a number of Online girls in our study experienced the pleasure of bending gender and rebelling against the conventions of both emphasized femininity and hegemonic masculinity. They found, however, that gendered boundaries online are more heavily policed than they had perhaps anticipated. Nevertheless, a few participants claimed that the alternative femininities that they were able to practice online had contributed positively to their personal growth. Rose told Shauna that before she role played online, she was more shy and "giggly." As she played her character on the *Buffy the Vampire Slayer* site, she learned from her character's interactions with others to "talk totally differently from what I used to" and to engage in repartee. "Some people are really funny naturally, and so if you read like their stuff on the Internet, you kind of ... pick it up," she explained. "And if you are constantly improving your character and you make them really cool, then you also kind of pick it up." Similarly, Nina felt that she had become more "extroverted." She claimed that being online "brought out another personality, which, therefore, gives me the chance to be the person I really want to be," namely, "a very aggressive girl who likes to voice my opinions."

## UPDATING THE RULES OF ROMANCE

> Marcia: I can talk more freely to boys, and I know more boys [online]. If it wasn't for MSN, I would know no boys. [laughter] That's a guarantee.
> Candy: Same as me. Like, I've become more comfortable after knowing someone maybe a bit better on MSN. And you can confront people better.

As we have seen, some girls were aware of and could identify the "tragic romance" storyline, and a few were attempting to rewrite it. Taking our wider study as a point of comparison, many girls were still living within that dominant storyline, which authorized a relatively passive role for them in the area of heterosexual relationships. Many agreed with Pete that most girls were still "stuck in the stereotype that guys ask girls out." They split over whether this rule represented an annoyance or a relief, with most girls expressing the latter. For example, GG and Forsyth were among girls who preferred the passive role: "People expect the guys to make the first move [asking a girl to dance], and I think that's what is good about being a girl—you don't have to do that!" (GG). "It's fun [being a girl] because you get to get all dolled up and you get to be all girly. Guys have to approach you—you don't have to approach a guy" (Forsyth). Added Jordan, who was being interviewed with Forsyth, "You're just there to look pretty." Even girls who were critical of a conventional, passive role were quick to blame girls rather than to identify the double standards at work. For example, Brenda complained that "girls don't have enough guts" to ask guys out.

Rarely did girls spontaneously label this boys-as-initiators-girls-as-there-to-look-pretty ideology as a sexist double standard. Instead, they essentialized this double standard by reasoning that boys "naturally" have more "confidence." This reasoning obscured the power relations (based not only on gender, but also age, class, "race," sexual orientation, and ability) that enable some to display confidence across a variety of settings, but particularly in romantic or sexual encounters. It is significant, therefore, that a number of Online girls, including Mia and Reese, used the Internet to practice taking more initiative in potentially romantic heterosexual relationships. However, while we see this initiative as signaling a positive boost in their self-confidence, we also characterize these practices as updating the rules of romance rather than challenging them.

Instant messaging played an important role in girls' claims to newly found confidence. Using instant messaging, girls were adept at screening boys online whom they might be interested in getting to know. Mia and Reese, along with Beverly, Vera, and Anna, all were online "members" of AsianAvenue (AA). Unlike the case of gaming and role play, AA members created their own web page which usually included their picture, as well as a description of themselves and their interests, and a guest book. Members then surfed around, signing the guest books of those who interested them. Mia and Reese looked for "cute" guys whose "thoughts" they liked:

> This might be kind of shallow, but on AA, looking through like pages, if it's a particularly good-looking guy, I guess then you'd want to talk to him, get to know him, right? ... But it's also someone who ... if they write their thoughts in their page about anything in general, life ... and you like what they wrote. [If] you share the same outlook, then it's kind of nice, 'cause then you know you have something really different to talk about, right? (Mia)

In the guy's guest book, the girls might write "Oh, hey, add me on ICQ or MSN." Similarly, guys from AA would sign their guest books, inviting them to join their MSN friends list. Once in instant messaging or e-mail contact, they could get to know each other better online, which sometimes led to phone chats and meetings in public places accompanied by friends.

Instant messaging afforded girls more control because they could mask feelings of shyness and embarrassment, express emotions, or simply communicate with a boy, which some found difficult to do face to face. Anna, for example, liked a boy at school. Her friend Vera assured her that the boy liked her. Despite this reassurance, the normally outgoing Anna would "try not to look at him" if she happened upon the boy at school. Online, however, she found she could talk to him: "You're not going to be tense about how you look, or are you looking frustrated or flushed or something." As Cheryl also testified, "On MSN there's no awkward silence." This is because with MSN, claimed Marcia, "you can kind of think about like a good comeback or something." Alana and Cherry expressed similar feelings. "I get kind of shy when I meet new people face to face," explained Cherry. "And like once I get to know them, I turn into like the goofy self that I am. But over MSN it's just kind of like I can be myself without having to like be embarrassed because I'm not like standing there." Alana agreed: "Over MSN you can take your time and like process thoughts. ... And so you don't sound like a complete goon."

Instant messaging did more than simply give girls time to think about what they wanted to say, however. Because friendship circles of girls were often logged on to MSN at the same time, they were afforded the opportunity to quickly rehearse their lines in front of a friendly audience and to consult each other (via private IM notes) about what exactly to say and how to say it to a guy they might be interested in romantically:

Cheryl:   Say the guy you like is on [MSN], you can always plan what you're going to say. And like make it perfect. ... And then you can send it to your friends and be like, "Can I say this? Is this okay?"

Veronica: Yeah, 'cause you have your friends that you're having a conversation [with], then you're like, "What do I say now?"

Conversely, the boys they were communicating with were not physically present and with their own male friends, as they often were at school. School settings were thus more awkward than online situations for girls (especially the younger ones) who wanted to initiate communication with a boy. Rose, for example, recounted a time she simply greeted a boy at school, and then continued walking down the hall. Her greeting sparked ridicule from one of his male friends, who said in a loud voice, "Oh, lady killer now, are we?" Girls also said that boys were under pressure from male peers at school not to reveal any emotional vulnerability they might actually be feeling about, say, girlfriends. Some of these conditions were changed online. As a result, some girls felt more in control of social interactions with boys. "Boys, when they're around their friends, are like Big Macho Man," explained Marcia, "But when they're by themselves [with girls], they're, like, more nice and stuff." So she and her friend Candy preferred to "talk to a boy online" rather than in front of peers.

Although it is not clear whether the online practices of girls taking more initiative actually challenged the underlying sexism of conventional rules of romance, a number of participants felt their confidence had improved and had influenced their everyday lives in positive ways. Mia for example claimed that chatting with, and getting to know, boys via instant messaging helped her "to become more outgoing":

> Because you can speak a lot more and be more open-minded. You can maybe realize that you can be like that in person, too. ... When you've met some-one online and become really good friends with them—and still are to this day—then that's something special, because it's really hard. That's really hard to find actually.

In a similar vein, Vera claimed, "[when] you talk to people online, it's like you know them in reality" and you "get closer." And Alana, "So the next time you see each other like in real life, right, it's sometimes easier to talk to them. I've definitely gotten to be more comfortable around guys." Anna, who immigrated to Canada from the Philippines only 3 years before she was interviewed, explained that "Before I came here, I'm not really much of a socializing person. But then when I got online, I found out that ... people don't really care how you speak or stuff. And then I tried that here [in school]. [Now] I have friends." In her case, it would appear that playing online enabled Anna to success-fully navigate language-based boundaries among the peer cultures at her school.


## CHALLENGING SEXUAL HARASSMENT

As much as being online was a social space of interaction where "you can say anything" (Mia) and "grow your friends" (Candy), it was also a space to be "flamed" (the recipient of deliberately hostile or insult-ing messages) or propositioned for "cyber sex." All of our participants mentioned either the chilling effect of offers to "cyber" or examples of boys harassing them online. This finding is supported by a number of other studies. Valentine and Holloway (2002: 312), who studied the online and offline social networks and identities of both girls and boys, found that "Only girls referred to experiences of harassment or their fears about the strangers they might meet online." This finding is supported by Rodino (1997: 2), who reports that when users online are assumed to be female, they are subject to sexual harassment (also see Roberts and Parks 1999).

Although online sexual harassment was a fact of life, Online girls in our study (often in pairs or small groups) did not accept it passively; they reported numerous instances of confronting boys and men, both those known to them, as well as anonymous chat room users, about it. In the case of persistent offers from strangers to cyber, girls were no doubt emboldened to take these strangers to task, knowing that the strangers could not locate or harm them physically. Amy described her most "powerful online experience" this way:

> Amy: Oh, some jerk was like, "Hey, let's have sex." And I was like, "No, screw you! What's wrong with you? Why do you do this?..." I felt really good afterwards because I totally like yelled at him. It was like, "It's stupid like asking young girls to do things like that. So do the police know you're doing this? Should I tell them?"
> Shauna: You went for it.
> Amy: Yeah. I was just like really pissed off. I was having a bad day, too.
> Shauna: Right, so he got the brunt of your anger.
> Amy: Of course, I was like, "Go away." ... It's like I have saved some poor innocent girl from a pedophile.

It is noteworthy that Amy felt it worth mentioning that she was "pissed off" and "having a bad day." Similarly, Cheryl reported being "mad" one day when she decided to tell off strangers in a chat room wanting to cyber by positioning them as loners. "So I go in and I'm like, 'You guys have no lives. Go read a book.'" In response she got "so many mean little messages, like 'You're just sad because you can't get me.'" Refusing to be positioned as sexually unattractive, Cheryl responded by repositioning herself as a person concerned with learning and substance. It may be that the attacks that Cheryl and Amy launched, even if directed at strangers in cyberspace, placed them enough outside the boundaries of conventional femininity that they felt the need to explain that they were not quite themselves that day.

Girls also described confronting boys online who had been "mean" to them or their friends, either online or offline. Anna reported coming to the defense of a friend being harassed by a guy offline and online. Anna's friend had been pursued by a guy who was "coming on to her so strong that she doesn't really like him at all." Then the guy started to say:

stuff about her behind her back, like she's ugly, she's fat. Then one time they both went on [to an AOL chat room] at the same time, and my friend needed backup. It was like, "Anna, like get an account. Come in here with me." And I backed her up. But like he was saying bad stuff about her, and I'd say that they're not true.

Cherry and Alana told Shauna that boys they knew called them "ugly" and swore at them online. When asked how they responded, Cherry replied, "First I tell them off, and then I block them." (MSN allows a user to block any individual she designates from her friends' list, but the block is not revealed to the person who has been blocked.) Similarly, Candy and Marcia said they blocked boys who insulted them. Instant messaging also gave them the time to develop good "comebacks" when boys flamed them, which, at first, Marcia said they never would have said to a boy face to face. Then she changed her mind: "If someone insults me, I'm going to insult them back." This power to respond to insults is significant in light of research showing that girls and women still appear to be more vulnerable to sexual insults, because boys and men have available to them diverse sources of strength and status (not just attractiveness, but athletic and technical abilities, for example; see Francis 1997).

That girls in our study were practicing their counter-attacks and refusing to be positioned as sexual objects, often with the support of friends online, strikes us as a positive development. Overall, however, doing gender online could have contradictory effects. On the one hand, as "girls" our participants were vulnerable to pedophiles and flaming in cyberspace; if this was their main online experience, it could position girls as passive. Yet the "anonymity" of cyberspace afforded some girls the opportunity to fight back or to avoid situations that subjected them to sexual harassment, especially when supported by girlfriends. This experience positioned girls as strong (even when vulnerable) and discerning. It must be noted that the girls' efforts to fight back against "annoying" requests for cyber sex and "teasing" by boys would have been strengthened if they had had access to a feminist discourse of sexual harassment, which insists that the harassment is based on unequal gendered power relations within and between the sexes. No girl in the study used the phrase *sexual harassment* (although a number spontaneously described some male actions as "sexism"). This is perhaps not surprising, given that at this moment in history, not all people would characterize the behavior described above as wrong, and antifeminist arguments have been developed that suggest feminists or women have abused charges of sexual harassment (Fraser 1992a; D. Holland et al. 1998).


## NO BOUNDARIES?

Theoretically speaking, cyberspace would seem to offer an opportunity to explore the malleability of gender; in the online activities of our participants, their identities were disembodied, present only as discursive constructions. It interested us that Online girls were drawn to activities like role play, that engaged participants in this way, allowing them to "experiment" with their social identities. We have seen above, however, that even in the absence of a physical body or other visual clues, gendering occurs online. In our study, girls could "see" gender operate, not through simply a user's choice of nicknames but also language-use and the behavior of characters they chose to play. At the same time, those who explored the pleasures of "gender bending" found that the boundaries they hoped to cross were heavily policed. While a few of the girls were able, at least temporarily, to transgress gender expectations, in our limited study girls were more successful in being accepted in a virtual community when they practiced girlhood in conventional ways.

Rose and Shale, two of the more "savvy" Online girls, actively challenged the heterosexism of other players. Although Shale chose a female character for role play, she quickly discovered that unless she adopted the persona of a highly sexualized player, she was totally ignored. At the same time, Nina's female character was perceived as too aggressive, leading her to masquerade—successfully—as a man. Based on these kinds of experiences, Rose and Shale claimed that in cyberspace: "Everything's much more extreme—like they'll get little cliques and they hate each other. And they'll go wage all out war. I mean like hack each other's pages and stuff." Within this context, while some girls explored new girlhoods, the dynamics of virtual communities worked largely to confine their online practices within the boundaries of their designated gender. Within these confines, a few of our participants made more "modest" gender interventions.

One example is found in the practice of girls who took more initiative in heterosexual encounters. In what might be seen as a reversal of the male gaze, girl members of AsianAvenue were able to "cruise" AA pages looking for "cute" guys whose "thoughts" they liked. From the safety of cyberspace where they did not have to confront boys face-to-face, these girls could leave messages for guys who interested them. It is worth noting that these initiatives typically occurred with support from their off-line community of practice. At the same time, the mediated nature of communication saved girls from feelings of shyness and embarrassment; in the words of Alana "you can take your time and like process [your] thoughts." This was especially the case when friends logged on together, consulting each other through private instant messaging notes. As a result, a number of girls claimed that use of the Internet had improved their confidence socially, especially when interacting with boys. This boost is perhaps most in evidence when girls like Amy and Cheryl fought back against sexual harassment on the Internet. Despite this action, Amy (like many of the other Online girls) did not identify her actions as feminist, although Cheryl and some others did.

Returning to our opening questions, in our research there was no unmarked, "abstract" Subject of cyberspace discourse. The girls in our study were adept at spotting online participants who misrepresented their gender. Moreover, girls like Rose and Shale, who did attempt to cross over, discovered that it was much harder to "pass" than they might have imagined. We do not attribute their difficulty simply to these girls' "inexperience." Their difficulties underscore what we have emphasized as the performativity of gender sustained by the sexualization of not only "real" but also fictional female bodies. While cyberspace can be inhabited by imaginary creatures, once human identities are invoked, they make sense only through those frames of intelligibility that govern social life. We should not be surprised, therefore, that popular Internet venues replicate dominant values (see Gailey 1993).

In closing, virtual communities of practice remind us that the theoretical utility of recognizing the discursively constructed nature of subjecthood does not negate the materiality of the Subject. As noted in Chapter One, while discourses "interpellate" (potential) Subjects they do not determine "Who we are." In order to have a "social" life, discourses must be activated by speakers and doers. At the same time, our identities are not malleable self-representations. As in the "offline" world, our gendered performances are accountable to an audience of "others"; no matter how much we may feel "in control," our identities are subject to unspoken rules that work to reconstitute gender in specific ways. Within this context, the study of discursive identities remains important for what it can tell us about the taken-for-grantedness of our everyday constructions.

In order to more fully understand girls' agency, in the following chapter we explore interviews with girls who consciously, and to some extent successfully, took advantage of the fissures and contradictions of prevailing discourses to move between specific communities of practice. By moving between groups in this way, these girls were able to forge positive, multiple, and shifting identities for themselves. What sustains their ability to do so? What limits the ability of other girls to exercise this kind of agency? By answering these kinds of questions, we can better understand "empowerment" as a de facto feminist practice that opens possibilities for all girls.

NOTES

1   An earlier version of this chapter appears as: Deirdre M. Kelly, Shauna Pomerantz and Dawn H. Currie (2006). "'No Boundaries?' Girls' Interactive, Online Learning about Femininities" *Youth and Society* 38(1): 3–28

2   Public concern appears to be mounting about "cyber-bullying," a term originally meant to capture children and youth using electronic means to threaten, humiliate, or harass other children or youth. Recently, however, the Canadian Teachers' Federation has broadened the term to include teachers as the victims of cyber-bullying, which the CTF defines as "the use of information and communication technologies to bully, embarrass, threaten or harass another. It also includes the use of these technologies to engage in conduct or behaviour that is derogatory, defamatory, degrading, illegal or abusive" (Canadian Teachers Federation 2008: para. 5). In its annual meeting the CTF voted unanimously to ratify a policy on cyber-bullying, which included a call to make it a separate Criminal Code offense (Morris 2008). The term is extremely broad (as is the root term "bullying"), and we are concerned that it invites or feeds into a moral panic. By the same token, the power of the Internet to reach wide audiences raises the stakes of any one "bullying" incident to more serious levels (e.g., compare the passing around of an embarrassing photo to posting one online). We agree with Froese-Germain that given "the link between bullying and racism, homophobia and sexism, another part of the solution must be anti-discriminatory education and the strengthening of other equity initiatives in public schools" (2008: 52). We also feel we need a wide continuum of nuanced policy responses and good professional judgment to be exercised in dealing with cyber-bullying, rather than sweeping zero-tolerance policies that have been proven to be applied in disproportionately harsh ways towards marginalized children and youth.

3   We acknowledge the role that the Internet has played in facilitating the consolidation of Riot Grrrl communities (see Riordan 2001; Harris 2003).

4    We have seen that it also shapes their understanding of boys' identity practices.

5    Here it is worth noting that video games are not "coincidentally" gendered as a masculine pastime: they emerged in the context of military applications of computer technology (see Herz 1997). In her study, Walkerdine (2006) found that the successful game playing subject is "masculine" (page 531). Playing video games was difficult for the girls in her study because it engaged them in "complex, covert negotiations of power," while appearing not to (page 532). In other words, to play competitively, girls had to disavow their femininity. This finding makes the game playing of girls like Grenn and Lexi all the more interesting. They mentioned making their own computer games using RPG Maker and were among the few who identified as "gamers."

6    None of the girls in our study used web cam, which would obviously "qualify" this claim. We are also aware of how sites such as "Facebook" and online dating services sustain an embodied presence in online social interaction.

7    For a discussion of girls building communities online, see Ashley D. Grisso and David Weiss (2005).

8    The brochure, titled *Cyber Girls!*, posed the following questions: "Are you a girl between 13 and 15 years old? Do you create websites? Do you know HTML? Are you into writing fan-fiction? Do you role-play online? Would you call yourself a 'computer girl?'" Given the sexualized connotations surrounding the term "cyber girls," we decided to call the girls in this chapter "Online girls."

# 7

# ON THE MOVE

GIRLS, GIRLHOOD, AND FEMINISM IN MOTION

T he preceding chapters explored the identity practices of two specific groups of girls who challenged the dynamics surrounding
heteronormative girlhood: we referred to these participants as
constructing Skater and Online girlhoods. By characterizing their practices as "girlhoods," there is the danger of implying that we see embodied identities as unified and stable, seamlessly organized around
the dominant frames of intelligibility in ways that we find theoretically problematic. On the contrary, Chapters Five and Six are meant
to destabilize the notion of girlhood as a generic, monolithic category.
In order to explore how various girlhoods are accomplished as lived
presence, we focused on specific communities of practice and the discourses of girlhood that these communities sustained. Girls' identity
practices often demonstrated relationships to the identity categories of
school-based cultures, however, that were much more complex than
these chapters may imply. For example, Zoe claimed that she and her
Park friends moved "in between" what she called "the studying group"
and the skaters. This "dual" affiliation allowed them to resolve the dilemma of avoiding the "mean" set of Popular skaters while remaining
distinct from the "goody-goody" students who focused on academics
and were labeled "geeks" by the Populars. Zoe acknowledged that, as
Skater girls, she and her friends were "respected." They were seen as

fun loving and open minded, yet, because they were girls and good students, they avoided the stereotypes associated with boy skaters—as "into drugs," "punky," and "tough."

In moving between groups, the Park Gang (whether consciously or not) seized on a contradiction within skater discourse in a way that seemed to generate goodwill among their peers toward them. Skater culture tends to deride pop music and mass consumerism while simultaneously valuing individuality and authenticity. The Park Gang felt relatively free to select what they liked from mainstream or popular culture, and they turned their eclectic taste (in music, clothing style) into a mark of their individuality. Zoe took delight in telling Shauna, "like around skaters—we can tell them that we don't really care, even if they don't think that's cool." Pete elaborated: "Yeah. Like I'm not afraid to say that I like N'Sync [a popular boy band]."

Other girls in our study also moved between social groups. Madeline moved between membership in both skater girl and academic communities of practice to powerful effect. At her large, inner-city but gentrifying high school, she described knowing "so many people from different groups [academic students, French Immersion students, the Asian 'fashionable group,' and the skaters] that I can basically go in to any group and … hang around." Being a hardcore skater girl helped to offset the "smart student" stigma of having received the top academic achievement award at her school for two years running. Among these girls—whom we dub "in-betweeners"—Sara was proud of the fact that other kids positioned her as "weird" or "different" within peer culture. Describing herself as a "chameleon," she boasted:

> I can sometimes be very mainstream, sometimes I can be like more dark, and sometimes I can be punk. Uhm, right now I'm wearing plaid (laughs)! Plaid pants and a black studded shirt. I'm also into like studded belts and studded collars, and I have a bike chain around my bracelet… Yeah, I'm really into safety pins. Uhm, I'm not really sure. I guess purple is my favorite color. I wear black a lot. Uhm, I have spiked whore boots (laughs). Like up to the knee, with big platforms.

Sara claimed: "I can just hang out with the poppy people and be really ditzy and like 'ah hah hah,' and then I can hang out with the intellectual people and be very like deep and 'blah blah blah,' and hang out with the skaters and be a moron."

Vanessa, the only working-class in-betweener in our study, described the social scene at her small, urban, largely working-class and immigrant school as consisting of the "popular people" ("the girls that are airheads and anorexic, and the guys that play basketball and try to score with the anorexic girls"); the "geeks" ("the people who study at home constantly"); the "punk kids" (who "make a lot of trouble and make a lot of noise in the halls and they're sort of off the beat, and they have friends that wear all black clothes and wear goth makeup, and they sort of get picked on, but people sort of accept them at the same time because they're pretty cool"); and the "immature, nerdy people." Vanessa described liking school, loving and excelling at sports such as volleyball, joining the dance club, and having "a lot of friends." These friends were members of the Popular as well as the punk crowds, while Vanessa did not display full membership in either group. Her punk friends (all girls) "listen to music like the Ramones and Bikini Kill [all-female punk band]… One of them, she shops at like Value Village for all the like vintage clothes and stuff like that. And they dye their hair like funky colors, like blue or purple." When probed about this, Vanessa observed, "My personality is more like them [the punk friends]; the way I look [dress] is probably not." In her words, she was an "in-between," and Vanessa raised the possibility that being an in-betweener might even constitute its own community of practice:

> I'm sort of an in-between…but a few people [are]—like, I'm not just like that by myself. There's quite a few people who are sort of in-betweeners as well— that's actually another group I should have mentioned… You [as an in-betweener] can sort of get along with everybody, and you don't really have any enemies or get into fights.

Vanessa revealed that she had a high grade point average and was known as "the smart one" but not as "nerdy." She attributed this reputation to the time she spent visibly "making the scene" in her neighborhood with various friends. For example, she often shot pool at a downtown establishment and played games such as Counter-Strike in Internet cafés. As a result:

> Yeah, the thing is that I spend a lot of time with my friends, [I'm seen to be] hanging out and going outside. What helps, like when you do well in school, so I have like a really good memory, so I often don't have to study or anything—I just do well.

The girls who described themselves as being able to move successfully between social groups at school bear some resemblance to a group described by Laura Sessions Stepp, a staff writer for the *Washington Post*, as "gamma girls" (Stepp 2002). Gammas differ from "alphas" (described in Chapters Two and Four as Popular mean girls) and "betas" (seen in Chapter Four as wannabe Popular girls). The gammas are achieving in numerous arenas and, according to *Newsweek's* cover story (entitled "In Defense of Teenage Girls"), gammas eschew the pursuit of Popularity and are "just plain nice" (Meadows 2002, para. 3). Without explication, *Newsweek's* pop anthropology sidebar profiling the "gammas" associates them with an alternative or resistant femininity by listing such items as:

> FAVE MOVIE: "Ghost World"
> IN HER DISCMAN: Ani DiFranco
> READS: *Jane*

To take these examples in turn, "Ghost World" (Clowes 2001) is a critically acclaimed art-house film; as described in Chapter Two, it features eighteen-year-olds Enid and Rebecca—both white and working-class—as smart and angry misfits who disparage conformity to the mainstream and draw power from their refusal to surrender willingly to consumer culture (for further analysis, see Kelly and Pomerantz, in press). Ani DiFranco is a well-known independent (self-produced) singer-songwriter, feminist, and political activist whose Righteous Babe Foundation supports such causes as abortion rights. *Jane* magazine is pitched at "irreverent" young women as a successor to *Sassy* and has covered such topics as the Riot Grrrl movement.

Gamma girls appear to be girls who have benefited from feminism, even if they do not all identify as feminists. While popular media representations gesture toward girl-style rebellion against emphasized femininity (as our study's in-betweeners did via skateboarding and punk), the gamma girls featured in *Newsweek* also seem to fit what Anita Harris (2004) calls the "can-do" or "future girl." As noted in our introductory chapters, within the current neoliberal social and economic order, the girlhood embodied by these young women is being constructed to signal freedom, personal choice, and self-improvement, with little to no acknowledgment of persistent gender and other inequalities.

While we are not identifying the in-betweeners in our study as gamma girls, they interest us because in their narratives we detected the capacity of these girls to flexibly fashion Selfhoods. They were able to do so because they (at least tacitly) recognized and consciously navigated multiple, competing discourses, including the dominant discourse of emphasized femininity. These girls described the ability to move between more than one peer-based community of practice at school in a way that allowed them to forge positive, multiple, and shifting identities for themselves. The question raised for us is how these girls are able to consciously negotiate competing, available Subject positions to their advantage. Their ability to do so seems to signal an exercise of power in ways intended by the feminist-inspired "girl power" programs mentioned in Chapter One. In the remainder of this chapter, we explore what makes this expression of "girl power" possible and consider its relation to feminism.

## CONSTRAINED MOBILITY: RE/INVENTION WITHIN LIMITS

While we highlight in-betweeners in this chapter, we do not intend to imply that all girls can adopt flexible Selfhoods—on the contrary. In our (limited) study, developing the discursive and social repertoire to recognize and enact several distinct ways of being, based on interaction with others in particular contexts, depended on a certain material privilege (that is, economic and cultural resources from home). With the exception of Vanessa, it was middle-class girls who strategically negotiated girlhood in this way. Their interviews offer some important lessons for rethinking the nature of girls' agency. In this section, we speculate[1] about the constraints on girls' abilities to freely move between and among what are otherwise often "competing"[2] communities of practice. Our focus is the limits on girls' ability to re/invent girlhood.[3]

As suggested in Chapter Five, we found that our participants practiced being Skater girls in different ways in different contexts (for example, in the diverse spaces of school, neighborhood, and home), depending partly on their social locations. Within the context of school, for example, working-class girls who attended working-class or class-divided schools more strongly identified with the "underground culture" of skateboarding, which they saw as diametrically opposed to "preppy culture." For them, being a skater was more likely to be an all-encompassing, nonconformist identity. Reflecting this position, Grenn evinced a clear class antagonism when she made clear, *"I hate sports! Skateboarding is not a sport!"* As mentioned in Chapter Five, for working-class Skater girls like Grenn, to call skateboarding a "sport" mistakenly associates it with middle-class (school) conformity. In skater circles, "Skateboarding is not a sport" is a rallying cry; hardcore skaters believe that there are no rules in skateboarding, and unlike a sport, there are no winners and losers. By contrast, as we have seen, middle-class girls were more likely to combine skater discourse with other discourses, including school-conforming ones. We can thus see how the school—bound up as it is in classifying and ranking students not only on academic "merit," but also according to such class-based characteristics as demeanor and social skills—works as a constraint on certain practices of femininity.

Working-class girls in our study were also more likely than girls with professional or middle-class parents to report that their families tried to exert control over their dress style and appearance. Kate and Christine, for example, complained:

> Kate:      My grandparents and my uncles, they're also trying to get me to wear dresses and everything, and that's just not who I am.
> Christine:  Even my parents used to be like, "Why do you always wear the same thing like that? Like, wear a skirt!" This whole like, "You gotta look really pretty and wear all this" —
> Kate:      —so you look like a girl.

When asked directly, neither Kate nor Christine had heard of feminism and asked Shauna what it meant. In fact, the working-class and immigrant girls in our study were less likely to report having had access to feminist discourse or to have an accurate sense of the meaning of feminism (sometimes confusing it with femininity, as when Beverly guessed that it meant "girlie girl").

As also seen in Chapter Six, even in cyberspace where role playing may seem to invite "experimentation," girls experienced constraints on their ability to "play" with gendered identities. Online girls described harassment and other forms of violence as limiting their online practices of gender-bending and rebellion against both emphasized femininity and hegemonic masculinity. A number of participants had created powerful, gender-bending female characters online, for example, but they also described getting expelled from or being ignored in chat rooms, being flamed or insulted, and labeled as inauthentic. Recall from Chapter Six that when Shale posted a picture meant to represent her in the chat room, Vampire Desecrated Cathedral, she was kicked out because her chosen avatar Self was not sexy enough. Shale learned that garnering attention online as a girl or woman was bound up with sexual objectification, a form of symbolic violence.

These social constraints on girls' ability to reconfigure their identities show that re/inventing girlhood cannot happen one girl at a time. The girls in our study talked about the importance of support from friends and others in practicing alternative or resistant girlhoods—their stories testify to the importance of their community of practice. As seen in Chapter Five, members of the Park Gang benefited from the support they could give each other. This support was important given that, in the words of Jessica, "We're really different from other groups." She went on to explain: "You know, there are some groups that are—really enjoy shopping and looking for clothes and boy hunting and all that stuff. But with us, it's just whatever we want to do. So if we're tired, we will just sit around at lunch or, you know, we're all really nice to each other, like there's no backstabbing in our group whatsoever." In these words and practices, we discerned the importance of girls supporting one another when performing girlhood in ways that, in defiance to conventional femininity, gave them a sense of control over their lives. It is in this collective agency that we explore girls' relationship to feminism. Like girls, is feminism "on the move"? Do we discern the emergence of a youthful feminism, one that can enlarge girls' opportunities to explore and expand the boundaries of what it means to be "a girl"?

## RE/INVENTING GIRLHOOD, RE/INVENTING FEMINISM(?)

In this chapter, we can see the need to view youth and their cultural practices as dynamic or in motion; in other words, girls produce identities and cultural meanings that draw from and reconfigure cultural notions of youthful femininity (or masculinity), improvising upon established notions, and sometimes challenging them. Analytically speaking, "community of practice" helps us see "collective" as well as individual agency. It thus acts as a mediating concept that brings together the personal and the social. With Levinson and Holland (1996), we "argue that local analyses must retain a critical perspective on political economy and dominant socio-ideological formations, without losing sight of the particular contingencies and cultural dynamics which characterize local sites" (page 22). In other words, as a mediating concept, "community of practice" brings the social relations of broader society into consideration. This is not to say that racialized or classed processes (for example) determine the identity practices of girlhood in specific communities. Rather, these "structural" processes give various girls differential access to the material and symbolic resources that are the "raw materials" for meaning-making. Thus working-class girls in our study often held part-time jobs in order to acquire the material "props" favored by powerful classmates from middle-class households. Conversely, middle-class girls could purchase goods that signify transgression of their class of origin. For example, girls talked about "hobo shopping" in secondhand clothing stores.

In considering the agency of the in-betweeners in our study, we argue that feminism must likewise stay on the move if it is to remain attuned to girls' on-the-ground political struggles, such as battling the male-domination of space in skate parks or dealing with sexual harassment and flaming in cyberspace. Consistent with our view of culture as practice and as "what people do in everyday life, informed by implicit and shared knowledge" (Levinson 2000: 4; also Misciagno 1997), we see feminism as praxis. Drawing on Misciagno (1997) in Chapter Five, we argued that, in the context of late modernism, feminism can be seen in individual and small group practices of girls and women. It thus needs to be explored in these contexts rather than in the large-scale social action and explicit political agendas that characterized second-wave feminism. Misciagno's (1997) de facto feminism arises from the everyday efforts of individual girls and women to grapple with the various inequities and contradictions in their lives. De facto feminism thus can be seen to embrace the practices of girls in our study who do not necessarily explicitly identify as feminists but whose everyday actions create greater freedom for girls and women generally. One lesson for us is that becoming a feminist is a much more complex and ongoing process than typically acknowledged. It is not simply a matter of asking girls whether they adopt the identity as "feminist." At the same time, we do not therefore claim that every expression of Selfhood that transgresses normative femininity constitutes de facto feminism. Pushing against the boundaries of what constitutes acceptable femininity does not necessarily mean that gendered power inequalities are being challenged, let alone transformed. In the final analysis, we identify political agency when people, interacting in groups, develop shared meanings that enable them to identify an issue or structure of inequality that becomes the conscious target of resistance and propels people to act collectively. We refer to this effect as *transformative agency*; as we argue in Chapter Eight, it takes girls' actions beyond transgression as a way of doing girlhood that can, in fact, reaffirm the boundaries of heteronormativity.

The Park Gang's successful boycott of the male-dominated skate park (described in detail in Chapter Five) is a case in point of what we call transformative agency. The girls involved in this boycott retreated to a safe space where they were not being monitored, honed their skateboarding tricks, and then remerged—triumphant. Through the boycott, the Park Gang challenged the skater boys' power and the ways in which girls are constructed through sexist and oppressive discourses. Before the boycott, skater boys treated the Park Gang as posers, flirts, and interlopers. After the boycott, the girls altered how the boys thought of them and, more significantly, how they thought of themselves. Through this political struggle, the Park Gang carved out a space for girls where none previously existed. They felt they had opened the doors for other girls to use the park.

What interests us is that not all members of the Park Gang identified as feminist, despite our view of their boycott as de facto feminism. While Skater girls can be credited with resignifying girlhood, in the final analysis, their actions are feminist in *effect* rather than *intent*. Like Misciagno (1997), we are open to the idea that feminism is being resignified through the actions of girls and women who struggle to redefine the parameters of girlhood and womanhood; this idea enables us to think about feminism as in a constant state of becoming. Nevertheless, it interests us that most of these girls distance themselves from feminism as a discourse that has the potential to support their actions and help sustain the kinds of changes that they were able to achieve as a relatively small, local collective. In considering why this might be so, we found that, ironically, feminist-inspired projects based on popular notions of "girl power" can themselves work to distance girls from feminism. In conclusion to not only this chapter but also our book, we revisit feminist-inspired discourses that encourage girls to express "authentic" Selfhoods in the name of their "liberation" from the socially constructed constraints of conventional femininity.

## PENGUINS AMONG THE SHEEP: CONSTRUCTING ALTERNATIVE GIRLHOODS

Skater girls in Chapter Five initially drew our attention because of the way that they mocked their Popular classmates:

> Grover: We call them "bun" girls… [because] they used to all like wear hair buns and like, tight jeans, and stuff like that.
> Sandy: But not just—they wear these really tight tank tops. And they all look the same. But it's not, you know. I mean it's also just the way that they act too. It's not just how they dress.

Sandy complained, "They're like 'eeeaah' and like act stupid when they're really smart or something." Zoe and Pete also found Popular girls annoying. For Zoe, the problem was that "They're always the same, sort of. Like they talk the same, they always dress the same. And it gets annoying after a while." Agreeing, Pete claimed that "their main goal in life—at least it looks like to me—is to be 'cute.' It's all they care about… I think it's just totally wrong to live your life like that." Gauge and Spunk ridiculed the conformity of Popular girls, whom Gauge called "sheep": "They're sheep, and we're like penguins. Sheep [pause] all do the same things and penguins are cooler [both laugh together]." Being "penguins" earned Gauge and Spunk the label "weird" among their peers. They attributed this label to the fact that their group is "outgoing and doesn't listen to pop music."

Importantly, these girls rejected the informal rules that governed girls' dress and comportment at school. According to Spunk, these rules entailed "tight jeans, obviously. Always. Always. And, I don't know. Just brand names. A shirt that has a brand name on it is 'cool.'" At the time of their interview, Gauge was wearing a skater T-shirt and baggy pants, while Spunk was dressed in black and sported a shaggy haircut. Spunk called herself "punk rock": "I don't know. It's mostly—that's what people call me. I wear a lot of black and I have a lot of chains and I have a dog collar and—I don't know. I just like that kind of stuff." Both girls talked about themselves as "alternative looking." As we have argued in Chapter Five, their skateboard antics illustrate how dress does not simply signal "girlhood" as an identity label, but shapes what it is possible for girls to "do." While Zoe indicated that "skater clothes aren't slutty, so that's real cool," she went on to say, "That really tight stuff—those can get really annoying after awhile, and you can't do *anything* on a board in it."

To be sure, some of the girls whom we characterize as engaged in de facto feminism claimed a feminist identity.[4] Among them was Gracie, who defined feminism as "just making sure there is equality," reasoning that "Like if there weren't feminists, then we would go backwards. And men would get back the power. Feminism is just like making sure that there is always that equal power." In the final analysis, however, feminism was not the prevailing discourse that we heard in the talk of girls who defied school-based gender conventions. While very few talked about "being feminist," it was common for girls to invoke a discourse emphasizing the importance of "being *yourself.*" Sara, for example, was emphatic: "Popularity is not important to me, but just being acknowledged. Being known as *a person.* Like *Sara.* When I die, what are people going to look back and see? 'Oh yeah. That girl that I went to school with.' Or, am I going to be, you know, 'This character who had *personality.*'" This kind of talk resonates with that used by adults to encourage teenagers to resist "peer pressure" by "being yourself."

We were drawn to the self-assertiveness of these girls in a context where other participants lamented competition over boys' attention and the "meanness" of girls policing that competition. In her critique of the pursuit of Popularity, Onyx reasoned that "if you keep adjusting yourself to fit in," you could lose yourself, a problem that she claimed as "the center of teenage problems":

> Not finding yourself again. Not knowing what you're worth. Thinking that you are only good if someone else finds you to be who they think you should be. And I think this is a time when, this is a big time for kids like our age to either go one direction or the other.

Knowing "who I am" allowed Onyx to assert, however tentatively: "I think I know what I want. Well, I have direction. I mean, I know how I am going to get there and what I am going to have to do." Included in what she wanted was "to go on to university and become—I'm not sure what yet, but I have choices and I'm trying not to limit them." Onyx's reasoning was shared by Grover when she exclaimed, "I know who I am and I am confident with who I am!":

> I think you should just let someone, you know, express themselves the way they want to be expressed. And I am against people, you know, saying, "You shouldn't look a certain way" like that because, you know, "it's not pleasing," "it's degrading," or something like that.

This discourse that legitimates a search for authenticity interests us because we heard it in the work of writers who equate empowerment with girls' (re)discovery of their "inner" Self, an approach we criticized in earlier chapters. In contrast to our theoretical rejection of this discourse, "authenticity" was repeatedly invoked by girls to dismiss the emphasized femininity performed by Popular girls: "They think they are real, but to everyone else they look fake... They are not really their *own* person" (Onyx). Consciously distancing herself from the conformity required for Popularity, Onyx reasoned that "I think everyone's unique, and if you change that, you wouldn't be unique anymore. You'd just be like wanting to be something else. And that's not *you*."

To be sure, we are not claiming that Popular girls would not claim authenticity (although this discourse did not emerge in their interviews with Shauna). Rather, when employed by girls performing alternative or resistant identities, a discourse of authentic Selfhood enabled them to reject the performance of girlhood in ways that disempowers them. Although the term "disempower" is problematic, we use it to signal loss of power rather than to assume that girls do not/cannot exercise power until they have become "empowered." It gave the girls discussed above an ability to consciously negotiate the kind of meaning they assigned to "girlhood." However theoretically problematic for us, in interviews, a discourse of "authentic Selfhood" signaled possible awareness on the part of girls about femininity as a socially constructed—hence malleable—identity. It thus promised to open up girlhood to the kind of critical introspection that we associate with feminist subjectivity:

Sandy:   Well, I guess fifteen, sixteen is kind of like—
Onyx:    The age where you separate yourself from maybe other people.
Sandy:   Yeah. You're more like—I think it's more like you're independent, es-
         pecially from your parents. I think you become—like you think the
         way you want to more and like, you know, you're more social. And
         I don't know. You just kind of know yourself better than when you
         were younger… You know yourself and you've been around longer
         so like you just make better decisions and—
Onyx:    It's like between wanting to be a woman and realizing that you are
         one. Maybe that's what this age is all about.

Realizing "you are a woman" is important because, in the words of
Sandy, fifteen is "the 'breaking age" of like where you are trying to
figure out like who you are. And what you want to do. And stuff like
that." Despite their descriptions of life at school as complex and stressful, Sandy and Gracie celebrated girlhood because it gave them a freedom to explore "who you really are" with girlfriends:

Sandy:   You think it seems like—not like this is true—but it seems like you
         [girls] think more [than boys], and like you care more about things
         and you're more—you try to be more involved. Maybe.
Gracie:  I think probably it's better being a girl because you can be like more
         "who you are" because the guy, you have to—I don't know, you can't
         really talk about things that much. And with girls, like your friends
         are usually like really important to you. And you can always just talk
         to your friends if you want to. And I don't think that it is the same for
         guys. I mean, they have friends, but they can't be, like call their guy
         friend up and be like, "Oh, I have a problem."

While we might not share their perceptions about boyhood, given that
Sandy and Gracie both believed that "girls have a lot more stuff to deal
with," the freedom they associate with being able to explore girlhood
is important. Most of the girls in our study would agree with Grenn:
"You're supposed to be a certain way. The other girls expect you to be
that way. You go against them, then they *hate* you." Why do so many
of these girls, then, distance themselves from feminism as a movement
that made resistance to gender subordination initially "thinkable" and
today offers girls a discourse that enables them to challenge the socially
constructed nature of their subordination?

In exploring this quandary as feminists, we suggest that, although
encouraging girls to "be themselves," the discourse of "authenticity"
that supports their transgressions can also limit the transformative po-

tential of girls' agency. This is because the confidence to speak oneself into an "alternative" existence required the Speaker to believe in her ability to do so. According to Sara, for example:

> We're equal, as equal as we're going to get. And it's just the way that you carry yourself. And they think—I think they [classmates] have less self-esteem and they feel that they don't have that much power and that's what makes—that's why they think they should be feminist, because they feel that men have more power. I don't feel that men have more power, and so I don't think I should have to be a feminist.

Implicit in Sara's thinking is a trump discourse of postfeminism, a widely accepted view that gender equality has been achieved and, as a consequence, young women are "freed" from the kinds of constraints on self-actualization that made second-wave feminism necessary. Accordingly, rather than reiterate a victimized subjecthood, young women should get on with their self-constructions. Within this discourse, girls are not dismissing feminism; rather, as McRobbie (2004) argues, postfeminism invokes feminism in order to argue that it is no longer needed: because gender equality has been accomplished, feminism is a "spent force" (page 4). This kind of thinking led Gauge to claim that, in fact, feminism works against girls' self-expression:

> Some of it's [feminism] silly. I mean, like, you're not allowed to wear tight clothes. You have to wear baggy sweaters and absolutely no makeup and your hair has to be, like, just *normal* and— You've just got to be *who you are.* You shouldn't, you know, just try to be someone you're not just based on things that people [feminists] say.

Here Gauge consciously placed herself against what she understood as the "rules" governing the behavior of anyone identifying as "feminist." While this move supported her search for a unique, authentic Self, it placed Gauge outside discourses that can help make the socially constructed nature of girlhood visible.[5] This is because the abstract individualism that makes "authenticity" possible requires the individual to see herself as unique, separate from the social world, and apart from history. Within this discourse (and its associated practices), feminism becomes associated with conformity and the pursuit of authentic individualism with "resistance." The reflexivity that attracted us to interviews with girls performing alternative or resistant girlhoods can thus have an ironic twist.

By rejecting feminism, these girls also reject a discourse that can help them better understand the dynamics that they resist. These dynamics arise from the social imperative to take up a girlhood that sustains gender inequality at the extra-local as well as personal level. As a result, the reasoning of girls like Sara could appear contradictory. Despite Sara's claims that "we're equal as we're going to get," she gave everyday examples of sexism but then immediately added: "It bothers me a little bit, but I think they're [the guys] being jackasses. And it has nothing to do with the truth. It's just the way they feel. And we can't change the way they think. Uhm. We can prove them wrong." This kind of thinking allowed girls in our study to sustain the claim that, while feminism might have been necessary "in the past" when women faced barriers to equality, it is no longer needed. In fact, Pete maintained that "sometimes feminism is brought too far: [There is] 'Yeah, I want to be equal to the men. Get paid the same wage for doing the same job.' And there is 'I'm going out and be a firefighter just for the sake of having women on the force.'"

In the final analysis, what we heard in girls' talk is what we call "postfeminist essentialism" as an emergent discursive formation. While sustaining belief in feminine and masculine identities as necessary for social stability, this essentialism is "feminist" in the sense that it acknowledges rather than denies the legitimacy of second-wave feminism. It concedes that gender subordination, historically, reflects mistaken beliefs about gender—particularly about womanhood. It is "postfeminist," however, by maintaining that the "social misconstruction" of gender that sustained women's subordination is something "in the past." In the present, social harmony is threatened by continuing demands for social change. This (contradictory) discourse resonates with, and becomes a hybrid of, contemporary neoliberalism. Neoliberalism maintains that individuals have been "freed" from the traditional constraints that, historically, acted as barriers to Self-fulfillment. Individuals are now able to begin—and hence must take responsibility for—fashioning Selfhoods. Neoliberalism thus positions girls to construct new girlhoods. As promoted in commercial and popular culture, changing norms for how gender, the body, and sexuality can be represented in public have opened space for new expressions of gender in relation to sexuality. Within this space, "normative femininity is coming more and more to be centered on woman's body—not its duties and obligations or even its capacity to bear children, but its sexuality, more precisely its presumed heterosexuality and appearance" (Bartky 1988: 81). In this way, the re/invention of girlhood remains bounded by the heterosexual matrix that continues to make our identity practices intelligible. One problem for us is the way in which this matrix supports a postfeminist essentialism that makes gender inequality much more difficult to name and, hence, criticize.

By operating as "common sense," the claims supported by postfeminist essentialism escaped girls' conscious interrogation. It often encouraged girls to attribute what they described as "complications" of life at school to something inherent in girlhood. For example, while Pete and Zoe recognized girls' negotiations as complicated and contradictory, they located the problem in girls themselves:

| Pete: | Guys seem to be more logical at this age. They kind of see things for what it's for. And girls seem to be more twisty about it and— |
| Shauna: | "Twisty?" |
| Pete: | Like they kind of turn things less logically, and they're into their feelings. And they kind of consider a lot of different areas that affect whatever it is they're trying to decide or see. |
| Zoe: | Yeah. It's true because at this age we are all into how we feel. And they're—the guys, aren't like that. They're just— |

Despite claims of personally constructed Selfhoods, this kind of essentialism about girlhood was widely shared, but not surprising when one considers its prevalence in mainstream culture. As noted by Tasker and Negra (2007), postfeminism resonates with girl power slogans meant to personally empower girls. Popular culture itself celebrates both girls and "girlishness," constructing feminism as "other": as rigid and having the propensity to "take things too far" (page 19). While a discourse of postfeminist essentialism thus legitimates girls' claims to authentic Selfhood "as girls"—and thus might seem to be "empowering"—it also works to limit their understanding of "who they can become."

Hearing such a discourse in interviews with girls performing alternative or resistant girlhoods tells us that transgressing the rules of normative girlhood does not necessarily signal girls' belief in their ability to be "anything" they want to be. On the contrary, transgression can work to reaffirm boundaries when it establishes meaning through "difference" from what is "normal." As noted by Tori, for example, the commodification of skateboarding enables "rich kids" to buy the signifiers of a once underground culture. In this example, the signifiers of transgression are not accompanied by the transformation of class relations. Through commodification, "difference" is bounded by the very regulatory processes that give rise to "resistance."

Along similar lines, Weeks (1998: 126) warns us, "girlhood" cannot be transcended through "Selfhood," no matter how "alternative," because Selfhood is mediated by the very constructions that feminists expect girls to resist. In the final analysis, the empowerment one might expect to hear from a cohort of girls raised in the cultural context of "girl power" requires girls to position themselves against the very discourses that bring them into existence in their peer cultures. Although one of the most taken-for-granted notions of everyday life, the concept of "Self" has an unacknowledged social pedigree that implicates it in the constitution of a normative order based on inequality. The discourse of inner personal qualities "belonging" to individuals emerged at the turn of the last century, along with new disciplines such as psychology (see Lesko 2001). As argued in Chapter Four, it allowed an emergent bourgeois class to claim moral superiority because its newly achieved status was characterized as the result of personal effort. Unlike the landed aristocracy, the bourgeoisie could claim the virtue of hard work. At the same time, the laboring classes—which included immigrant populations of "others"—were not seen as capable of self-development, because they put their hopes for social improvement in collective endeavors like trade unions or socialism. Cultivating Selfhood became a credential for proper self-governance (hence political enfranchisement).[6]

No matter what their class or race, however, women were denied Selfhood because they were deemed to lack the rationality necessary for self-control. Women's behavior came under the direct and strict control of men—first fathers (and often brothers), and then husbands. Women's conduct and appearance thus reflected on their families' status and became signifiers of moral dis/order. Within this order, young women (and later, schoolgirls) signified "purity" and innocence, an idealization that continues into the present through the sexual double standard. In other words, the notion of Selfhood itself works as a regulatory impulse, constructing girlhood in particular ways. While Selfhood may have the common sense feeling of being open, of being available to all, historically it gained ascendancy by aligning identity with the values and mores of a white middle class.

Within this context, feminization of the "new subjectivity" discussed in Chapter One—the "flexible, individualized, resilient, self-driven, and self-made" Subject—continues rather than challenges this legacy (see Gonick 2006). As a result, the contemporary context that celebrates Selfhood[7] complicates feminist notions of "empowerment." We are reminded that, like girls' agency, girls' relationship to feminism is more complex that we initially conceptualized. Even though many participants distanced themselves from feminism, to be sure most of them implicitly recognized themselves as beneficiaries of feminism. When Sara, for example, claimed "we're as equal as we're going to get," she is invoking the notion that women must now take responsibility for getting what they want. Rather than dismiss this view as "naive," we draw attention to the way in which it is informed by a sense of women's entitlement. While Budgeon (2001: 18) also found that young women's search for Selfhood may engage them in discourses that distance them from feminism, she points out that their sense of entitlement can be a source of agency at the micro level of everyday practices. This appears to be the case when Sandy and Grover suggested that even Bun girls have the confidence to believe in rights "as girls":

> Sandy: Well, I think today—in *their* kind of like "time era" [feminists] were more aware of things. We are able to express our emotions more than we used to be. And we get somewhere by doing it. And I think—I mean most girls are like "for feminism" and they're not—even if they're not like rallying or something.
> Grover: But they will be angry if something like—if something antifeminist—
> Sandy: Yeah. Like they will stand up for themselves if—
> Grover: Go do something.
> Sandy: Even the Bun girls I think would... And be confident. And really like make sure they're like, you know, believing in themselves.

Drawing attention to this kind of talk in her interviews with young women, Budgeon (2001) maintains that what she heard is not an outright rejection of feminism as much as feminism "in process," a feminism wedded to individualism.

We agree with Budgeon that if feminism is to be relevant to young women today, it must resonate with its sociocultural context. As she notes, today these conditions include a mandate for girls to "choose" their Selfhood. In the short span of about three decades, we have witnessed a transformation of struggles by women to gain control over "Who they are" into a mandate for women to take responsibility for the new choices they face, in a postfeminist context devoid of cultural evidence that "race, class, and gender" matter. In their place, social differences are coded and read as "lifestyles" exercised through participation in a marketplace of "choices." Thus we agree with Budgeon that girls' struggles for self-discovery are not so much a celebration of a depoliticized individualism as they signal a more general transition within late modernity that directs youth towards self-actualizing Selfhoods (Budgeon 2001: 22). To be critical of the latter does not require us to be critical of the ways girls incorporate this modern individualism into their identity practices. We elaborate on the pedagogical implications of this position in Chapter Nine.

In this chapter, the feminist praxis demonstrated by many of the girls in *"Girl Power"* does, indeed, bode well for the future of feminism. The challenge is to understand how the struggle to construct alternative or resistant girlhoods (as well as womanhoods) can explode rather than redraw the boundaries of what it means to be female. We take up this challenge in the concluding chapter. In order to foreshadow these conclusions, Chapter Eight revisits how we answer the questions that inspired our research: How do girls make sense of themselves "as girls?" What does their meaning-making tell us about the operation of power through everyday identity practices that bring gender into existence? And what does it tell us about the relevance and role of feminism in the lives of girls today?

NOTES

1   We say "speculate" because of our relatively small sample and the fact that our study was not based on sustained participant observation (while we do have observational data of the Park friends at the community center where they skated and hung out, most of our data consist of girls' self-reporting on what they said and did within various communities of practice).

2   We say "competing" because these peer groups very often construct meaning through "difference" from other youth groups. The operation of "difference" can signal deliberated opposition, or it can work to re-establish normative ways of being.

3   As a limitation of our study, we can say very little about processes that positively facilitate their mobility.

4   Feminists in this chapter include: Jessica, Gracie, Rose, Shale, Vanessa, and Anna. Girls who did not claim feminist identity when asked directly include: Sandy, Zoe, Pete, Sara, Spunk, and Gauge.

5   While we are not implying that becoming feminist is simply a matter of "knowing" feminism, we are reminded of Spender's (1982) observation that feminist knowledge about women's oppression, historically, has been lost "between generations" and thus has required continual rediscovery.

6   Along with the notion of "citizenship," the feminist struggle for women to claim "identity" began in their struggle to be included in the rights of citizenship. In Canada, women were granted legal "personhood" only in 1929, and even then this personhood did not include women of Asian descent or aboriginal women (see Errington 1988). As we argue for the notion of "Selfhood," this project of female citizenship was classed and racialized from the onset.

7   Here we add the celebrity worship that characterizes popular culture, especially commercial culture aimed at youth.

# 8

# *"GIRL POWER"* REVISITED

In Chapter Seven, we have seen how practices of "Selfhood," paradoxically, can work to limit girls' sense of "who they are" and "who they might become." Given that *"Girl Power"* is framed in terms of "understanding Selfhood" as practiced by girls, it seems necessary to revisit what we have learned about the transformative potential of girls' identity practices in the context of competitive individualism and postfeminism. In this chapter, we review the analytical lessons of our research; in Chapter Nine, we explore the practical implications of our work.

Our focus on Selfhood as the organizing principle of *"Girl Power"* is motivated by our commitment to recognize girls as "individuals" and cultural producers in their own right rather than miniature "women in the making." Influenced by writers such as Simone de Beauvoir, who characterized girlhood as the formative years between childhood and adulthood, until the 1990s, adolescent femininity was studied primarily as preparation for womanhood: academic interest in girls—feminist and otherwise—was driven by theoretical investment in understanding the identities of adult women. While this interest contributed to the recognition that womanhood is a malleable identity, ironically, it naturalized adolescent femininity by characterizing it as a universal, transitory period of "maturation."[1] Against this view, we join Girls' Studies scholars in treating girls as Subjects in their own right. Because we see girls as actively creating their social presence "as girls," we view their identity practices as bringing girlhood into existence: girlhood is not out there, waiting for female children to grow into (see Driscoll 2002). As a culturally and historically changing social identity, girlhood is being constantly rewritten by girls themselves, albeit within limits. In exploring girlhood in the process of being rewritten in this way, the challenge for us has been to interrogate Selfhood without re-inscribing compulsory individualism (see Gonick 2007). We took up this challenge by treating identity as embodiment of the social and cultural processes that frame everyday practices (see Smith 1987). This approach allows us to see the operation of power at the micro, everyday level but connects the personal power of individual girls to social investments in girlhood.

Throughout *"Girl Power"*, we use "girlhood" to signal that, no matter how unique the identities of individual girls may seem, the meaning of their practices of Selfhood is mediated by cultural definitions of what it means to "be a girl" (including those given by adult researchers). Although grounding our work in the identity practices of individual girls, we are interested in extra-local social processes that work to constitute girlhood in specific ways. Indeed, we have seen that girlhood is not "innocent and unburdened." Popular discourses generated by advertising, entertainment media, and adult "experts" testify to social investment in what it means to be "a girl." They also remind us that girls' ability to rewrite girlhood is what Lalik and Oliver (2007: 49) call a "limited potentiality." Rather than advance a vision of what we imagine girls can "become," our goal is to help identify how girls' potentials are enabled and yet, at the same time, circumscribed. Thus our inquiry is organized around girls' agency as an attempt to understand the character of relations that are sustained by girls' identity practices while affirming the possibilities these practices embody for social change.


## GIRLHOOD AS CONTESTED TERRAIN

During the 1990s, public interest in girlhood crystallized in the girl-oriented popular culture described in Chapters One and Two. While the postwar years were characterized by a commercial culture of girlhood propagated through magazines targeting girl readers, the 1990s witnessed a culture about girlhood, produced for girls and, in some cases, *by* girls. Keying off feminist-inspired empowerment programs, this culture incited girls to be "anything they want to be." It thus worked to signify girls as historical agents and girlhood as a metaphor for social change. Inheritors of the second wave of women's liberation, young women came to symbolize the new millennium, through the trope of what Harris (2004) calls "future girl." Evidence for their succession came from girls' educational success-es, fashion that celebrated girlhood and girlish sexual assertiveness, and young women's apparent rejection of institutionalized feminism, even as they embraced what feminism helped make possible: professional ambi-tions and delayed motherhood (see Harris 2004: 17). "Future girls" thus testify to the historically contingent nature of what it means to be a girl. As Nielsen (2004: 11) points out, while contemporary girls may still long for feminine beauty and the pleasures of male attention, today they are also incited to act as rational, self-controlled, and autonomous Subjects in ways historically associated with their male counterparts.

Reflecting these changes, some contemporary commentators maintain that gender equality has "arrived." This claim was encouraged by Riot Grrrl bands of the early 1990s. These bands initiated a discourse of "girl power" that troubled the "natural innocence" conventionally associat-ed with girlhood. "Softening" its message, the Spice Girls rendered girl power more accessible to everyday girls and more acceptable to adults. Girl power music offered girls and adults alike new ways to think about "who girls are" and "who they might become." The term "girl power" was taken up by advertising media and soon became associated with a range of girl-positive activities, including adult-initiated projects to save girls from the perils of adolescence. Encouraging girls to follow their "inner voices," these projects presupposed an "authentic girlhood" si-lenced by the patriarchal mandate of male approval. "Voice" became a metaphor for a social movement that would empower girls to reclaim girlhood. By the turn of the twenty-first century, "girl power" entered everyday lexicon. As cited in Chapter One, as an everyday expression, "girl power" signals "a self-reliant attitude among girls and young women manifested in ambition, assertiveness, and individualism" (*Ox-ford English Dictionary*, page 3). In the final analysis, this "movement" gave girls access to girl-positive messages through a depoliticized ver-sion of girl power. While it enabled them to think about alternative and resistant girlhoods, for the large part these alternatives took the form of cultural rather than political engagement (see Taft 2004).

In the context of mass consumption, "taste" and "lifestyle choices" have become increasingly important markers of "being someone." Culturally, identities have become malleable; middle-class girls in our study talked about "hobo shopping," for example, or participants described white classmates as "wiggers."[2] It is therefore interesting that, at the same time that gender is claimed as "irrelevant" in terms of future success, and girlhood came to represent a historical force, girls themselves became a focus of public censure. Beginning in about the mid-1990s, the media began to resignify girl power as an emerging social menace. This resignification occurred through the kinds of images we have seen in Chapter Two: girls dedicating their existence to undermining female competitors, girls as sexually aggressive exhibitionists and relentless, butt-kicking heroines. A number of writers have pointed out that the anxiety embedded in these constructions is not entirely new: Worrall (2004: 44; also see Kelly 2000) reminds us that girls who are sexually active, get drunk, or act "unruly," historically have been constructed as threats to the moral fabric of society. One difference is that, in the past, these behaviors were seen to be associated with working-class and immigrant girls, or girls from "broken" homes. It is now white middle-class Subjects of girl power culture who are seen to "exceed" the boundaries of normative girlhood, destabilizing a gendered order that requires females to be chaste until they marry, bear children, and organize their lives around domestic responsibilities. As we began our research, popular media was invoking "girl power" to support the notion that feminism for girls is dangerous: we encountered both "girlhood" and "girl power" as contested terrain. To us, what seemed to be at stake is not the future of girls as much as the future of patriarchy, hence we organized our research to include questions about how feminism figures into the lives of contemporary girls.

As researchers, our interest lies in the ways that competing discourses surrounding girlhood and girls' bid for Selfhood cohere as social knowledge, gelling together into a narrative that is symptomatic not of girls but of social investments in girlhood. By making this distinction, we draw attention to the difference between "girlhood" as the construction of social thought about girls—a construction through which we come to think about girls, talk about them, and categorize them for purposes of intervention—and actual girls. Once constructed as natural and inevitable, "girlhood" operates as common sense, working to conflate the culturally constructed category "girlhood" and embodied girls (see Driscoll 2002).

Framed by a medically authorized discourse of "puberty," girlhood operates as if it "has always been there," existing in the same way across time and place—as physical and social maturation out of the innocence of childhood into the (hetero)sexuality of womanhood. When embodied girls trouble societal expectations surrounding this transition,[3] they are seen as aberrations of a "natural" gender order.

Given what is at stake for girls, we view discourses surrounding girlhood and girl power as a vehicle of power, thus a terrain of political intervention. This is because, in the words of Davies (1997: 10–11):

> The active taking up of oneself as male or female, dominant or passive, is a complex process that must be understood if we are to recognise and deconstruct the binaries in our own lived experience of them. That is, if we want to read the ways in which the culture inscribes itself on the inner and outer body, and if we want to read against the grain, that is, discover other than dominant truths embedded in our experience and in the possibilities the culture holds open to us, we must look again, and more closely, at how discourse works to shape us as beings within the two-sex model.

As Davies notes, while discourse is productive in the Foucauldian sense, as it enables Selfhood to happen, discourses also have the ability to delimit our sense of "who we are" and "who we can become" as social Subjects. Because we view agency as a capacity for action that historically specific relations enable and create, we differentiate between girls' agency, as expressed in their everyday practices of Selfhood, and power, as those processes that shape girls' agency in historically and culturally specific ways. In order to retain girls' active role in giving girlhood an embodied presence, we refer to our participants as "doing girlhood."[4] While girls talked to us about doing girlhood, understanding power required us to identify discourses expressed through their actions but not necessarily in their talk. In other words, although the focus of our attention is deliberated practices of individual girls, we are interested in what makes these practices possible and sustains girls' investments in particular ways of doing girlhood. Treating discourse as one such enabling process, our goal is to identify how specific discourses work to make certain girlhoods thinkable—hence do-able—but others not. Thus we ask how girls understand their actions and their social worlds. What kinds of discourses sustain their meaning making? And how might feminism (as both a cultural and a social practice) open new possibilities for how both young people and adults think about girlhood?

## GIRLHOOD AS A SOCIAL PRACTICE

By focusing on discourse, we do not mean to imply that gender is a purely cultural formation. As much as it is constructed through ideas, talk, and representations, girlhood is also constructed through and within the material practices of institutions like the media, school, medicine, social sciences, and so on. We are interested in how discourses sustaining the identity practices of embodied girls in local sites are connected to these institutionalized processes. In our work, discourse mediates individual identity practices and the social order, enabling us to connect the micro level of everyday gender dynamics to the social operation of power. We return to the institutional context of our participants' agency in Chapter Nine; for the moment, we are interested in the local sites of girls' identity practices.

In our work, the specific micro level site of interest is all-girl groups. As noted by previous researchers, the same-sexed groupings of school-based cultures are an important venue through which both girls and boys "practice" social identities. Recognizing the influence of same-aged classmates, conventional youth researchers have favored the notion of "peer pressure." As noted in Chapter Four, one problem is that this notion portrays young people as "acted upon" by their friends. Moreover, the term "pressure" characterizes this influence as a "negative" factor in the lives of youth, obscuring the ways in which young people support each other in positive ways.[5] To some extent, feminists have criticized this approach (often implicitly) in their study of all-girl cultures as friendship networks fostering connection and support rather than competition. Research has shown that girls have uniquely different relationships with each other than boys do among themselves; girls are reported to have smaller groups of friends, have more exclusive relationships, and engage in more intimate sharing than boys. Because psychologists associate such relationships with positive developmental outcomes, some writers have romanticized girls' friendships as a "haven of warmth and support, intimate self-disclosure and trust" (Frith 2004: 357; also see Code 1991).

As we have seen in Chapter Four, against this view, girls can act in ways that are personally hurtful and socially harmful. As documented by others, in our study, girls often formed alliances with other girls—typically more powerful peers—in order to exclude or publicly humiliate targeted classmates, in some cases purported "friends." Even girls who disapproved of this behavior frequently "went along" with these dynamics, making boys' propensity for physical violence seem more "honorable" because it is direct and open. In recognizing this contradiction between feminist representations of girls' friendships and how girls themselves experience friendship, like Hadley (2003: 378) we question what it is about long-held gender stereotypes and feminist ideals that is being challenged by recognizing girls' "not so nice" behavior. Gonick (2004) warns that by implicitly accepting an imputed "innocence" of girlhood and altruism of femininity, feminism can become complicit in the kinds of moral tales described in Chapter Two. Without an interrogation of girls' agency, their aggression can become symbolic of social decay, supporting claims that feminist empowerment is "not good" for girls.

In an attempt to address this problem, in *"Girl Power"* we explore all-girl peer cultures as local communities of practice. In our study, a community is sustained through performance of a shared identity category. While a community of practice can include friends, as an analytical category it tells us much more about the social context of girls' lives at school. Coming at a point when young people are carving out identities independent from the endorsement of adult parents, relatives, and teachers, these communities can exercise a strong hold on both girls and boys, because membership signals acceptance by those with whom young people, involuntarily, spend a significant amount of time. As Emily informed us in Chapter One, "most people don't define us for who we are, but for who we hang out with." Participation in communities of practice can thus help young people answer questions concerning, "Who am I? What can I do? And not do? How do I want to be seen by others? And who might I become?"

Like friendship, a community of practice entails interpersonal relations. While members of any local community may indeed be "friends," membership may require girls to "give up" friendships in order to demonstrate group loyalty. Moreover, membership in a community may not require face-to-face interaction: by sharing a socially recognized identity, girls can be united across dispersed local sites of action without ever meeting each other. Such communities have been enhanced by everyday access to the Internet. Members adhere to similar rules of self-presentation and share affinity to an entire set of values, attitudes, and beliefs expressed through distinctive ways of talking, dressing, and behaving—what is commonly referred to as "style."

188 "GIRL POWER" | Currie, Kelly, & Pomerantz

The styles of youth cultures cohere around body image and demeanor, as well as argot (Brake 1985), reflecting how the body and its presentation have become what Pomerantz (2008) calls "social skin." In our work, style is the most obvious, but not most significant, characteristic of local communities of practice. It is important for us, because it demarcates the boundaries of specific communities that could be strictly policed, especially by a group's trendsetters. Our goal is not simply to identify the styles of different girlhoods, however, but to identify the consequences that different ways of doing girlhood have for both individual girls and girls more generally. For the Populars in Chapter Four, for example, minor "infractions" of unspoken dress codes could have major implications for those involved. For the Park Gang, style was not only a conscious rejection of the pursuit of Popularity, it enabled girls to engage in the traditionally male pursuit of skateboarding. However inconsequential youthful dress codes may appear to adults, the importance given to "style" in youth culture reflects the paucity of venues through which young people can creatively express "who they are."

Since about the 1960s, youth culture has become a subject of academic interest as researchers attempt to better understand the often audacious style of teenagers. One potential problem with ethnographic focus on youth style is that some adult interpretations have tended to obscure the heterosexist practices that can sustain youthful rebellion (see Hey 1997: 16, 17). For example, a girl's adoption of clothing that her parents deem "inappropriate" may signal resistance to adult attempts to mute her emerging sexuality, but it could at the same time align her identity practices with principles of male desire. For this reason, while we see "style" as an observable expression of girls' agency—and potentially, resistance—we treat it also as an expression of power relations. In order to do so, we do not focus on the various styles visibly associated with different girlhoods, but rather on the relations sustained by the shared meaning making that specific styles express.

In summary, as our site of investigation, a community of practice offers an activity-based approach to exploring individual identity that retains the social character of meaning making, hence of girls' gender performances. Our participants made sense of both themselves and their classmates through participation in and contributions to these communities (or exclusion from socially significant ones). While we recognize that our participants were members of many communities, each working to constitute contextually specific identities, they participated in each of these communities "as girls." In other words, while we see gendered identities as contingent and thus unstable, we are interested in why gender is nevertheless such an important principle in the operation of everyday social life. In youth cultures, the categories "femininity" and "masculinity" do more than sustain personal identities; they are critical elements in the social ontology of life at school (see Bartky 1988).

By "ontology" we refer to a framework through which the world makes sense; it identifies what is important, what belongs, what to ignore and what is not possible. Despite the claims advanced by neoliberal, postfeminist discourses that individuals are now "freed" from tradition as a "dead weight of history," we have seen how conventional meanings surrounding gender persist to inform this ontology. Because they operate as common sense, heterosexism can be hard for girls to articulate—not because it is hidden (or because they have no experience of it), but because it is such a naturalized aspect of so many aspects of girls' lives, especially popular culture. As we have seen, even girls who rejected the "trappings" of conventional hetero-femininity in order to perform "alternative" or "resistant" ways of being were "judged" according to established expectations surrounding girlhood. What this tells us is that, although a space for youthful experimentation of ideas, styles, and practices, communities of practice cannot be understood in isolation of their broader context; no matter how creative their experimentation, young people's meaning making is mediated by the belief systems, values, and knowledge of extra-local cultures expressed in commercial culture, adult talk, and scientific "wisdom."

## POWER REVISITED: PRODUCING "GIRLED" SUBJECTS

In short, communities of practice are *semi-autonomous* sites of creative meaning making. In our research, they enable us to witness the operation of power at the everyday, micro level without losing sight of the *social* nature of individual agency. Thus, while we have been inspired by Foucauldian notions of the Subject as constituted in local sites, analytically we do not treat individual Subjects as the "terminal form" of power. In our work, social practices, and not individual bodies, are the "terminal form" that power takes. Gender practices—conformist and transgressive—are produced by the circulation of power through the everyday discourses that bring us into existence. Unlike (some) other writers, as we direct our attention to girls' resistance to conventional practices of girlhood, we do not interpret their transgression as necessarily transformative. Chapters Four, Five and Six explore how power operates to shape girls' agency without presupposing that power produces either compliance or resistance. This is because the notion of a community of practice helps us study how power circulates at the everyday micro level but avoids celebrating individualism, even when expressing alternative or resistant girlhoods such as those described in Chapter Seven.

What all this means to us is that whether or not transgressive expressions of Selfhood can be claimed as feminist politics is more complicated than we might have expected. While dissent is perhaps a basic political emotion, in itself transgression does not contribute to sustained social change that "frees" girls from patriarchal investments in girlhood. Thus we cannot simply read "politics" off styles that reject conventional school-based norms. Are we arguing then that, as feminists, we would not encourage girls to pursue practices that sustain a sense of unique Selfhood? On the contrary, *"Girl Power"* is predicated on the importance, if not necessity, of such a process, given that Selfhood is the historically specific way that individuals participate in Canadian society. At the same time, however, we recognize that this participation is also predicated on a specific form of Subjecthood—one that is classed and racialized as well as gendered. In the final analysis, while girl power discourses may promise a future for some girls—for the most part, white middle-class girls—they can foreclose that future for others. Clearly, the dilemma for feminists remains that while existing discourses surrounding girlhood may produce girls as subordinate to male desire, it is also true that girls cannot sustain a gendered presence outside the discourses that are available to produce "girled" Subjects. While these discourses carry the danger of reinscribing the competitive individualism that characterizes patriarchal interests, they produce Subjects who can speak "as girls." However contradictory this positioning may appear to be, speaking "as girls" remains important, because it embodies the potential to "speak back" to these interests. The operative word here is "potential." We thus direct our analytical attention to the question of how power works through discourse in ways that connect the cultural, social, and embodied elements of girlhood.

DISCOURSE REVISITED: ENABLING AND DELIMITING
GIRLS' POTENTIALS

Schools are not the only site for the performance of gendered identities
or gendered relations; neither is everything that happens in the school
the result of schooling alone. As noted by Epstein and Johnson (1998:
108, 109), whether expressed as compliance or resistance to cultural expectations, youth draw on the discursive repertoires that they live elsewhere, in ways that give these repertoires new, specific meaning in the
context of the school. In our research, specific meanings concern what is
"hot," who is "cool," what to pay attention to and what to ignore, who
to talk to, what to talk about, and so on. This kind of cultural knowledge takes the form of distinct ways of being that can operate as unspoken rules. Membership in any local community of practice is signaled
by talk, dress, and behavior that demonstrate both competence in this
knowledge and compliance to the rules governing that community. Understanding how this knowledge and accompanying "rules" come into
being and how they work to produce a specific community of "girls"
by coordinating their actions illustrates how power produces collective practices. Thus research must go beyond capturing the meaning
of any individual identity practice in order to ask how shared meaning
is sustained. It must bring to light the role that discourse plays in communities of practice, enabling us to see how gender is a characteristic
of collective action by analytically dispersing power across group processes without rendering girls' agency indeterminate.

Admittedly, identifying discourses that sustain particular ways of
doing girlhood was more challenging that we initially expected (see
Currie, Kelly, and Pomerantz 2007). One problem is that girls themselves often told Shauna that there was no available language to express what they experienced or to capture how they felt. A further
problem is that, in contrast to much theoretical work, discourses employed in the service of embodied action are typically an assemblage
of multiple and often competing discursive elements. Foucault himself
noted that, as a result, contradictory discourses can exist within the
same frame of reference, sometimes reconstituting but at other times
challenging the conditions that make them actionable. In other words,
girls did not simply adopt available discourses wholesale. Talking as
girls, about girlhood, and about their lives as girls required the "work"

of assembling various and often competing discursive elements; in many instances, what we heard as adult listeners was inconsistency and contradiction. It became a question not so much about what our participants said as to how the shared meaning that characterizes any community of practice becomes possible.

Our focus turned to the logic that sustains communication despite what, on first encounter, we heard as contradiction. We attributed this logic to "trump discourses." A trump discourse imparts context-specific coherence to a speaker's statements, no matter how contradictory her statements may seem to "outsiders." In the face of contradictory meanings, a trump discourse anchors meaning in a "higher-order" discourse. Trump discourses thus coordinate a world in motion; they help us understand why instability and contradiction do not necessarily invite novel forms of self-expression. Because trump discourses operate as "common sense" to members of a community of practice, they are more often than not "latent" in girls' talk. They sustain collective action while remaining unspoken. Trump discourses helped us identify ways of thinking and being that enable while they delimit girls' potentials; making power accountable for the individual actions of our participants required us to bring these foundational discourses into view.

In our study, one of the most striking trump discourses that operated in this way is that of gender essentialism. By "gender essentialism," we refer to the belief that girlhood is a natural rather than social construction; this thinking tied girls' understandings of themselves as gendered Subjects to the physicality of their existence by anchoring their understandings of girlhood in discourses surrounding their sex(ualiz)ed bodies.[6] The operation of discourses to naturalize their social worlds in this way is captured by Butler's heterosexual matrix: "a hegemonic discursive/epistemic model of gender intelligibility that assumes that for bodies to cohere and make sense there must be a stable sex expressed through stable gender ... that is oppositionally and hierarchically defined through the compulsory practice of heterosexuality" (Butler 1990: 151 note 6). In short, Butler reminds us that common sense demands that gender is sexualized, and that sexuality is gendered. As S. Jackson (2006: 107) notes, one result is that heterosexual femininity is not coterminous with heterosexual sexuality, because heterosexuality is not simply a form of sexual expression. In other words, heterosexuality is a gendered relationship that orders much more than sexual life. This is why a girl's sexuality rather than gender can be called into question if she violates the tenets of femininity by engaging, for example, in conventionally masculine pursuits. When employing the logic of this matrix, girls' talk often conflated sex, gender, and sexuality, shoring up the "heterosexual imaginary" of youth culture (Ingraham 1994).[7]

## GIRLS' (EM)POWER(MENT) REVISITED

As argued throughout "Girl Power", the heterosexual imaginary that predominates youth culture is not simply gendered but is also shaped by relations of subordination, including class, racialization, and colonialism. This is why practices that transgress the heteronormativity of school culture may be least risky for white, middle-class girls (see Ross 1997; Tanenbaum 1999). Working-class girls and girls of color—especially aboriginal girls—are already "marked" as "beyond" the conventions of normality; their transgression will be read differently from that of girls who, by virtue of their racialized and class privilege, can freely "choose" nondominant ways of being. As Walkerdine, Lucey and Melody (2001) have argued, investment in markers of conventional femininity may be more important for those girls whom feminists might identify as most in "need" of "empowerment": girls marginalized in school-based youth cultures by virtue of not being the "right" body size or being from working-class or non-Anglo families. In the absence of economic and social capital, these girls may have more to gain from investments in normative femininity than their more advantaged classmates: while they may hear girl power rhetoric that tells them they can "be anything," many of them face a future of dead-end, low-paying jobs. These girls may find the security offered by "romantic attachment" more appealing than the specter of a feminist struggle that cannot guarantee social reward. In short, we should not assume that girls who perform emphasized femininity do so "unconsciously," while those performing alternative or resistant femininities make conscious choices.[8] Instead, we need to ask, "What is gained by specific ways of doing girlhood? By whom? And in what kinds of contexts?" The problem is that within a postfeminist context, girls do not have access to a language and a discourse that enable them to raise, let alone answer, these types of questions. As a consequence, discourses that work to shape girls' understandings of themselves and of their social worlds remain unspoken; prominent among these "silent" discourses are those surrounding sexuality.

As Epstein and Johnson (1998: 108) note, in the school "sexuality is both everywhere and nowhere." Sex is implicit in the gendered identities of pupils but seldom spoken about in ways that affirm young people's understandings of gendered sexuality because, with few exceptions, such talk is disallowed from the formal curriculum. Moreover, the implicit sexuality embodied by youthful self-expression can become the target of adult censure; if adults read these expressions as explicit signals of sexual behavior, a moral panic can ensue that conflates sex, sexuality, and the heterosexualization of femininity. What is given less attention—if not outright ignored—is the double standard that genders sexuality. It is this double standard that gives coherence to adolescent identity practices while remaining an "unspoken" presence.[9] As we have seen, it placed girls in our study in a "no-win" situation: too much interest in boys could earn a girl the label "slut," while too little could make girls susceptible to being labeled as lesbian. As girls struggle to make sense of these gendered dynamics, the logic of essentialism encouraged them to attribute the social "complications" of their lives at school to something inherent in themselves "as girls." It smoothed over contradictions between their experiences of being treated as boys' subordinates and official rhetoric about gender equality and about the school as a site of meritocracy. When adults also treat Selfhood uncritically, as a "gender-neutral" category of existence now "open" to girls and boys alike, they contribute to this postfeminist essentialism.

In our study, essentialism "repackaged" through postfeminist discourse (see Chapter Seven) enabled girls to recognize that political transformation is possible—as evidenced by the successes of social movements of "the past"—but placed "natural limits" on social change. For example, while Sara acknowledged the existence of sexism, she concluded that things are "as equal as they are going to get." We also have seen girls who reasoned that, by challenging a "natural" order, feminism can "be brought too far" when advocating social (rather than personal) change: while feminism might have been necessary in the past, when things were "obviously" unfair for women, demands to take change further are "excessive." In this way, postfeminist gender essentialism not only limited girls' thinking about "who they are" but also their thinking about "who they might become."

Perhaps ironically, by empowering girls to claim a voice "as girls," feminism can contribute to the belief that gender equality has been accomplished, especially given that this way of thinking informs so much of commercial culture. Discourses of "girl power" likewise carry the danger of supporting postfeminism, not as a dismissal of feminism but as a discourse that actually "takes feminism into account" in order to discount its contemporary relevance (see McRobbie 2004). Feminism is granted legitimacy, but only in a previous time and place; thus associated with an older generation of adult women, it does not belong in the present moment. Where does this lead us in thinking about girls' "empowerment"?

It is not our intention to participate in a discourse that girls "need to be saved." On the contrary, we initiated our project in order to challenge debates that position girls as either "at risk" or as empowered "future girls." In our view, both positions convey a "little bit of truth." While femininity continues to be shaped by conventions that can silence girls and eclipse their futures, feminization of the liberal Subject as we begin the twenty-first century undoubtedly gives some girls an advantage. Whatever the case, in the wake of the women's liberation movement, it has been more necessary for contemporary girls than for boys to ask "who I am" and "who I can become." Researchers and social commentators alike have drawn attention to changes in the Subject positions available to girls and, correspondingly, to the emergence of a "new kind of girl": one who relates actively, critically, and reflexively to the world around her, having no problem in "raising her voice" in public (Nielsen 2004: 10). To be sure, such girls participated in our study, highlighted in Chapters Five, Six, and Seven. These girls reflexively engaged in identity practices that allowed them to creatively explore new embodiments of girlhood in ways that feminist-inspired "girl power" slogans promise. The question for us is why this ability to negotiate such a Selfhood was not characteristic of all our participants.

In our study, it was relatively advantaged girls who were most able to negotiate competing discourses to their benefit. Middle-class girls like Zoe,[10] Madeline, and Sara were able to employ skater culture as a way to distance themselves from the sexism of mainstream school-based culture and, if academically high achievers, to be seen as fun rather than as ploddingly diligent; these girls were able to move between and among cliques at the schools. They were flexible adaptors

with a sense not only of "who they are" but also of what they want for
their futures. But what about other girls in our study? We have in mind
girls like Riva, critical of the competitive dynamics of her school culture
but enjoying the attention of popular girls without being able to articulate "why." It is possible[11] that her behavior has something to do with
her racialized identity as Persian. We remember Amelia, a white working-class girl who had spent time in foster care and was designated as
"learning disabled." When Shauna asked Amelia if she could "move in
and around different groups" at school, Amelia spoke of feeling confined to one peer group "because most of the people don't really like
me; usually they think that I'm like a dirty little person or something."
And then there were Sally and Marie, both white and middle-class
"wannabes" who described their life at school as stressful because "it
costs a lot of money" to keep up with the latest trends in order to fit into
school culture.[12] To ignore these girls in order to celebrate the agency
of their more advantaged classmates would align us with those who
contribute to a discourse of postfeminism that sustains the inequalities
we position our work against.

Beyond our desire to interrupt "either/or" debates about the current
status of girlhood, similar to other research our study suggests that
girls' social lives at school are much more stressful than they need to
be. As educators, we do not accept the view, often expressed by girls
themselves, that the dynamics generating competition, sexual aggression, and hetero-normativity are simply "high schoolism." It is not a
matter, however, that the girls have "got it wrong." Such a view implies
that "correct" knowledge will "liberate" girls' thinking, hence futures.
While we have criticized the way in which essentialism limits girls'
thinking, we also recognize that it authorizes them to claim an identity
"as girls"—precisely what girl advocates encouraged throughout the
1990s. In the final analysis, when refracted through the heterosexual
matrix of postfeminist popular culture, "girl power" discourses do not
necessarily foster girls' transformative agency; they can just as likely legitimate pleasure in the competitive display of girls' hetero-sexed bodies in a social world devoid of gender politics.

In the final analysis, girls are correct in their recognition that their
sexed bodies are social capital. Within popular culture we are witness-
ing the "girling" of femininity (Tasker and Negra 2007: 18); women of
all ages are being referred to as "girls," reflecting the way that markers

of "age" itself are being erased through the commodification of beauty products (including cosmetic surgery). Within this context, girls' bodies have become a cultural site for public display and sexual self-representation. As "display," youthful sexuality is a cultural marker independent from sexual practice; we thus should not be surprised when girls signify their Subjecthood through practices that objectify them in public. Moreover, girls are sexual Subjects with their own desires, however censored these desires might be by adults or distorted by the gendering of heterosexuality. The challenge is to support girls' sexual expression in ways that enhance their understanding of the role it plays in terms of both "liberation" and gender subordination. While we do not claim to have clear answers to this challenge, we would be remiss to ignore the practical lessons that can be drawn from our research. In Chapter Nine, we conclude *"Girl Power"* by discussing implications of our analysis of how power operates in school-based peer cultures to shape girls' thinking about "who they are" and "who they might become."

NOTES

1    Although the 1995 Beijing Platform for Action contains an objective concerning "the girl child," it exhibits this process of naturalization by framing the well-being of girls in terms of their future roles as wives and mothers.

2    "Wiggers" refers to white kids adopting the "style" of black musicians, especially black rappers and hip-hop artists. See Roediger (1998).

3    For example, by "growing up too fast" or being too sexually precocious (see Cook and Kaiser 2004).

4    Review footnote 7, Chapter One. The notion of "doing gender" allows us to treat gender as practiced and never fixed.

5    Perhaps because, as noted by Bibby and Posterski (1992: 203, 204), parents feel a loss of influence as friends become more significant in the lives of young people.

6    We say "girlhood" because girls seemed more likely to recognize a social pressure on boys to "be boys."

7    We are aware that, because we avoided talk about sexuality in our interviews, however unintentionally, our study contributed to this process. As noted in Chapter Three, footnote 10, we did not want student assistants to assume responsibility for dealing with difficult or overly sensitive issues. Moreover, the institutional context of our research encouraged us to avoid topics that had the potential to become controversial once the research gained public attention.

8    At the same time, feminist devaluation of normative femininity risks becoming reactionary, because it can engage girls in discourses that value masculine ways of thinking and thus sustain male privilege (Reay 2001: 162).

9   It also accounts for the extent of homophobic practices; when sexuality is not openly practiced, homophobic teasing can be a way of asserting one's heterosexuality.

10   Here we note the aboriginal ancestry of Zoe. While her middle-class position can be seen to provide relative advantage, her position with respect to race relations can be seen to provide relative disadvantage. We are not saying that membership in these social groups (or any other) determines one's personal identity in any straightforward fashion, but certainly one's positioning within various social groups does shape possibilities and constraints. Individuals make their identities within these constellations of power.

11   Given that Riva's school was highly multicultural, we do not want to impose our interpretation that her behavior signals internalized racism.

12   Sally and Marie were "wannabes" in terms of Popular girlhood. Noncommercialized skater attire would have allowed them, for example, to opt out of the "fashion race."

# 9

# SHAPING GIRLHOOD

LESSONS FOR THE CLASSROOM, SCHOOL, AND BEYOND

Education either functions as an instrument that is used to facilitate the in-
tegration of the younger generation into the logic of the present system and
bring about conformity to it, or it becomes the "the practice of freedom," the
means by which men and women critically and creatively engage with reality
and discover how to participate in the transformation of their world.
—Shaull in Freire, 1989, page 15

Our interest in youth has been fuelled by our roles as educators as well as mothers and aunts. In these roles, we have witnessed young people grapple with the kinds of questions that
girls raised in Chapter Three: "Who am I? What can I do? And not do?
How do I want to be seen by others? And who might I become?" It is
thus important to us that our research speaks to parents and teachers
as well as researchers. We conclude *"Girl Power"* with a consideration
of the practical lessons that can be drawn from our work. More specifically, we tease out the implications for policy and practice of various
concepts and lines of argument that we have developed in the book: a
social constructionist view of girlhood and Selfhood, trump discourses
such as postfeminism and gender essentialism, the centrality of peer
cultures to the construction of gender differences, and how power operates in all-girl and other communities of practice to shape girls' beliefs
about who they might become. In general, we argue that many current
policy and program interventions are insufficient (e.g., personal em-

powerment programs, traditional media literacy) and, in some cases, misguided (e.g., assertiveness training, admonitions to "be yourself" and to "just say 'no' to peer pressure"). We hasten to acknowledge that our social constructivist and group-oriented suggestions for teachers and other adults working with youth—outlined in sections to follow—cannot be translated from theory into practice in any direct manner, given the diverse and complex contexts within which our suggestions may apply. We do, however, hope to open up understandings in ways that facilitate working with girls and adults to create pedagogical opportunities, policies, and programs based in a social constructivist perspective on girlhood.

The kinds of thinking and activities that the girls in our study engaged in as they participated in informal and relatively unsupervised spaces can be seen to mediate formal or school-based curriculum and pedagogy. A focus on this mediation, particularly as it relates to girls' learning about gender identities and gendered relations, helps to bring certain, more formal aspects of learning into sharper relief, spotlighting points of possible intervention. In this chapter, we identify how the obverse is also true: namely, the formal practices associated with the institution of schooling and beyond (e.g., to neoliberal government policies) mediate what happens in informal spheres of learning about femininity (and masculinity).

## BEYOND LIBERAL INDIVIDUALISM: SELFHOOD AS SOCIAL ACCOMPLISHMENT

How can adult girl-advocates help to enhance the potential future of girls? In addressing this question, we are interested in girls as a social group—an interest that takes us beyond personal empowerment for girls. Does our critique of compulsory individualism mean that we would not encourage girls' search for Selfhood?

Despite our critique of the individualism that underlies many attempts to empower girls, we recognize that autonomy is a historical and cultural prerequisite for participation in liberal democracies, including the political movements for social justice that these democracies inspire. For us, the point is to interrupt the competitive individualism that sustains a subjectivity that, while accomplishing a social presence, forestalls a social collectivity that embraces the diversity and different characteristic of the student body. As noted by Gonick (2007: 18), if adult-initiated projects of girls' empowerment adopt slogans of "can-do" feminism based on the expectations for white, middle-class girls, they can act as a technology of Self that ranks girls as "winners" and "losers." Such an effect sustains the kinds of inequalities that, as feminists, we struggle against in our everyday professional and personal lives. In its place, we advocate ways of thinking about Selfhood that sustain the autonomy required for young women to exercise control over their personal lives without losing sight of their relation to others and the social context of their lives. Such thinking raises challenges for the way in which individualism is currently constructed in both the formal pedagogy of the school and in popular culture.

Individualism is the philosophical foundation of Western democracies, hence an unexamined principle of liberal education. Viewing individuals as separate, rational agents, liberal philosophy "frees" individuals to pursue their best interests, based on reason as a guide to morality and values. Historically, this ability to reason was constructed as characteristic of men, and as absent in women. As a result, one of the most important gains of feminism (beginning with the "first wave" of women's liberation during the nineteenth century) has been formal recognition of women as moral equals to men. Transformed into neoliberalism, the ideal Subject embodies a mix of both masculine and feminine traits: independence, competition, and risk-taking are accompanied by the feminine propensity for flexibility, conscientiousness, and reflexivity (see Francis and Skelton 2005). The idealized result is reflexive Self-construction that maximizes individual performance in a free market. Within a context of competition, Self-realization sets the individual against society. One of the challenges within this approach is how then to foster loyalty to a group whose social character has been "erased" because both Selfhood and market competition are treated as natural occurrences, the taken-for-granted nature of social life.

For us, one problem with neoliberalism as the pedagogical foundation of contemporary education is that it teaches young people that Self-determined action is constitutive of the social world. The underlying assumption is that human individuals are the basic constituents from which social groups are composed; individuals are ontologically prior to society (Jaggar 1983: 29). Incorporated in projects to "empower" girls—typically by enhancing their skills for independence and risk-taking—this approach to Selfhood incites girls to make themselves into "whatever they want to be." The basic premises, which we share, are that girls are as capable as boys, and that girls have the right to make claims on the future. And yet, in *"Girl Power"* we have seen how the context of postfeminist discourse places limits on girls' aspirations. Without access to discourses about the socially constructed nature of gendered inequalities, girls are encouraged to think about their feminine identities through a heterosexual matrix that renders only a limited range of specific, culturally mandated practices of girlhood—and subsequently womanhood—intelligible.

In contrast to this liberal view of Selfhood, social justice advocates situate individuals within collectivities, so that membership in a social group cannot be ignored when thinking about the nature of the Subject. This approach recognizes that our experience of Selfhood "as if" it is the primary unit of social life is an historical and cultural construct. Moreover, within this social constructionist view, there is no inevitability of human character, hence of practices, that constitute us as gendered Subjects. While we do indeed "make ourselves," this approach does not ignore how our making occurs within a cultural "moment" characterized by its own historically specific gender politics and other forms of subordination. As a social, not individual, accomplishment the gendered, racialized, and classed nature of Subjecthood remains in view. This position thus raises questions about "whose interests" are served by the current social order. As an antiessentialist position, it invites interrogation of the conditions under which we "do gender." By making the operation of power visible in projects of Selfhood, possibilities for what we have called transformative agency are opened.

Within this way of thinking about Selfhood, "individuality" replaces individualism. Individuality is an expression of our creative capacity for self-construction; it differs from individualism by giving primacy in our thinking to the social context within which we "do" Selfhood. Because this approach thus recognizes the contingent nature of what we come to assume is inherent, it interrogates the socially imposed limits to our being "who we are" and "who we might become." This kind of thinking informs what many teachers identify as "critical pedagogy."[1] In an antiessentialist approach to gender, an overriding principle is to help girls "see" how conventional femininity is constructed through media images, for example, that set unrealistic standards for girls and naturalize inequalities between women and men. We discuss this protectionist[2] approach to "media literacy" below. While we have ourselves participated in this kind of exercise, we would take its "ideological critique" further. We say "further," in part because we would not only interrogate the way that media shape our thinking about girlhood, but ask how these media can destroy outdated gendered conventions at the same time as reconstituting new forms of oppression. For example, in Chapter Two, we have seen that while girls may no longer be idealized in commercial media as "passive and compliant," "nice" girls are being displaced by competitively mean and sexually predatory girls—both in need of adult intervention and correction. The point is that while gender oppression can "disappear" from public consciousness—because it can be, and has been, erased from the cultural sphere of gendered representations—as argued in Chapter One, it is being reconfigured in the social sphere, especially in areas of adult employment and domestic life not yet experienced by girls. This "disappearance" of gender inequality can make the neoliberal, self-fashioning Subject attractive to girls, especially when feminist alternatives can be interpreted as ending one's social life at school (Tamake 2001).

## RETHINKING "CRITICAL PEDAGOGY"

The challenge of a critical pedagogy is to help girls identify the socially constructed nature of everyday gender dynamics and yet affirm possibilities for social change by supporting an individuality fostering girls' creative self-expression. As Fiske (1996: 6) argues, "Discourse continues its work silently inside our heads as we make sense of our daily lives." His position gives urgency to Weedon's (1987/99: 121) injunction to strategize "how to disrupt discourses" by "identifying how they are articulated." When working with girls, this pedagogy often takes the form of "media literacy." As noted above, this protectionist approach hopes to "inoculate" girls against negative cultural representations by teaching them how media images of adult femininity construct unrealistic beauty standards that align girls' aspirations with damaging investments in femininity. These standards are seen as a source of girls' dissatisfaction with their bodies, fostering disordered eating among girls and lowering their self-esteem as they experience the sexual maturity of puberty. As an "antidote" to media messages, girls are often told by adults attempting to be "supportive" that "looks are not as important as the kind of person a girl is," because "beauty is something inside you."

In general, we are sympathetic to these kinds of efforts. However, as a "solution" to the kinds of dilemmas that girls must negotiate within school-based peer cultures, this approach is not without problems. The first problem is that while girls can be told that they "can be anything they want to be," their everyday lives testify to the importance of being "not fat," "pretty," and popular among peers. The message to ignore this mandate is not helpful; on the contrary. Telling girls to ignore the rules that dominate adolescent interaction can have the opposite effect than intended, because ignoring these rules runs the risk of positioning girls on the margins of peer culture. Moreover, as noted in Chapter 8, research indicates that pedagogical criticisms of femininity can silence girls, especially working-class, racialized minority, ethnic, and immigrant girls (Gonick 2007). This silence reflects the way in which "doing femininity" through "adult" (read: sexualized) ways of dressing and doing makeup can be pleasurable for girls. In our study, dressing for school was a source of stress, but also what many girls cited as a positive aspect of being a girl. Girls like Rose and Sara, for example, enjoyed dressing for school because they treated style as a creative act of self-expression. Brooke echoed the sentiments of many girls when she argued that feminists have labeled these kinds of pleasures as "bad." Such a sentiment about feminism can enhance the appeal of popular media that, by contrast, is experienced as positive for many girls, as offering harmless "fun." It is perhaps ironic that at the same time as criticizing processes that limit girls' thinking about "who they are" and "who they might become," feminist discourse can unwittingly contribute to the problems feminists are attempting to address materially.

Finally, we have found relatively little published work on how middle school or high school teachers might enhance girls' media literacy about the kinds of narratives about girlhood that we analyzed in Chapter Two—and in a fashion that complicates the protectionist approach.

While some researchers have begun to point the way to an alternative set of media literacy practices (discussed below), these do not appear to have filtered into teacher education; nor have many school teachers published accounts of excavating popular culture texts (and the cultural practices of youth that are linked to pop culture) as rich pedagogical resources (but see Christensen 2007). Given that the images in the films we discussed in Chapter Two claim to represent girls today—as a point of fact, *Thirteen* gained "authenticity" through collaboration with a thirteen-year-old girl—critical engagement with these images may better resonate with girls' experiential knowledge of their social world than media images of adult femininity. This might also include films produced by girls (see Kearney 2007) or documentaries like "Emoticons" (Honigmann 2007), a film about teenaged girls and their relationships with, through, and beyond the Internet. In this sense, media literacy could begin from where girls are at rather than where adults worry that they might be going.

## TOWARD A CRITICAL SOCIAL LITERACY

> With critical social literacy oneself becomes a shifting, multiple text to be read. The construction of that self through discourse, through positioning within particular contexts and moments and through relations of power, is both recognised and made revisable. Critical social literacy involves the development of a playful ability to move between and amongst discourses, to move in and out of them, to mix them, to break their spell when necessary (Davies 1997: 29).

As we have seen, the context of girls' thinking about and doing girlhood is characterized by claims that gender equality has been achieved. As a result, girls often claimed that while feminism was necessary "in the past," it is no longer relevant. Given that their everyday experiences were often shaped by sexism and other forms of discrimination, one result could be what Pete called "twisting thinking" on the part of girls struggling to make sense of their social world. Another could be the claim that girls are, by nature, more "emotional" than boys, who (to the girls) seemed to be able to deal more easily with the stresses of life at school. In this way, contradictory messages can strengthen the appeal of the kinds of "trump discourses" that encourage what we have called "postfeminist essentialism." For example, an unspoken sexual double standard not only works to "naturalize" the way that sexuality is gendered, it can give the appearance that girls have "all the power." According to Sara, "Girls have more power [than boys] because we have tits! Guys have to work their butts off just to get a number."[3]

In order to be effective, critical literacy must help girls themselves recognize and interrogate this kind of "contradictory" thinking rather than simply "correct" such thoughts. Instead of teaching girls *what* is "right" or "wrong" about the social world, they can benefit from frank discussion about *how* the social world operates to construct various ways of thinking and being. Included in this approach—what we call, following Davies (1997), "critical social literacy"—is discussion of how the body itself is a cultural product. As such, girls' experiences of their bodies, as much as their minds, are sites for self-invention. Bordo's (2003) analysis of media images that construct a "culture of body 'enhancement,'" and of differential readings of media effects, provide one example of critical social literacy in action.

Bordo does not claim to be exempt from the "empire of images," noting that many second-wave feminists "still believe it is possible to 'just turn off the television.' They are scornful, disdainful, sure of their own immunity to the world I talk about" (page B7). Her undergraduate students comprehend that one can be savvy about advertising and the culture industry while still "hating their own bodies for failing to live up to computer-generated standards" (page B7). Bordo writes that she does not preach what she does not practice; she does not admonish young people to "love their bodies" or to refuse to partake in commercialized media culture; rather she tries to "disrupt, if only temporarily, their everyday immersion in the culture. For just an hour or so, I won't let it pass itself off simply as 'normalcy'" (page B9).

High school language arts teacher, Linda Christensen (2007), provides another example of critical social literacy. As well as incorporating poetry and literature into her classroom curriculum, her students write about the importance of clothing, shoes, or haircuts in their own lives. This kind of assignment encourages young people to recognize markers of social class in order to think about how, and why, dominant North American culture equates success with wealth and self-worth with the "appropriate" consumer goods. Christensen stresses the importance for students to read their own stories aloud to each other: "It is the public airing of these stories that helps us excavate those private feelings of doubt, that helps develop the ability to question why our society pushes us to look a certain way, to question *why* we believe that the right clothes or shoes or address will make us a better person" (para. 31). (We return to the importance of young people creating their own stories below.)

We believe that young people have the capacity for this kind of critical reflection and, in fact, already critically interrogate the social world as they negotiate "who they are" and "who they might become." We found both explicit and implicit critiques of conventional femininity in girls' talk; the question for us has been how those critiques become "contained" and distanced from feminism through the logic of essentialism, belief in the self-made individual of neoliberalism, and the paucity or absence of a language and discourse that encourage girls to think of alternatives. We have identified these kinds of limits to girls' thinking by looking at the informal learning that takes place outside of the classroom, within local communities of practice. It is these communities that bring "girls" into existence.

More research is required on the local communities wherein young people learn how to be "somebody," how to navigate the social world, how to exercise power over others in order to gain status, and sometimes how to exercise power with others in order to accomplish group goals.[4] These skills are required for the adult world; they can be acquired only as a social practice. Following from this, a critical social literacy based on an understanding of group dynamics rather than individual behavior can be effective in opening up girls' thinking about "who they are" and "who they might become."

Along these lines, our study highlights the central role that peer cultures play in the construction of gender differences. Educational researchers have begun to document how peer group investments do not develop suddenly, with the onset of puberty, but gradually build from early childhood. As a result, Hickey and Keddie (2004) argue that school-based adults need to recognize and engage "with the collective investments of young people" (page 57). This means, for example, that critical social literacy practitioners need to attend carefully to the social and interpersonal dynamics of classrooms as well as the peer-based investments of children and youth's engagement with media. Buckingham, an expert in media education, argues that children's espoused judgments about media allow them to claim particular social identities, both in relation to their peers and to adults (2003: 48). "For example, girls' frequent complaints about the 'unrealistic' storylines or events in action-adventure cartoons often reflect a desire to distance themselves from what are seen as boys' 'childish' tastes, and thereby to proclaim their own (gendered) maturity" (page 45). When engaging girls in critical discussions of our mediated world, therefore, educators need to bear in mind that critical social literacy "is an interpersonal phenomenon, in which social interests and identities are unavoidably at stake" (Buckingham 2003: 48).

## EMPOWERMENT AS PRACTICE

Our work aligns us with practice theorists who maintain that learning is much more dynamic than implied by socialization theory. Children do not simply "grow" into adults; competence as an autonomous social Self is gained through the repeated performances that bring adult identities into being. Children are active in the process of culturally producing their identities; they are not just passively taught ideas and values by adults, as portrayed in socialization theory. Connolly (2006) has shown, for example, how boys aged five and six appropriated discursive resources (including improvising upon racist ideas and practices) to construct gendered identities and regulate the behavior of their peers. Renold (2003, 2006) has documented how boys aged ten and eleven engaged in practices of sexual harassment, homophobia, and misogyny to construct "heterosexualized masculinities" within the primary school setting.

Viewing identity as something that is practiced rather than "taught" is an argument against the view that adults can impose behavioral change and bypass peer dynamics. Rather than take choice away from girls by "pathologizing" their performances of gender, we suggest that, as teachers, we engage students in activities that are oriented toward transformation of the practices that give young people a sense of "who they are" in relationships with others. To return to the example provided by Christensen, she notes the importance of starting "a little to one side" rather than focusing dead center on the influences of consumer culture and social class on her students' identity formation. "By using literature and their lives, I set the scene for them to make their own discoveries, to learn their own lessons without teacher lectures ..." (2007: para. 9). More generally, educators can encourage youth to produce their own artifacts, such as creating their own media messages to counter commonly used stereotypes in the corporate media, writing a protest song (see Blackwell and Knight 2005), or collaborating with adults to create short videos on social issues of mutual interest (Stack in press).

In other words, we do not believe that closing off choices for adolescents by prohibiting specific forms of self-expression—for example, through codes that attempt to regulate dress and conduct—will necessarily make young people more responsible citizens. In fact, as we suggested in terms of girls' self-expression, outright "opposition" by adults to youthful expressions of Selfhood can foster resistance. We are confronted with the dilemma that, because girlhood comes into existence through the operation of power, girls' capacity for agency is constituted by precisely what it must struggle against in order to be "free." Moreover, as Underwood (2004: 374) points out, any approach that discourages girls from expressing anger or aggression may simply remind them of their subordinate position in society. It is tempting to suggest, as indeed Underwood does, that instead of teaching girls to behave in "better" ways, we might consider helping girls to become more "assertive" and straightforward in resolving interpersonal difficulties. This approach gained popularity due to the common sense appeal of socialization theory. Employed in assertiveness training and date rape prevention programs, it rests on a top-down socialization model that is premised on an assumption that, without appropriate intervention, girls are victims and dupes (see Frith and Kitzinger 1998). The "remedy" is for girls and young women to practice saying "no" in a direct and repetitive way. Unfortunately, as Kitzinger (2000: 178) argues, this strategy does not reflect "the reality of how refusals are [normatively] done." Thus we would go further than Underwood by giving girls access to discourses that help them locate their anger, frustration, or confusion in its context of gender subordination. While the injunction to say "no" helps to construct a speaking Subject, it does not necessarily help girls, as speakers, to recognize, interrogate, or negotiate the underlying power dynamics.

We would also think about how to engage young people in classroom practices oriented to constructive group dynamics. This is because the individual empowerment of students can result in a sense of personal entitlement that favors white, middle-class students, a sentiment that is encouraged in a context where the market is experienced as the source of Self-realization. An example of collective empowerment would be classroom practices based on democratic rather than competitive behavior (e.g., cooperative learning, student collaboration on assessment of their work, discussion and critical examination of teacher-student power dynamics and questioning of the image of the teacher as infallible or always the expert, non-tokenistic student involvement in setting classroom ground rules and school policies, and so on). Perhaps ironically, one measure of success would be students' resistance to the regimented practices and top-down authority relations that prevail between school adults and children and youth in conventional schooling. While it may strike some readers as perverse to encourage students to resist conventional schooling practices, encouraging their participation in decision-making about what and how they learn is vital if we expect schools to prepare young people for democracy. In other words, we cannot perpetually prepare children and youth until they reach the age of legal adulthood, at which point they actually "do" democracy; they need to experience democracy by having opportunities to practice it in their daily lives in meaningful, not token, ways that augment their individual and collective self-determination.

Because we think that girls and boys benefit from the kind of association that their local communities of practice can offer, we would support communities of practice that offer girls collaborative ways of interacting and ways of experiencing their sexed bodies that impart the kind of "thrill" that we heard in the talk of girls from the Park Gang as they learned new skateboarding skills. Skater girls enacted the kind of risk-taking and self-determination promised by girl power slogans; because these enactments are not in service of a femininity that takes meaning from Butler's heterosexual matrix, we see the potential for new definitions of girlhood in their practices. Much more research—particularly through critical ethnography—is needed to help adults better understand how local communities of practice are formulated and how they might sustain the kind of critical consciousness that prepares young people for the challenges of living in an increasingly complex and competitive world.

## CRITICAL DECONSTRUCTION OF GENDER DIFFERENCES

Children do not enter school as blank slates. They "bring with them a myriad of perceptions of difference that they have taken up from their families, peers, the media, and other social sources and negotiated in the representations of their own identities" (Robinson and Jones Diaz 2006: 4). Girls may notice, for example, that some boys treat all girls as second-class citizens. Boys may notice that they are ridiculed by boys and girls alike if they do, say, or like anything associated with femininity. They may hear adults downplay these perceived gender injustices by attributing them to their age, maturity level, brain chemistry, and so on. Within common sense thinking and popular culture, gender is constructed as a relational and hierarchical binary that embraces mutually exclusive categories. Masculinity is defined as the opposite of femininity and usually as the superior category. When particular subject areas, literacy, or the ideal learner become gender coded in the school curriculum, underachievement can result. This influence of gendered stereotypes can be seen at an early age. In a study of first graders in four schools in Vancouver, for example, researchers found that both boys and girls actually preferred to read stories or a combination of stories and information books to the same degree. Yet boys and girls perceived that boys in general prefer information texts and girls in general prefer storybooks (Chapman et al. 2007).

Over time, many children become inured to inequalities that structure their daily lives; they cease complaining about the unfairness of gendered expectations. With the social construction of gender thus naturalized, it becomes difficult for students, teachers, and administrators alike to perceive gender inequities. In a study of a school committed to gender equity, researchers Spencer, Porche, and Tolman (2003) found that teachers as well as students perceived their school to be gender fair. Yet classroom observations and student interviews revealed significant differences in how seventh-grade boys and girls behaved and were treated in their classrooms. The students interpreted these differences as reflecting natural differences between boys and girls; thus, they described their experiences as equitable. The researchers joined a growing number of others studying gender, achievement, and schooling to call for more explicit teaching about gender. Francis and Skelton (2005), for example, argue that "The only way to influence pupils' gendered learning identities is through actively deconstructing traditional stereotypes" (page 149; see also Arnot 2006). In the remainder of this section, we provide some concrete suggestions for deconstructing gender (and other) stereotypes. In total, our suggestions explore: how students can use the Internet to identify and challenge stereotypes; how teachers can mine popular culture as a classroom resource; and how teachers (and parents) can engage youth in cultural production by rewriting dominant narratives.

## ONLINE GENDERING AND REGENDERING

Educators concerned to make visible the socially constructed nature of gender might draw lessons from our study of how girls learned about and practiced gendered identities online. As noted in Chapter Six, online social interactions often allow young people more time to think about how to represent themselves and what to say compared to offline social situations. Recall that girls often did MSN together in the same room or privately text messaged each other as they crafted messages to boys they liked; or recall how they enlisted help from friends (either from school or their virtual communities) to contest those disrespecting them in cyberspace. These actions were possible because there is more room to be deliberative—an ideal learning condition. Because online communications are textual, they are "frozen," thus more open to girls' critical interrogation over time.

Although, as shown in Chapter Six, online interactions are gendered just as surely as they are offline, it may be easier to see gendering online because of cyberspace's recent history. As Rodino (1997) argues, "The modes of gender construction may be less naturalized in computer-mediated than in FTF [face-to-face] communication and thus, the practices of gender construction in CMC [computer-mediated communication] may be more critically approachable" (page 17 n. 28). Nevertheless, the social construction of gender online is not immediately obvious. Our findings suggest that teachers might need to structure learning opportunities to highlight and address gender and power issues directly, because the online experiences of the girls in our study did not necessarily prompt them to inquire into the sexist standards that police boundaries between acceptable versus rebellious gender performances. For example, Anna explained the lack of strong female characters in her favorite *Yu Yu Hakusho* RPG as due to the fact that the show was made "a long time ago." "At that time," she reasoned, "women were not really that strong, like now." As a point of fact, *Yu Yu Hakusho* was created in 1990—not "a long time ago" to three researchers who variously span second- and third-wave feminism; perhaps so, however, to a member of the cybergeneration for whom 1990 predates the mass use of the Internet. We see Anna's tendency to filter out the ongoing production of sexist imagery in popular culture as evidence of the recuperative tendencies of the prevailing gender order (in particular, the widespread rhetoric of gender equality).

In order to prompt deeper reflections about the social construction of gender, teachers might ask students to keep a journal of their on-line experiences. Students could be asked to note what happens during role-playing, in chat rooms, or during instant messaging, how they feel about those happenings, and why. They could conduct informal comparative experiments similar to the one Shale conducted in the "vampire desecrated cathedral" by presenting different images of themselves and noting responses. They could look for avatars that do not bear obvious markers of conventional femininity or masculinity, investigate the level and nature of women's participation in the software industry (and more specifically, computer game creation), or research the activist and educational game design context in Canada (see, for example, de Castell and Jenson 2005) and in the USA (see, for example, Flanagan 2005). Students could inquire into how other forms of oppression shape the representation of various social groups, rather than only girls and women, including racism and white supremacy, heterosexism, ableism, classism, adultism, and xenophobia.

A teacher could ask: "What might it mean to adopt an unconventional or indeterminate gender online?" They could inquire into the use of non-male and non-female gender within the social virtual environment LambdaMOO, which "offers a choice of eight additional designations beyond male and female–spivak, neuter, either, splat, egotistical, plural, second [person], and royal" (Roberts and Parks 1999: 525). What would these alternative genders look like in practice? Students could switch genders online and then reflect on their successful and unsuccessful attempts. What assumptions did the student bring to their cross-gender performance? What assumptions did the people s/he was interacting with online bring to the interaction? What difference, if any, do the specifics of the online context make in the students' cross-gender performances (e.g., location, type of virtual environment, discussion topics)? As Kenway (1997: 270) notes, "The value of this approach is that it has the potential to avoid both the boredom and the authoritarian preaching which feminist pedagogies often involve and which often provoke student resistance." At the same time, we recognize the pleasure girls experience while engaged in interactive online activities outside of extensive adult monitoring and thus urge educators to tread with some caution when attempting to turn something fun to explicitly pedagogical purposes.

## MINING POPULAR CULTURE AS A PEDAGOGICAL RESOURCE

As argued above, popular culture provides an invaluable resource for critically analyzing the social construction of gender. Often, young people are immersed in pop culture; it provides resources for girls and boys as they shape their identities. It is a prime arena where ideas about gender circulate and understandings of social inequalities (and equalities) form, get challenged, and are modified. In critically analyzing pop culture, teachers can invite the same interrogation as they would with literary texts: encourage students to make alternative interpretations beyond the obvious themes intended by the author/s; inquire into whether some stereotypes were challenged while other stereotypes may have been introduced or reinforced; ask students to consider that no interpretation, no matter how implicitly and explicitly privileged, is neutral; prompt students to inquire into how being male or female, aboriginal and non-aboriginal, and so on might position them differently in the text and whether this leads them to interpret it differently (as Ellsworth [1997] asks, "Who does this film or TV show think you are?"). These kinds of questions aim to help young people learn to see what Bronwyn Davies (1993) calls the "constitutive force of text" and to "read against the grain" (pages 158–159).

Middle school teachers might consider using *Archie* comic books, for example, as a springboard to examine the social construction of gender and discuss ideas of masculine/feminine desires and sexuality. *Archie* has the advantage of still being widely available and read, primarily by six- to twelve-year-olds (who constitute 78% of its audience) and by both boys and girls (45% and 55% of its readership, respectively).[5] Ready connections can be made in most North American school jurisdictions between *Archie* themes and prescribed learning outcomes in areas such as relationships and health, where health is defined broadly to include the social determinants of health.[6] Researchers have found that preteens, even in highly multicultural cities like Vancouver where over half of the inhabitants are first generation immigrants and half of the population speaks a first language other than English or French (Statistics Canada 2007), are familiar with *Archie* and that many of its stories provide rich entry points for discussion of the social construction of gender. Moffatt and Norton (2008) surveyed and then interviewed students in grades 5 to 7 about their *Archie* reading habits and their interpretations of gender relations and sexuality in a particular story they had been asked to read. Participants in their study held "somewhat complex ideas of gender relations" (i.e., most espoused both feminist and patriarchal views concurrently); by contrast, recognition of diverse sexualities was virtually absent (i.e., the preteens did not imagine characters in *Archie* could be gay, lesbian, bisexual, questioning, or queer).

As any seasoned reader of *Archie* knows, a central theme in the long-running comic book series is the rivalry between Betty Cooper and Veronica Lodge for the attention and affection of the lead character, Archie Andrews. A teacher might ask students to read *Archie* looking for cultural patterns that recur across stories, to note what prompts which characters to become jealous, to describe sources of power imbalances (e.g., in gender relations) between and among characters, to provide examples of stereotypes (i.e., sexist, heterosexist, racist) or patriarchal assumptions, and to identify dominant storylines as well as possibilities for alternative identities that the texts might offer. A teacher might ask students to imagine that Betty and Veronica are tired of competing with each other for Archie's affections; imagine that the young women "talk back" to the comic artist or writer, expressing their boredom or frustration with the who-will-be-Archie's-date-to-the-prom (or any other) storyline. Students might be asked to assume the characters of the now resistant Betty and Veronica, to work in small groups to brainstorm alternative storylines, and develop and share new endings with each other. A next step in this proposed set of lessons might be to introduce feminist or other oppositional texts and to invite students to create their own texts (written, visual, digital) that "disrupt certainties and open up new possibilities" (Davies 1993: 159).

## SCHOOLING GIRLS

In the preceding sections, we have highlighted how educators might draw upon, and build from, the learning that goes on in informal arenas and what we might see as informal, alternative curricula (e.g., popular culture). In this section, we note that the school is a key institution in most children's lives and spotlight how schooling practices mediate girls' identity practices within and beyond the school. As practice theorists, we draw attention to the ways in which the school itself embodies the relations of ruling through which social inequalities are not simply reproduced but reconfigured within the contemporary context. As such, the primary goal of most schooling is to help students "make sense" of dominant social arrangements. This meaning making occurs through the everyday practices of "education." Indeed, education (as schooling) involves the central practice of assessing, classifying, and ranking students. As teachers, we are often called upon to classify students as "winners" and "losers" according to their acceptance of—and fit with—the established social order. Thus student assessment and classification do not rest on purely scholastic "merit" but also on the demeanor and social skills of white, middle-class notions of appropriate Selfhood. In this sense, the school operates to shore up boundaries that separate what comes to be socially accepted as "normal" in contrast to "abnormal." We should not be surprised that the informal communities of youth engage in similar practices, employing many of the ranking categories embedded in the formal curriculum: age, gender, racialized identity, standards of "ability" that promote physical and mental "normality," command of English, and so on.

Central to this ordering is an ethos of competitive individualism that is necessary to sustain belief in a meritocracy. This belief is enhanced if we continue to maintain uncritically that girls (like boys) can be and can do anything. Within youth culture, this message of "being anything" can be transformed by an overriding sense of a properly gendered order. Girls, unlike boys, are judged according to their looks; girls, unlike boys, are seen to be emotionally rather than physically expressive; and girls, unlike boys, can be kept in line through labels that demean their sexual agency.[7] Within this context, a disjuncture is created between the rhetoric of equality espoused by the formal curriculum and the everyday reality of how girls are labeled and classi-

218 "GIRL POWER" | Currie, Kelly, & Pomerantz

fied outside the classroom. In sum, we cannot help but note how the competitive hierarchies of school-based peer cultures resonate with the official mandate of schooling; we draw attention to a growing body of research that explores: how school dances, especially "proms," function as a homogenizing mechanism structured around white, middle-class, heterosexual ideals, demanding conformity to dominant notions of femininity (Best 2000); how cheerleading not only emphasizes physical differences and abilities between girls and boys but tends to present these differences as natural (Bettis and Adams 2003, 2006; Bettis, Jordan and Montgomery 2005); and how formal dress codes construct girls as vulnerable and sexually out of control (Hyams 2000; Pomerantz 2007). To this research we add the complaints by many girls about physical education as a compulsory activity for students that often reinforces notions of female physical inferiority (field notes, Currie 1999).

Other research has shown that sexual harassment (of both girls and boys) is so widespread as to be considered normal (Kehily and Nyack 1997; Kenway, Blackmore, and Rennie 1998; Smith, Bourne, and McCoy 1998; Chambers, van Loon, and Tincknell 2004; Robinson 2005). Boys target girls and nonconforming boys through humorous insults that produce and sustain heterosexist hierarchies in peer cultures (Kehily and Nyack 1997) as well as homophobic and racist discourses of power. A recent provincial survey in British Columbia, involving some 30,000 pupils from grades 7 to 12, reports significant levels of sexual abuse among youth; those identifying as lesbian and bisexual in particular reported high levels of rejection, discrimination, and violence (cited in Creese and Strong Boag 2008: 40–41). Over 50% of lesbian and bisexual youth reported verbal harassment at school; about 50% purposeful exclusion; and 15 to 20% physical assault. Bisexual girls are five times more likely than heterosexual girls to consider suicide (cited in Creese and Strong Boag 2008: 40–41).[8]

Although we have focused in our work on how girls police the sexual double standard, other research has shown that boys hold to this standard more stringently than do girls, as many girls do not believe that it applies anymore (Risman and Schwartz 2002). Moreover, others have shown how the double standard operates in all-boys communities of practice through misogynist banter and homophobic teasing that sustains boys' performances of hegemonic masculinity (see Fineran and Bennett 1999; Renold 2002; Bamberg 2004). While we have limited our work to the identity practices of girls, we do not want to re-affirm a binary between girls' and boys' social worlds or imply that boys and girls are "the inverse of each other" (Hadley 2003: 373). While our interest has been directed to all-girl cultures and communities of practice, we believe that research similarly focused on boys' communities of practice would help teachers design gender curriculum directed specifically to boys.

Finally, beyond the school, various policies of government—funding cutbacks, encouragement of market forces, and a retreat from equity policies and supports—may be exacerbating gendered, racialized, and sexualized aggression; we include in this aggression girl-on-girl and girl-initiated violence. A renewed emphasis on testing has heightened competitive pressure in the lower grades and communicates a very narrow view of public schooling; the testing craze, along with various other neoliberal policies within and beyond education that promote compulsory individualism, threaten to undermine principles of social justice (see Kelly and Brandes 2008).

Government policy responses to violence frame it through an individualizing, pathologizing, and homogenizing discourse of "bullying." Under this broad umbrella, an analysis of sexism, sexual harassment, homophobia, and other forms of gendered violence disappears (for further discussion and analysis, see Moy 2008a, 2008b. Within the jurisdiction of our study, the British Columbia Ministry of Education's focus on bullying (e.g., 2001) fails to identify specific forms of violence and aggression—those fueled by inequalities of gender, sexuality, race, language, class, and ability—and obscures their gendered dynamics. Thus, gendered aggression—exacerbated by sexism and heterosexism—is subsumed under the broad banner of bullying and often lost or misunderstood as a result.

## TEACHING FOR SOCIAL JUSTICE

In closing, perhaps the most important lesson that we take from our research is how feminist interest in girls' empowerment must be connected to the broader goal of teaching for social justice. For us, teaching for social justice encompasses two important and interconnected dimensions: (1) strengthening participatory democracy, in part by creating and sustaining alternative or subaltern counterpublics, including feminist and other equality-seeking networks (Kelly 2003); and (2) practicing anti-oppression education (Kelly 2007). While we have focused on girls' empowerment in this book, by now we hope it is clear that we do not assume that "girls" are a homogeneous group. We recognize that girls identify along a spectrum of identities, and that gender is not always the most prominent one. Gender is a significant structure, but we need to be aware of how it intersects with other structures of oppression based on class, race, sexuality, and ability. These interlocking structures, in turn, create a complex array of social positionings that shape girls' agency, hence identity practices. For example, white middle-class girls from socially advantaged family backgrounds will likely have access to the resources—including social and cultural capital—that give them opportunities not available to other girls, especially those marginalized by their racialized or family backgrounds. Critical social literacy—whatever its form—must include these kinds of complexities in any discussion of "gender."

NOTES

1   We use "critical pedagogy" here as an umbrella term for various equity-oriented pedagogies (e.g., feminist, anti-racist, critical multicultural, queer, anti-oppressive, etc.). We recognize that there are multiple and contested meanings of the term, but to present a comprehensive overview of this complex field is beyond the scope of this book.

2   The field of "media literacy," or more broadly "media education," is complex and encompasses diverse approaches, some of which are at odds with one another (see Kellner and Share 2005; Stack and Kelly 2006). A consensus appears to be emerging (at least among critical media educators) that the field needs to move beyond the dichotomy of *protecting* young people from potential negative media influences versus *preparing* them for understanding and participation in the media culture, and instead pursue both aims. We align our approach with this latter position.

3   We are reminded of Walkerdine's (2006: 533) observation that what feels like an exercise of "personal power" can be, in a Foucauldian sense, deeply compromised because it is the way in which we are managed and regulated through projects of gendered Selfhood.

4   Wendy Johnson's dissertation (2009) documents how a group of high school students in a small city in British Columbia organized a sophisticated ten-month campaign to prevent their high school from being reconfigured into a middle school. It included protests, letters to the editors of the local newspapers, lobbying trustees, presentations at Board of Education meetings, and appearances on radio and television. Stephanie Higginson's MA thesis (2006) reports on the actions of a group of high school girls in Toronto to shape the "Girls' Nite" program to their own purposes, claim space within the wider school to negotiate gendered subjectivity, and challenge sexist attitudes among some boys and men teachers and administrators.

5    According to a 2001 survey commissioned by Archie Comic Publications, each issue of *Archie* reaches 4.7 million kids and makes over 44 million "reader impressions." Available at: http://www.archiecomics.com/acpaco_offices/presskit/2002%20New%20Media%20kit%20part%201%20Co%20Info.htm

6    In British Columbia, teachers could relate the suggested *Archie* comic activities to the prescribed learning outcomes for a grade-7 unit on "relationships": "identify characteristics of healthy relationships and unhealthy relationships (e.g., healthy relationships—respect, open communication; unhealthy relationships—jealousy, power imbalance, lack of empathy)"; "describe a variety of influences on relationships (e.g., peers, media, physical and emotional changes as a result of puberty)"; and "demonstrate behaviours that contribute to the prevention of stereotyping, discrimination, and bullying" (BC Ministry of Education 2006: 229).

7    We are aware that homophobia also plays an important role in boys' practices of hegemonic masculinity.

8    The McCreary Centre Society conducts the Adolescent Health Survey (AHS) in British Columbia periodically to gather information about physical and emotional health and factors that can influence health during adolescence or in later life; it is done via anonymous questionnaires filled out during school time. A number of school districts, large and small, have over the years refused to allow youth to take the survey due to concerns about parental opposition, particularly to questions about sexuality and drug use. We offer this as an example of avoidance that allows trump discourses to flourish.

# Description of Girls in the "Girl Power" Study

Alana—fourteen years old; white from an upper middle-class family; attended a private girls school; into MSN; friends with Cherry.

Amanda—fifteen years old; Chinese Canadian from a middle-class family; attended a large, urban, multicultural school; quiet and reserved; friends with Emily.

Amelia—fourteen years old; white from a working-class family; attended a large, urban high school; into "grungy" style; spoke of being "picked on" at school.

Amy—thirteen years old; Bangladeshi Canadian from an upper middle-class family; attended a private girls school; described her group of friends as "strangely intellectual"; into MSN; friends with Tatiana.

Anna—fourteen years old; Filipina Canadian from a working-class family; attended a large, urban high school; into computers, especially role-play, fan fiction, and anime; friends with Vera.

Beverly—fourteen years old; Chinese Canadian from a middle-class family; attended a large, urban high school; into computers, MSN, fan fiction, anime, and "gaming"; friends with Anna and Vera.

Brenda—fourteen years old; Chinese Canadian from a working-class family; attended a large, urban high school; lived with her dad; into youth mentoring, shopping, and computers; friends with Leanna.

Brooke—fifteen years old; white from an upper middle-class family; alternates living with her mom, then her dad; member of the popular clique at her large, middle-class urban school; friends with Forsyth, Lydia, and Jordan; belongs to a group dubbed "The Clan" by their friends.

Candy—thirteen years old; Chinese Canadian from an upper middle-class family; attended a private girls school; displayed a feminist consciousness; into MSN; friends with Marcia.

Casey—fourteen years old; Russian heritage from a working-class family; moved to Canada three years ago; attended a large, urban high school and was in an advanced math class; friends with Jess.

Cassandra—fourteen years old; Iranian Canadian from a working-class family; attended a large, suburban high school; friends with Rebecca, Nicole, and Jane.

Cherry—fourteen years old; white from an upper middle-class family; attended a private girls school; into MSN; friends with Alana.

Cheryl—fifteen years old; white from a middle-class family; attended a small, urban high school and was in an enriched academic program; friends with Veronica.

Christine—sixteen years old; white from a working-class family; attended a small, suburban high school; into sports, especially volleyball and soccer; into biking, surfing, snowboarding, and skateboarding; friends with Kate.

Dephy—fifteen years old; white from a working-class family; attended a large, suburban high school; member of the popular "preps"; friends with Tina and Susie.

Emily—fifteen years old; white from a middle-class family; attended a large, urban, multicultural school; quiet and reserved; friends with Amanda.

Emma—fifteen years old; white from a middle-class family; attended a large, urban high school; called herself "political"; into sports, particularly soccer.

Erin—fourteen years old; white from a middle-class, Jewish family with parents recently divorced; member of the popular clique at her "progressive" school; displayed a feminist consciousness.

Eve—eleven years old; Chinese Canadian from a middle-class family; attended an urban elementary school with a good reputation; confident, into martial arts, used to be unpopular but was now part of the popular clique in her grade; friends with Missy.

Forsyth—fourteen years old; white and African Canadian from a middle-class family; member of the popular clique in her large, middle class urban school; friends with Jordan and Lydia; belongs to a group dubbed "The Clan" by their friends.

Gauge—fourteen years old; white from a middle-class family; lives with her mom, dad, and sister; attended a large, urban high school and was in an academically enriched program; into skateboarding; called herself "alternative"; friends with Spunk.

Gerry—fourteen years old; Filipina from a working-class family; lived with her mom; attended an urban and multicultural high school; "quiet" and "shy"; friends with Sunshine and Lina.

GG (Ghetto Girl)—thirteen years old; white from a middle-class family; attended a large, urban school where she felt left out of the popular clique; assertive and bold; friends with Vicki.

Gracie—fifteen years old; white from a middle-class, British family; attended a large, urban, multicultural school; quiet and working on being "less shy"; into skateboarding; friends with Sandy, Pete, Grover, Onyx, and Zoë, a group we have dubbed the "Park Gang."

Grenn—fourteen years old; white from a working-class family; lives with her mom; attended a class-divided, suburban high school; into skateboarding, punk music, guitar, and Japanese anime; into computers and fan fiction writing; described herself as a "a freak" at school; friends with Lexi.

Grover—fifteen years old; Brazilian and Portuguese heritage from a middle-class family; attended an urban Catholic high school; "shy" and "quiet"; into skateboarding; friends with Sandy, Gracie, Zoë, Onyx, and Pete, a group we have dubbed the "Park Gang."

Ish—thirteen years old; white from a middle-class family; attended an urban high school with a good reputation; into computers, goth style, and *Buffy the Vampire Slayer*; unpopular within her school; friends with Rose, Shale, and Nikita.

Jane—fourteen years old, Yugoslavian Canadian from a working-class family; attended a large, suburban high school; friends with Cassandra, Rebecca, and Nicole.

Jess—fourteen years old; Bengali from a working-class family; moved to Canada six years ago; attended a large, urban high school and was in an independent creative program; friends with Casey.

Jessica—thirteen years old; white from an upper middle-class family; attended a private girls school; sporty style; displayed a feminist consciousness.

Jordan—fourteen years old; white from a middle-class family; member of the popular clique at her large, middle-class urban high school; friends with Lydia, Forsyth, and Brooke; belongs to a group dubbed "The Clan" by their friends.

Kate—fifteen years old; white and East Indian heritage from a working-class family; attended a small, suburban high school; into sports, especially volleyball and soccer; into biking and surfing, and skateboarding; friends with Christine.

Leanna—fourteen years old; Chinese Canadian from a working-class family; attended a large, urban high school; into youth mentoring, shopping, and computers; friends with Brenda.

Lexi—fourteen years old; white from a working-class family; lives with her mom; attended a class-divided, suburban high school; into skateboarding, punk music, and Japanese anime; into computers and fan fiction writing; described herself as a "freak" at school; friends with Grenn.

Lina—fifteen years old; Chinese Canadian from a working-class background; lived in foster care; attended a large suburban high school; friends with Sunshine and Gerry.

Liv—thirteen years old; white from a working-class, German family; attended an urban elementary school; into cheerleading and sports.

Lydia—fourteen years old; white from a middle-class family; belongs to the popular clique in her large, middle class urban school; friends with Jordan, Forsyth, and Brooke; belongs to a group dubbed "The Clan" by their friends.

Madeline—sixteen years old; white from a middle-class family; attended a large, urban high school and was in an academically advanced program; into skateboarding; described herself as a "floater" who had many different groups of friends.

Marcia—fourteen years old; white from a middle-class family; attended a private girls school; displayed a feminist consciousness; into MSN and "gaming"; friends with Candy.

Marianne—thirteen years old; white and First Nations from a middle-class family; lives with her mom; attended an urban Catholic high school; spoke of being "picked on" at school and feeling low self-esteem.

Marie—twelve years old; white from a middle-class family; attended an urban elementary school with a good reputation; friends with Sally.

Mia—fifteen years old; Chinese Canadian and Jewish from a middle-class family; lived with her mother and sister; attended an urban high school with a good reputation; friends with Reese.

Michelle—thirteen years old; white from a middle-class family; lived with her dad; attended a large, urban high school; was a sponsored amateur skateboarder.

Missy—eleven years old; white from a middle-class family; attended an urban elementary school with a good reputation; confident, into martial arts; used to be unpopular but was now part of the popular clique in her grade; friends with Eve.

Nicole—fourteen years old, white from a working-class family; attended a large, suburban high school; friends with Cassandra, Rebecca, and Jane.

Nikita—thirteen years old; white from a middle-class family; attended an urban high school outside of Vancouver; into computers, goth style, and *Buffy the Vampire Slayer*; unpopular within her school; friends with Rose, Shale, and Ish.

Nina—fourteen years old; white from a middle-class family; attended a large, urban high school; into computers, Japanese anime, and Wiccanism.

Onyx—fifteen years old; Chinese Canadian from a middle-class family; attended a large, urban, multicultural school; quiet but aware of her sexual power; into skateboarding; friends with Sandy, Gracie, Zoë, Onyx, and Pete, a group we have dubbed the "Park Gang."

Pete—fifteen years old; Chinese Canadian from a middle-class family; attended a large, urban, multicultural school; student council president, outgoing, "perfectionist"; into skateboarding; friends with Sandy, Gracie, Grover, Onyx, and Zoë, a group we have dubbed the "Park Gang."

Priscilla—fourteen years old; First Nations from a middle-class family; moves back and forth between her divorced parents; out of school for one year; attended a large, urban high school; into skateboarding; friends with Tori.

Rebecca—thirteen years old; Russian Canadian from a working-class family; attended a large, suburban high school; friends with Cassandra, Nicole, and Jane.

Reese—sixteen years old; Korean, Japanese, and Australian heritage from a working-class family; lived with her mother; attended an urban high school with a good reputation; English is her second language, Japanese her first; friends with Mia.

Riley—fourteen years old; white from a working-class family; was a member of the popular clique at her suburban school but got expelled from the group; friends with Tiffany.

Riva—fourteen years old; Iranian Canadian from a middle-class family; attended a large, suburban school with a mixed socioeconomic population; athletic and reserved.

Rose—thirteen years old; white from a middle-class family; attended a large, urban high school, was enrolled in a "creative" and "independent" program; into computers, goth style, and *Buffy the Vampire Slayer*; called herself "alternative"; friends with Shale, Nikita and Ish.

Sally—twelve years old; white from a middle-class family; attended an urban elementary school with a good reputation; friends with Marie.

Sandy—fifteen years old; Chinese Canadian from a middle-class family; attended a large, urban, multicultural school; confident and assertive; into skateboarding; friends with Gracie, Pete, Grover, Onyx, and Zoë, a group we have dubbed the "Park Gang."

Sara—fourteen years old; white from a middle-class Jewish family; attended a small, urban high school with a good reputation; saw herself as "religious" and was into goth/punk style and music.

Shale—thirteen years old; white from a middle-class family; attended a large, urban high school, was enrolled in a "creative" and "independent" program; into computers, goth style, and *Buffy the Vampire Slayer*; called herself bisexual; called herself "alternative"; friends with Rose, Nikita, and Ish.

Spunk—fourteen years old; white from a middle-class family; lives with her mom and sister; attended a large, urban high school and was in an independent, creative program; into skateboarding; called herself bisexual; called herself "alternative"; friends with Gauge.

Sunshine—fourteen years old; Filipina from a working-class family; lived with her mom; attended an urban and multicultural high school; into sports, especially basketball; friends with Gerry and Lina.

Susie—fifteen years old; white from a middle-class family; attended a large, suburban high school; member of the popular "preps"; friends with Dephy and Tina.

Tatiana—thirteen years old; Chinese Canadian from an upper middle-class family; attended a private girls school; described her group of friends as "strangely intellectual"; into MSN; friends with Amy.

Tiffany—fourteen years old; white from a working-class family; was a member of the popular clique at her suburban school but got expelled from the group when she became friends with Riley.

Tina—fifteen years old; white and First Nations heritage from a working-class family; attended a large, suburban high school; member of the popular "preps"; friends with Dephy and Susie.

Tori—fourteen years old; white from a working-class family; lives with her dad; attended various urban high schools off and on; into skateboarding and street culture; friends with Priscilla.

Vanessa—thirteen years old; white from a working-class family; lives with her mom; attended a small, urban high school; into computers, playing pool, sports, and dance; described herself as a "floater" at school who could move between the popular girls and the punks.

Vera—fourteen years old; Chinese Canadian from a working-class family; attended a large, urban high school; into anime fan fiction and computers; friends with Anna.

Veronica—fifteen years old; white from an upper middle-class family; attended a small, suburban high school; friends with Cheryl.

Vicki—thirteen years old; white from a middle-class family; her mother had recently died and she was clearly still grieving; attended a large, urban school where she felt left out of the popular clique; quiet and reserved; friends with GG.

Zoë—fifteen years old; white and First Nations heritage from a middle-class family; attended a large, urban, multicultural school; "happy" and "easy-going"; into skateboarding; friends with Sandy, Gracie, Grover, Onyx, and Pete, a group we have dubbed the "Park Gang."

REFERENCES

Aapola, Sinikka, Marnina Gonick and Anita Harris. 2005. *Young Femininity: Girlhood, Power and Social Change*. Houndmills, Basingstoke, Hampshire: PalgraveMacmillan.

Abraham, Yvonne. 1997. "Lipstick liberation" *The Worcester Phoenix*, May 30–June 6. Retrieved September 24, 2004, from: http://www.worcesterphoenix.com/archive/features/97/30LIPSTICK.html

Adams, Mary Louise. 1999. *The Trouble with Normal: Postwar Youth and the Making of Heterosexuality*. Toronto: University of Toronto Press.

Adams, Natalie G. 2005. "Fighters and Cheerleaders: Disrupting the Discourse of 'Girl Power' in the New Millennium" pp. 101–114 in Pamela J. Bettis and Natalie G. Adams (eds.) *Geographies of Girlhood: Identities in-between*. Mahwah, NJ: Lawrence Erlbaum Associates, Publishers.

Addison, Joanne and Michelle Comstock. 1998. "Virtually Out: The Emergence of a Lesbian, Bisexual and Gay Youth Subculture" pp. 367–378 in J. Austin and M. N. Willard (eds.) *Generations of Youth: Youth Cultures and History in 20th-century America*. New York: New York University Press.

Agrell, Siri. 2005. "Mean girls getting younger: U. S. psychologist says they are the result of years of empowerment" *National Post*, May 5. Retrieved July 18, 2005, from: http://www.canada.com

Allen, Louisa. 2004. "Beyond the birds and the bees: constituting a discourse of erotics in sexuality education" *Gender and Education* 16(2): 151–167.

Alloway, Nola and Pam Gilbert. 1998. "Video Game Culture: Playing with Masculinity, Violence and Pleasure" pp. 95–114 in Sue Howard (ed.) *Wired Up: Young People and the Electronic Media*. London: UCL Press.

Alphonso, Caroline. 2003. "Girls take top honours in world's classrooms" *Globe and Mail*, September 17: A3.

Alvesson, Mats and Kaj Skoldberg. 2000. *Reflexive Methodology: New Vistas for Qualitative Research.* London: Sage Publications.

Anzaldua, Gloria. 1987. *Borderlands/La Frontera: The New Mestiza.* San Fransisco: Spinsters/Aunt Lute.

Arnot, Madeleine. 2006. "Gender equality, pedagogy and citizenship: affirmative and transformative approaches in the UK" *Theory and Research in Education* 4(2): 131–150.

Askew, S. and C. Ross. 1988. *Boys Don't Cry: Boys and Sexism in Education.* Philadelphia, PA: Open University Press.

Attwood, F. 2007. "Slut and riot girls: female identity and sexual agency" *Journal of Gender Studies* 16(3): 233–247.

Bakker, I. 1996. *Rethinking Restructuring: Gender and Change in Canada.* Toronto: University of Toronto Press.

Bamberg, Michael. 2004. "'I know it may sound mean to say this, but we couldn't really care less about her anyway': form and function of 'slut bashing' in male identity constructions in 15-year-olds" *Human Development* 47: 331–353.

Barcella, Laura. 2007. "Full frontal feminism [interview with Jessica Valenti]" *AlterNet*, April 24. Available from: http://www.alternet.org/story/50843/

Barron, Christie L. 2000. *Giving Youth a Voice: A Basis for Rethinking Adolescent Violence.* Halifax: Fernwood Publishing.

Bartky, Sandra Lee. 1988. "Foucault, Femininity, and the Modernization of Patriarchal Power" pp. 61–86 in Irene Diamond and Lee Quinby (eds.) *Feminism & Foucault: Reflections on Resistance.* Boston: Northeastern University Press.

Bassett, Caroline. 1997. "Virtually Gendered: Life in an Online World" pp. 537–550 in K. Gelder and S. Thornton (eds.) *The Subcultures Reader.* London: Routledge.

Beal, Becky. 1995. "Disqualifying the official: an exploration of social resistance through the subculture of skateboarding" *Sociology of Sport Journal* 12: 252–267.

Beal, Becky. 1996. "Alternative masculinity and its effects on gender relations in the subculture of skateboarding" *Journal of Sport Behavior* 19(3): 204–220.

Beauvoir, Simone de. 1953. *The Second Sex*. Trans. H. M. Parshley New York: Bantam Books.

Beck, Ulrich. 1992. *Risk Society: Towards a New Modernity*. London: Sage.

Bellafante, Gina. 1998. "Feminism: it's all about me!" *Time*, June 29: 54–60. Retrieved March 28, 2000, from: http://www.time.com/time/maga zine/1998/dom/980629/cover2.html

Best, Amy. 2000. *Prom Night: Youth, Schools and Popular Culture*. New York: Routledge.

Best, Steven and Douglas Kellner. 2003. "Contemporary youth and the postmodern adventure" *Review of Education, Pedagogy, and Cultural Studies* 25: 75–93.

Bettie, Julie. 2003. *Women without Class: Girls, Race and Identity*. Berkeley: University of California Press.

Bettis, Pamela J. and Natalie G. Adams. 2003. "The power of the preps and a cheerleading equity policy" *Sociology of Education* 76: 128–142.

Bettis, Pamela J. and Natalie G. Adams (eds.). 2005. *Geographies of Girlhood: Identities in-between*. Mahwah, NJ: Lawrence Erlbaum Associates, Publishers.

Bettis, Pamela J. and Natalie G. Adams. 2006. "Short skirts and breast juts: Cheerleading, eroticism and schools" *Sex Education: Sexuality, Society and Learning* 6(2): 121–133.

Bettis, Pamela J., Debra Jordan and Diane Montgomery. 2005. "Girls in Groups: The Preps and the Sex Mob Try Out for Womanhood" pp. 69–83 in Pamela J. Bettis and Natalie G. Adams (eds.) *Geographies of Girlhood: Identities in-between.* Mahwah, NJ: Lawrence Erlbaum Associates, Publishers.

Bibby, Reginald W. and Donald C. Posterski. 1992. *Teen Trends: A Nation in Motion.* Toronto: Stoddart Publishing Company Ltd.

Blackwell, Karen and Adrianna Knight. 2005. *Rage against the Machine.* Burlington, ON: Halton District School Board.

Borden, Iain. 2001. *Skateboarding, Space and the City: Architecture and the Body.* Oxford: Berg.

Bordo, Susan. 2003. "The empire of images in our world of bodies" *Chronicle of Higher Education,* December 19: B6–B9.

Bouchard, Pierette, Isabelle Boily and Marie-Claude Proulx. 2003. *School Success by Gender: A Catalyst for Masculinist Discourse.* Ottawa: Status of Women Canada.

Bowlby, Rachel. 1993. *Shopping with Freud.* London: Routledge.

Brake, Michael. 1985. *Comparative Youth Culture: The Sociology of Youth Cultures and Youth Subcultures in America, Britain, and Canada.* London: Routledge and Kegan Paul.

Breazeale, Kenon. 1994. "In spite of women: *Esquire* magazine and the construction of the male consumer" *Signs: Journal of Women in Culture and Society* 20(1): 1–15.

Bright, Robin M. 2005. "It's not just a grade 8 girl thing: aggression in teenage girls" *Gender and Education* 17(1): 93–101.

British Columbia Ministry of Education and British Columbia Ministry of Public Safety and Solicitor General. 2001. *Focus on Harassment and Intimidation: Responding to Bullying in Secondary School Communities.*

Victoria: British Columbia Ministry of Education and British Columbia Ministry of Public Safety and Solicitor General.

British Columbia Ministry of Education. 2006. *Health and Career Education K to 7 Integrated Resource Package 2006.* Victoria: British Columbia Ministry of Education. Available: http://www.bced.gov.bc.ca/irp/hcek7 .pdf#nameddest=ca_model

Brooks, David. 2001. "The organization kid" *The Atlantic Monthly,* April: 40–54.

Brown, Lyn Mikel. 1998. *Raising Their Voices: The Politics of Girls' Anger.* Cambridge, MA: Harvard University Press.

Brown, Lyn Mikel and Carol Gilligan. 1992. *Meeting at the Crossroads: Women's Psychology and Girls' Development.* Cambridge, MA: Harvard University Press.

Brumberg, Joan Jacobs. 2000. "When girls talk: what it reveals about them and us" *The Chronicle of Higher Education,* November 24: B7–B10.

Buckingham, David. 2003. *Media Education: Literacy, Learning and Contemporary Culture.* Cambridge: Polity Press.

Budgeon, Shelley. 2001. "Emergent feminist (?) identities: young women and the practice of micropolitics" *The European Journal of Women's Studies* 8(1): 7–28.

Budgeon, Shelley. 2003. *Choosing a Self: Young Women and the Individualization of Identity.* Westport, CT: Praeger.

Bulbeck, Chilla. 1998. *Re-orienting Western Feminisms: Women's Diversity in a Postcolonial World.* Cambridge and New York: Cambridge University Press.

Burr, Vivien. 1995. *An Introduction to Social Constructionism.* London: Routledge.

Butler, Judith. 1990. *Gender Trouble: Feminism and the Subversion of Identity*. New York: Routledge.

Butler, Judith. 1992. "Contingent Foundations: Feminism and the Question of 'Postmodernism'" pp. 3–21 in J. Butler and J. W. Scott (eds.) *Feminisms Theorize the Political*. New York: Routledge.

Butler, Judith. 2003. *Bodies that Matter*. New York: Routledge.

Campbell, Susan. 2006. "'Get a nice bikini butt!' Is there any hope for magazines aimed at young women?" *Vancouver Sun*, June 29: A19.

Canadian Advisory Council on the Status of Women. 1992. *We're Here, Listen to Us! A Survey of Young Women in Canada*. Ottawa: CACSW.

Canadian Teachers' Federation. 2003. Kids' take on media: Summary of findings. Ottawa: Canadian Teachers' Federation. Retrieved June 15, 2005, from: http://www.ctf-fce.ca/en/projects/MERP/summary -findings.pdf

Canadian Teachers' Federation. 2008. Cyberbullying in schools: National poll shows Canadians' growing awareness. Press release, July 11. Retrieved August 6, 2008, from: http://www.ctf-fce.ca/e/news/news .asp?id=-873341035

Chambers, Deborah, Estella Tincknell and Joost Van Loon. 2004. "Peer regulation of teenage sexual identities" *Gender and Education* 16(3): 397–415.

Chapman, Marilyn, Margot Filipenko, Marianne McTavish and Jon Shapiro. 2007. "First graders' preferences for narrative and/or information books and perceptions of other boys' and girls' book preferences" *Canadian Journal of Education* 30(2): 531–553.

Chesney-Lind, Meda and Katherine Irwin. 2004. "From Badness to Meanness: Popular Constructions of Contemporary Girlhood" pp. 45–56 in Anita Harris (ed.) *All About the Girl: Power, Culture and Identity*. New York: Routledge.

Christensen, Linda. 2007. "'Can't buy me love': teaching about clothes, class and consumption" *Rethinking Schools* 21(4). Available: http://www.rethinkingschools.org/archive/21_04/love214.shtml

Cimitele, Anna Maria. 2002. "Feminism today: revolution, genealogy, borderwork" *European Journal of English Studies* 6(3): 273–288.

Clark, Lynn Schofield. 2005. "The Constant Contact Generation: Exploring Teen Friendship Networks Online" pp. 203–221 in Sharon Mazzarella (ed.) *Girl Wide Web: Girls, the Internet, and the Negotiation of Identity*. New York: Peter Lang.

Clegg, Sue. 2006. "The problem of agency in feminism: a critical realist approach" *Gender and Education* 18(3): 309–324.

Code, Lorraine. 1991. *What Can She Know? Feminist Theory and the Construction of Knowledge*. Ithaca, NY: Cornell University Press.

Collins, Patricia Hill, Lionel A. Maldonado, Dana Y. Takagi, Barrie Thorne, Lynn Weber, and Howard Winant. 2002. "Symposium on West and Fenstermaker's 'Doing Difference'" pp. 81–94 in Sarah Fenstermaker and Candace West (eds.) *Doing Gender, Doing Difference: Inequality, Power, and Institutional Change*. New York: Routledge.

Conlin, Michelle. 2003. "The new gender gap: from kindergarten to grad school, boys are becoming the second sex" *BusinessWeek online*, May 26. Available: http://www.businessweek.com/magazine/content/03_21/b3834001_mz001.htm

Connell, R. W. 1987. *Gender and Power*. Stanford, CA: Stanford University Press.

Connell, R. W. 1995. *Masculinities*. Berkeley: University of California Press.

Connell, R. W. 2002. *Gender*. Cambridge, UK/Malden, MA: Polity.

Connell, R. W., and James W. Messerschmidt. 2005. "Hegemonic masculinity: rethinking the concept" *Gender and Society* 19(6): 829–859.

Connolly, Paul. 2006. "The masculine habitus as 'distributed cognition': a case study of 5- to 6-year-old boys in an English inner-city, multi-ethnic primary school" *Children & Society* 20: 140–152.

Cook, Daniel Thomas and Susan B. Kaiser. 2004. "Betwixt and be tween: age ambiguity and the sexualization of the female consuming subject" *Journal of Consumer Culture* 4(2): 203–227.

Cook, Sharon and Joel Westheimer. 2006. "Introduction: democracy and education" *Canadian Journal of Education* 29(2): 347–358.

Cooper, Joel. 2006. "The digital divide: the special case of gender" *Journal of Computer Assisted Learning* 22(5): 320–334.

Corbett, Christianne, Catherine Hill and Andresse St. Rose. 2008. *Where the Girls Are: The Facts About Gender Equity in Education*. Washington, DC: American Association of University Women.

Cotterill, Pamela. 1992. "Interviewing women: issues of friendship, vulnerability, and power" *Women's Studies International Forum* 15(5/6): 593–606.

Creese, Gillian and Veronica Strong-Boag. 2008. *Still Waiting for Justice: Provincial Policies and Gender Inequality in BC 2001–2008*. Vancouver: Centre for Women and Gender Studies, University of British Columbia.

Cronin, Anne M. 2000. "Consumerism and 'Compulsory Individuality': Women, Will and Potential" pp. 273–287 in Sara Ahmed, Jane Kilby, Celia Lury, Maureen McNeil and Beverley Skeggs (eds.) *Transformations: Thinking Through Feminism*. London and New York: Routledge.

*Culture Jam: Hijacking Commercial Culture*. 2001. Directed by Jill Sharpe. Vancouver, BC: Moving Images.

Currie, Dawn H. 1997. "Decoding femininity: advertisements and their teenage readers" *Gender and Society* 11(4): 454–478.

Currie, Dawn H. 1999. *Girl Talk: Adolescent Magazines and Their Readers*. Toronto: University of Toronto Press.

Currie, Dawn H. 2000. "Dear Abby: advice pages as a site for the operation of power" *Feminist Theory* 2(3): 259–281.

Currie, Dawn H. and Deirdre M. Kelly. 1999. "Girl Power": A study of adolescent decision-making and the empowerment of women. A research proposal submitted to (and funded by) Social Sciences and Humanities Research Council of Canada.

Currie, Dawn H., Deirdre M. Kelly and Shauna Pomerantz. 2007. "Listening to girls: discursive positioning and the construction of self" *International Journal of Qualitative Studies in Education* 20(4): 377–400.

Davies, Bronwyn. 1989. *Frogs and Snails and Feminist Tales: Preschool Children and Gender.* St. Leonards, Australia: Allen & Unwin.

Davies, Bronwyn. 1993. *Shards of Glass: Children Reading and Writing Beyond Gendered Identities.* Cresskill, NJ: Hampton Press.

Davies, Bronwyn. 1997. "Constructing and deconstructing masculinities through critical literacy" *Gender and Education* 9(1): 9–30.

Davies, Julia. 2004. "Negotiating femininities online" *Gender and Education* 16(1): 35–50.

de Castell, Suzanne. 2002. "No place like home: final research report on the Pride House Project" Jennifer Jenson, Collaborator. Burnaby, B C: Simon Fraser University.

de Castell, Suzanne and Mary Bryson (eds.). 1997. *Radical In(ter)ventions: Identity, Politics, and Difference/s in Educational Praxis.* Albany: State University of New York Press.

de Castell, Suzanne and Jennifer Jenson. 2005. "Videogames and digital game play—the new field of educational game studies" *Orbit* 35(2): 17–19.

DeBell, Mathew and Chris Chapman. 2003. *Computer and Internet Use by Children and Adolescents in 2001.* (NCES 2004-014). Washington DC: US Department of Education, National Center for Education Statistics.

Deitz, T. 1998. "An examination of violence and gender role portrayals in video games: implications for gender socialization and aggressive behaviour" *Sex Roles* 38(5/6): 425–442.

Delany, Paul (ed.). 1994. *Vancouver: Representing the Postmodern City.* Vancouver, BC: Arsenal Pulp Press.

Deutsch, Francine M. 2007. "Undoing gender" *Gender and Society* 21(1): 106–127.

DeVault, Marjorie L. 1999. *Liberating Method: Feminism and Social Research.* Philadelphia: Temple University Press.

Dillabough, Jo-anne. 2004. "Class, culture and the 'predicaments of masculine domination': encountering Pierre Bourdieu" *British Journal of Sociology of Education* 25(4): 489–506.

Douglas, Susan. 1994. *Where the Girl Are: Growing Up Female with the Mass Media.* New York: Random House Inc.

Dowd, Maureen. 2002. "Mean, nasty and missing" *New York Times,* February 27. Available: http://www.nytimes.com/2002/02/27/opinion/27DOWD.html?ex=1015839488&ei=1&en=1632e0907eae069e

Downes, Lawrence. 2006. "Middle school girls gone wild" *New York Times,* December 29. Available: http://www.nytimes.com/2006/12/29/opinion/29fri4.html?ex=1325048400&en=705773ca836fc865&ei=5088&partner=rssnyt&emc=rss

Driscoll, Catherine. 1999. "Girl culture, revenge and global capitalism: cybergirls, riot girls, spice girls" *Australian Feminist Studies* 14(29): 173–195.

Driscoll, Catherine. 2002. *Girls: Feminine Adolescence in Popular Culture and Cultural Theory.* New York: Columbia University Press.

Driver, Susan. 2005. "Out, creative and questioning: reflexive self-representations in queer youth homepages" *Canadian Woman Studies* 24(2/3): 111–116.

Duncan, Neil. 2004. "It's important to be nice, but it's nicer to be important: girls, popularity and sexual competition" *Sex Education: Sexuality, Society and Learning* 4(2): 137–152.

Ebert, Teresa L. 2005. "Rematerializing feminism" *Science & Society* 69(1): 33–55.

Eckert, Penelope. 1989. *Jocks and Burnouts: Social Categories and Identity in the High School*. New York: Teachers' College Press.

Eckert, Penelope and Sally McConnell-Ginet. 1999. "New generalizations and explanations in language and gender research" *Language in Society* 28: 185–201.

Eder, Donna with Catherine Collins Evans and Stephen Parker. 1995. *School Talk: Gender and Adolescent Culture*. New Brunswick, NJ: Rutgers University Press.

Eder, Donna and David A. Kinney. 1995. "The effect of middle school extracurricular activities on adolescents' popularity and peer status" *Youth & Society* 26(3): 298–323.

Eisenhauer, Jennifer. 2004. "Mythic Figures and Lived Identities: Locating the 'Girl' in Feminist Discourse" pp. 79–90 in Anita Harris (ed.) *All About the Girl: Culture, Power, and Identity*. New York and London: Routledge.

Ellsworth, Elizabeth. 1997. *Teaching Positions: Difference, Pedagogy, and the Power of Address*. New York: Teachers College Press.

*Emoticons*. 2007. Directed by Heddy Honigmann. Netherlands: Films Transit International.

Epstein, Debbie and Richard Johnson. 1998. *Schooling Sexualities*. Buckingham: Open University Press.

Erikson, E. H. 1950. *Childhood and Society*. New York: Norton.

Erikson, E. H. 1968. *Identity: Youth and Crisis*. New York: Norton.

Errington, Jane. 1988. "Pioneers and Suffragists" pp. 51–79 in Sandra Burt, Lorraine Code and Lindsay Dorney (eds.) *Changing Patterns: Women in Canada*. Toronto: McClelland & Stewart.

Faludi, Susan. 1992. *Backlash: The Undeclared War against Women*. London: Vintage.

Fanon, Frantz. 1967. *Toward the African Revolution*. [1964] Trans. Haakon Chevalier. New York: Monthly Review Press.

Fanon, Frantz. 1986. *Black Skin: White Masks*. [1952] Trans. Charles Lam Marmann. London: Pluto.

Featherstone, M. 1991. *Consumer Culture and Postmodernism*. London: Sage.

Fine, Michelle. 1988. "Sexuality, schooling and adolescent females: the missing discourse of desire" *Harvard Educational Review* 58(1): 29–53.

Fineran, Susan and Larry Bennett. 1999. "Gender and power issues of peer sexual harassment among teenagers" *Journal of Interpersonal Violence* 14(6): 626–641.

Fiske, John. 1996. *Media Matters: Everyday Culture and Political Change*. Minneapolis: University of Minnesota Press.

Flanagan, Caitlin. 2006. (January 17) "Are you there God? It's me, Monica" (review of *Rainbow Party* by Paul Rudtis) *Atlantic Monthly*. Available: http://www.theatlantic.com/doc/200601/oral-sex

Flanagan, Mary. 2005 (June 16–20) Troubling "games for girls": Notes from the edge of game design. Paper presented at the Digital Games Research Association (DiGRA) conference: Changing views—worlds in play, Vancouver, BC.

Foucault, Michel. 1972. *The Archaeology of Knowledge and the Discourse on Language*. Trans. A. M. Sheridan Smith. New York: Pantheon Books.

Foucault, Michel. 1977. *Discipline and Punish: The Birth of the Prison.* Trans. A. Sheridan. London: A. Lane.

Foucault, Michel. 1990. *The History of Sexuality. Vol. 1* Trans. Roberts Hurley. New York: Vintage.

Francis, Becky. 1997. "Power plays: children's constructions of gender and power in role plays" *Gender and Education* 9(2): 179–191.

Francis, Becky. 1999. "Modern reductionism or post-structuralist relativism: can we move on? An evaluation of the arguments in relation to feminist educational research" *Gender and Education* 11(4): 381–393.

Francis, Becky and Christine Skelton. 2005. *Reassessing Gender and Achievement: Questioning Contemporary Key Debates.* London: Routledge.

Fraser, Nancy. 1992a. "Sex, lies and the public sphere: some reflections on the confirmation of Clarence Thomas" *Critical Inquiry* 18: 595–612.

Fraser, Nancy. 1992b. "The uses and abuses of French discourse theories for feminist politics" pp. 177–194 in N. Fraser and S. L. Bartky (eds.) *Revaluing French Feminism: Critical Essay on Difference, Agency and Culture.* Bloomington and Indianapolis: Indiana University Press.

Frenette, Marc and Simon Coulombe. 2007. Has Higher Education Among Young Women Substantially Reduced the Gender Gap in Employment and Earnings? (Research paper 11F0019MIE) Ottawa: Analytical Studies Branch Research Paper Series, Statistics Canada.

Friedan, Betty. 1963. *The Feminine Mystique.* New York: Norton.

Frith, Hannah. 2001. "Young women, feminism and future: dialogues and discoveries" *Feminism and Psychology* 11(2): 147–151.

Frith, Hannah. 2004. "The best of friends: the politics of girls' friendships" *Feminism Psychology* 14(3): 357–360.

Frith, Hannah and Celia Kitzinger. 1998. "'Emotion work' as a participant resource: a feminist analysis of young women's talk-in-interac-
tion" *Sociology* 32(2): 299–320.

Fritzsche, Bettina. 2004. "Spicy Strategies: Pop Feminist and Other Em-
powerments in Girl Culture" pp. 155–162 in Anita Harris (ed.) *All About
the Girl: Culture, Power, and Identity*. New York and London; Routledge.

Froese-Germain, Bernie. 2008. "Bullying in the digital age: using technology to harass students and teachers" *Our Schools/Our Selves* 17(4):45–54.

Fuchs, Cynthia. 2003. "So alluring, but toxic: interview with Catherine
Hardwicke, co-writer and director of *Thirteen*" *PopMatters*, September
3. Available: http://www.popmatters.com/film/interviews/hardwicke
-catherine-030903.shtml

Gailey, C. W. 1993. "Mediated messages: gender, class and cosmos in
home video games" *Journal of Popular Culture* 27: 81–97.

Gee, James Paul. 2002. *An Introduction to Discourse Analysis: Theory and
Method*. London and New York: Routledge.

*Ghost World*. 2001. Directed by Terry Zwigoff. Los Angeles: United Artists.

Giddens, Anthony. 1991. *Modernity and Self Identity: Self and Society in
the Late Modern Age*. Oxford: Polity Press.

Gilbert, R. and P. Gilbert. 1998. *Masculinity Goes to School*. New York: Routledge.

Gilligan, Carol. 1982. *In a Different Voice: Psychological Theory and Wom-
en's Development*. Cambridge, MA: Harvard University Press.

Gilligan, Carol, Nona P. Lyons and Trudy J. Hanmer. 1990. *Making Connections: The Relational Worlds of Adolescent Girls at Emma Willard School*.
Cambridge, MA: Harvard University Press.

Gilligan, Carol, Janie Victoria Ward and Jill McLean Taylor (eds.). 1988.
*Mapping the Moral Domain*. Cambridge, MA: Harvard University Press.

Gittins, Diana. (1998). *The Child in Question*. London: MacMillan.

Gleeson, Kat and Hannah Frith. 2004. "Pretty in Pink: Young Women Presenting Mature Sexual Identities" pp. 103–114 in A. Harris (ed.) *All About the Girl*. New York: Routledge.

Goldman, Robert. 1992. *Reading Ads Socially*. London: Routledge.

Gonick, Marnina. 2001. "What's the 'problem' with these girls? Youth and Feminist Pedagogy" *Feminism and Psychology* 11(2): 167–171.

Gonick, Marnina. 2003. *Between Femininities: Ambivalence, Identity and the Education of Girls*. Albany: State University of New York Press.

Gonick, Marnina. 2004. "The 'mean girls' crisis: problematizing representations of girls' friendships" *Feminism and Psychology* 14(3): 395–400.

Gonick, Marnina. 2006. "Between 'girl power' and 'Reviving Ophelia': constituting the neoliberal girl subject" *NWSA Journal* 18(2): 1–23.

Gonick, Marnina. 2007. "Girl Number 20 revisited: feminist literacies in new hard times" *Gender and Education* 19(4): 433–454.

Grisso, Ashley D. and David Weiss. 2005. "What Are gURLS Talking About? Adolescent Girls' Construction of Sexual Identities on gURL.com" pp. 31–49 in S. R. Mazzarella (ed.) *Girl Wide Web*. New York: Peter Lang.

Grossberg, Lawrence. 1996. "On Postmodernism and Articulation: An Interview with Stuart Hall" pp. 151–173 in David Morely and Kuan-Hsing Chen (eds.) *Stuart Hall: Critical Dialogues in Cultural Studies*. New York: Routledge.

Hadley, M. 2003. "Relational, indirect, adaptive, or just mean: recent work on aggression in adolescent girls part I" *Studies in Gender and Sexuality* 4(4): 367–394.

Hall, Stuart. 1973. "Encoding and Decoding in Media Discourse" Stencilled Paper 7. Birmingham Centre for Contemporary Cultural Studies.

Hall, Stuart. 1996. "Who Needs Identity?" pp. 1–17 in S. Hall and P. Du Gay (eds.) *Questions of Cultural Identity*. London: Sage.

Hames-Garcia, Michael R. 2000. "'Who Are Our Own People?' Challenges for a Theory of Social Identity" pp. 102–129 in P. M. L. Moya and M. R. Hames-Garcia (eds.) *Reclaiming Identity: Realist Theory and the Predicament of Postmodernism*. Berkeley: University of California Press.

Hancunt, Maren. 2001. "Full Frontal Confrontation" pp. 237–251 in A. Mitchell, L. Bryn Rundle and L. Karaian (eds.) *Turbo Chicks: Talking Young Feminisms*. Toronto: Sumach Press.

Harris, Anita. 1999. "Everything a teenage girl should know: adolescence and the production of femininity" *Women's Studies International Forum* 15(2): 111–124.

Harris, Anita. 2001a. "Dodging and weaving: young women countering the stories of youth citizenship" *International Journal of Critical Psychology* 4: 183–199.

Harris, Anita. 2001b. "Revisiting bedroom culture: new spaces for young women's politics" *Hectate* 27(1): 128–139.

Harris, Anita. 2003. "gURL scenes and grrrl zines: the regulation and resistance of girls in late modernity" *Feminist Review* 75: 38–56.

Harris, Anita. 2004. *Future Girl: Young Women in the Twenty-First Century*. New York: Routledge.

Havrilesky, Heather. 2002. "Powerpuff Girls meet world" *Salon.com*, July 2. Available: http://dir.salon.com/story/mwt/feature/2002/07/02/powerpuff/index.html

Hawkesworth, Mary. 2004. "The semiotics of premature burial: feminism in a postfeminist age" *Signs: Journal of Women in Culture and Society* 29(4): 961–985.

Hebdige, Dick. 1979. *Subculture: The Meaning of Style*. London: Methuen.

Hebidge, Dick. 1988. *Hiding in the Light: On Images and Things*. London: Routledge.

Heinecken, Dawn. 2003. *The Warrior Women of Television: A Feminist Cultural Analysis of the New Female Body in Popular Media*. New York: Peter Lang.

Helford, Elyce Rae. 2000. "Postfeminism and the Female Action-Adventure Hero: Positioning *Tank Girl*" pp. 291–308 in Marleen S. Barr (ed.) *Future Females, the Next Generation: New Voices and Velocities in Feminist Science Fiction Criticism*. Lanham, MD: Rowman & Littlefield.

Henry, Astrid. 2004. *Not My Mother's Sister: Generational Conflict in Third-Wave Feminism*. Bloomington: Indiana University Press.

Herz, J. C. 1997. *Joystick Nation: How Videogames Ate Our Quarters, Won Our Hearts, and Rewired Our Minds*. Boston: Little, Brown and Company.

Hesse-Biber, Sharlene. 1996. *Am I Thin Enough Yet? The Cult of Thinness and the Commercialization of Identity*. New York: Oxford University Press.

Hey, Valerie. 1997. *The Company She Keeps: An Ethnography of Girls' Friendships*. Buckingham, UK: Open University Press.

Hickey, Christopher and Amanda Keddie. 2004. "Peer groups, power and pedagogy: the limits of an educational paradigm of separation" *Australian Educational Researcher* 31(1): 57–77.

Higginson, Stephanie. 2006. "We are not just painting our toenails and having pillow fights": Adolescent girls questioning gender and power within a secondary school setting. Unpublished MA thesis, University of British Columbia, Vancouver.

Hodkinson, Paul. 2002. *Goth: Identity, Style and Subculture*. Oxford, UK: Berg.

Holland, Dorothy C, William Lachicotte, Jr., Debra Skinner and Carole Cain. 1998. *Identity and Agency in Cultural Worlds*. Cambridge, MA: Harvard University Press.

Holland J., C. Ramazanoglu, S. Sharpe and R. Thompson. 1991. *Pressured Pleasure: Young Women and the Negotiation of Sexual Boundaries.* London: Tufnell Press.

Holland, J., C. Ramazanoglu, S. Sharpe and R. Thomson. 1998. *The Male in the Head: Young People, Heterosexuality and Power.* London: The Tufnell Press.

Holloway, Sarah L., Gill Valentine and Nick Bingham. 2000. "Institutionalizing technologies: masculinities, femininities, and the heterosexual economy of the IT classroom" *Environment and Planning* 32(4): 617–633.

Hudson, B. 1984. "Femininity and Adolescence" pp. 31–53 in A. McRobbie and M. Nava (eds.) *Gender and Generation.* Basingstoke, UK: Macmillan.

Hyams, Melissa S. 2000. "'Pay attention in class...[and] don't get pregnant': a discussion of academic success among adolescent Latinas" *Environment and Planning* A 32: 635–654.

Ingraham, Chrys. 1997. "The Heterosexual Imaginary: Feminist Sociology and Theories of Gender" pp. 275-290 in R. Hennessy and C. Ingraham (eds.) *Materialist Feminism: A Reader in Class, Difference, and Women's Lives.* New York, London: Routledge.

*It's a Girls' World.* 2004. Directed by Lynn Glazier. Montréal: Canadian Broadcasting Corporation and National Film Board of Canada.

Jackson, Carolyn. 2006. "'Wild' girls? An exploration of 'ladette' cultures in secondary schools" *Gender and Education* 18(4): 339–360.

Jackson, Carolyn and Penny Tinkler. 2007. "'Ladette' and 'Modern Girls': 'troublesome' young femininities" *The Sociological Review* 55(2): 252–272.

Jackson, Stevi. 2006. "Gender, sexuality and heterosexuality: the complexity (and limits) of heteronormativity" *Feminist Theory* 7(1): 105–121.

Jaggar, Alison. M. 1983. *Feminist Politics and Human Nature.* Sussex: The Harvester Press.

Jenson, Jennifer, Suzanne de Castell and Mary Bryson. 2003. "'Girl talk': gender, equity, and identity discourses in a school-based computer culture" *Women's Studies International Forum* 26(6): 561–573.

Jiwani, Yasmin. 1999. "Erasing race: the story of Reena Virk" *Canadian Woman Studies* 19 (3): 178–184.

Jiwani, Yasmin. 2000. "The denial of race in the murder of Reena Virk" *Kinesis: News about Women That's Not in the Dailies.* Available: ttp://www.harbour.sfu.ca/freda/articles/denial.htm

Jiwani, Yasmin. 2006. "Racialized Violence and Girls and Young Women of Colour" pp. 70–88 in Y. Jiwana, C. Steenbergen and C. Mitchell (eds.) *Girlhood: Redefining the Limits.* Montréal: Black Rose Books.

Jiwani, Yasmin, Nancy Janovicek and Angela Cameron. 2001. *Erased Realities: The Violence of Racism in the Lives of Immigrant and Refugee Women of Colour.* Vancouver, BC: FREDA.

Johnson, Lesley. 1993. *The Modern Girl: Girlhood and Growing Up.* Buckingham: Open University Press.

Johnson, Wendy. 2009. Student voice: Creating possibilities for democratic citizenship. Unpublished Ed.D. dissertation, University of British Columbia, Vancouver.

Jones, Alison. 1993. "Becoming a 'girl': post-structuralist suggestions for educational research" *Gender and Education* 5(2): 157–167.

Kamen, Paula. 2000. *Her Way: Young Women Remake the Sexual Revolution.* New York: New York University Press.

Karlyn, Kathleen Rowe. 2006. "Film as cultural antidote: *Thirteen* and the maternal melodrama" *Feminist Media Studies* 6(4): 453–468.

Kearney, Mary Celeste. 1997. "The Missing Links: Riot Grrrl—Feminism—Lesbian Culture" pp. 207–229 in Sheila Whiteley (ed.) *Sexing the Groove: Popular Music and Gender.* London: Routledge.

Kearney, Mary Celeste. 2007. "Productive spaces: girls' bedrooms as sites of cultural production" *Journal of Children and Media* 1(2): 126–141.

Kehily, May Jane and Anoop Nayak. 1997. "Lads and laughter: humour and the production of heterosexual hierarchies" *Gender and Education* 9(1): 69–88.

Kehler, Michael D. 2007. "Hallway fears and high school friendships: the complications of young men (re)negotiating heterosexualized identities" *Discourse: Studies in the Cultural Politics of Education* 28(2): 259–277.

Kehler, Michael and Wayne Martino. 2007. "Questioning masculinities: interrogating boys' capacities for self-problematization in schools" *Canadian Journal of Education* 30(1): 90–112.

Kellner, Douglas and Jeff Share. 2005. "Toward critical media literacy: core concepts, debates, organizations, and policy" *Discourse: Studies in the Cultural Politics of Education* 26(3): 369–386.

Kelly, Deirdre M. 1993. *Last Chance High: How Girls and Boys Drop in and out of Alternative Schools*. New Haven, CT: Yale University Press.

Kelly, Deirdre M. 1997. "Warning labels: stigma and the popularizing of teen mothers' stories" *Curriculum Inquiry* 27(2): 165–186.

Kelly, Deirdre M. 2000. *Pregnant with Meaning: Teen Mothers and the Politics of Inclusive Schooling*. New York: Peter Lang.

Kelly, Deirdre M. 2003. "Practicing democracy in the margins of school: the Teen-Age Parents Program as feminist counterpublic" *American Educational Research Journal* 40(1): 123–146.

Kelly, Deirdre M. 2007. "Toward a more nuanced and reflective social justice discourse" *Professional Development Perspectives* [Canadian Teachers' Federation] 6(1): 8–12.

Kelly, Deirdre M. and Gabriella Minnes Brandes. 2008. "Equitable classroom assessment: promoting self-development and self-determination" *Interchange* 39(1): 49–76.

Kelly, Deirdre, Shauna Pomerantz and Dawn H. Currie. 2005. "Skater girlhood and emphasized femininity: 'you can't land an ollie properly in heels'" *Gender and Education* 17(3): 129–148.

Kelly, Deirdre M. and Shauna Pomerantz. In press. "Mean, wild, and alienated: girls and the state of feminism in popular culture" *Girlhood Studies*.

Kendall, Lori. 2002. *Hanging out in the Virtual Park: Masculinities and Relationships Online*. Berkeley: University of Berkeley Press.

Kenway, Jane. 1997. "Backlash in Cyberspace: Why 'Girls Need Modems'" pp. 255–279 in L. Roman and L. Eyre (eds.) *Dangerous Territories: Struggles for Difference and Equality in Education*. New York: Routledge.

Kenway, Jane, Sue Willis, with Jill Blackmore and Leonie Rennie. 1998. *Answering Back: Girls, Boys and Feminism in Schools*. New York: Routledge.

Kindlon, Dan. 2006. *Alpha Girls: Understanding the New American Girl and How She Is Changing the World*. Emmaus, PA: Rodale.

Kirsch, Ges A. 1999. *Ethical Dilemmas in Feminist Research: The Politics of Location, Interpretation, and Publication*. New York: State University of New York Press.

Kitzinger, Celia. 2000. "Doing feminist conversation analysis" *Feminism and Psychology* 10(2): 163–193.

Kitzinger, Jenny. 1995. "I'm sexually attractive but I'm powerful: young women's negotiation of sexual reputation" *Women's Studies International Forum* 18(2): 187–196.

Kling, Kristen, Janet Shibley Hyde, Carolin J. Showers and Brenda N. Buswell. 1999. "Gender differences in self-esteem: a meta-analysis" *Psychological Bulletin* 125(4): 470–500.

Kolko, Beth E. 1999. "Representing bodies in virtual space: the rhetoric of avatar design" *Information Society* 15: 177–186.

Kruger, Crystal, Natasha Lezard and Justina Easterson (eds.). 1994. *Just Talking About Ourselves: Voices of Our Youth*. Penticton, BC: Theytus Books Ltd.

Lalik, Rosemary and Kimberly L. Oliver. 2007. "Differences and tensions in implementing a pedagogy of critical literacy with adolescent girls" *Reading Research Quarterly* 42(1): 46–70.

Lamb, Sharon. 2001. *The Secret Lives of Girls: What Good Girls Really Do — Sex Play, Aggression, and Their Guilt*. New York: Free Press.

Lave, Jean and Etienne Wenger. 1998. *Situated Learning: Legitimate Peripheral Participation*. Cambridge: Cambridge University Press.

Leblanc, Lauraine. 1999. *Pretty in Punk: Girls' Gender Resistance in a Boys' Subculture*. New Brunswick, NJ: Rutgers University Press.

Lee, Jo-anne. 2006. "Locality, Participatory Action Research, and Racialized Girls' Struggle for Citizenship" pp. 89–108 in Yasmin Jiwani, Candis Steenbergen and Claudia Mitchell (eds.) *Girlhood: Redefining the Limits*. Montréal: Black Rose Books.

Lees, Sue. (1986). *Losing Out: Sexuality and Adolescent Girls*. London: Hutchinson.

Leonard, Marion. 1997. "'Rebel Girl, You Are the Queen of My World': Feminism, 'Subculture' and Grrrl Power" pp. 230–255 in Sheila Whiteley (ed.) *Sexing the Groove: Popular Music and Gender*. London: Routledge.

Lesko, Nancy. 2001. *Act Your Age! A Cultural Construction of Adolescence*. New York: Routledge Falmer.

Leventhal, Anna. 2005. "Broads on boards: Anna Leventhal rolls with the skirtboarders, Montreal's feisty all-female skate crew" *Shameless: For girls who get it* 24–27.

Levinson, Bradley A. U. 2000. "Introduction: Whither the Symbolic Animal? Society, Culture, and Education at the Millennium" pp. 1–11 in Bradley A. U. Levinson (ed.) *Schooling the Symbolic Animal: Social and Cultural Dimensions of Education*. Lanham, MD: Rowman & Littlefield.

Levinson, Bradley A. and Dorothy Holland. 1996. "The Cultural Production of the Educated Person: An Introduction" pp 1–54 in Bradley A. Levinson, Douglas E. Foley and Dorothy C. Holland (eds.) *The Cultural Production of the Educated Person: Critical Ethnographies of Schooling and Local Practice*. Albany: State University of New York Press.

Levy, Ariel. 2005. *Female Chauvinist Pigs: Women and the Rise of Raunch Culture*. New York: Free Press.

Lincoln, Sian. 2004. "Teenage Girls' 'Bedroom Culture': Codes versus Zones" pp. 94–106 in Andy Bennett and Keith Kahn-Harris (eds.) *After Subculture: Critical Studies in Contemporary Youth Culture*. Houndmills, Basingstoke: Palgrave Macmillan.

Lipka, Sara. 2004. "Feminine citique" *Chronicle of Higher Education*, May 21: A35–A36.

Liston, Delores D. and Regina E. Moore-Rahini. 2005. "Disputation of a Bad Reputation: Adverse Sexual Labels and the Lives of 12 Southern Women" pp. 211–230 in Pamela J. Bettis and Natalie G. Adams (eds.) *Geographies of Girlhood: Identities in-between*. Mahwah, NJ: Lawrence Erlbaum Associates.

Lorber, Judith. 2005. *Gender Inequality: Feminist Theories and Politics*. Los Angeles: Roxbury Publishing Company.

Lovell, Terry. 2000. "Thinking feminism with and against Bourdieu" *Feminist Theory* 1(1): 11–32.

Marshall, Barbara L. 2000. *Configuring Gender: Exploration in Theory and Politics*. Peterborough, ON: Broadview Press.

Martin, Caitlin Kennedy. 1999. "Girls, video games, and the traditional stereotype of female characters." Retrieved July 19, 2006, from: http://ldt.stanford.edu/ldt1999/Students/ckmartin/pdf/videoGames.pdf

Martin, Courtney. 2006. "Is overachieving bad for girls?" *Alternet*, November 16. Available: http://www.alternet.org/story/44267/

Martino, Wayne. 2003. "'We just get really fired up': Indigenous boys, masculinities and schooling." *Discourse: Studies in the Cultural Politics of Education* 24(2): 159–174.

McCabe, Janet. 2004. "Claire Fisher on the couch: discourses of female subjectivity, desire and teenage angst in *Six Feet Under*" *The scholar and feminist online* 3(1): 8. Available: http://www.barnard.columbia.edu/sfonline/hbo/mccabe_01.htm

McClintock, Anne. 1995. *Imperial Leather: Race, Gender, and Sexuality in the Colonial Conquest*. New York: Routledge.

McLeod, Julie. 2002. "Working out intimacy: young people and friendship in an age of reflexivity" *Discourse: studies in the cultural politics of education* 23 (2): 211–226.

McNay, Lois. 2000. *Gender and Agency: Reconfiguring the Subject in Feminist and Social Theory*. Cambridge: Polity Press.

McRobbie, Angela. 1978. "Working Class Girls and the Culture of Femininity" pp. 96–108 in Women's Studies Group, Centre for Contemporary Cultural Studies, Birmingham University (eds.) *Women Take Issue: Aspects of Women's Subordination*. London: Hutchinson.

McRobbie, Angela. 1999. "Shut Up and Dance: Youth Culture and Changing Modes of Femininity" pp. 65–88 in M. Shiach (ed.) *Feminism and Cultural Studies*. Oxford: Oxford University Press.

McRobbie, Angela. 2000. "Sweet Smell of Success? New Ways of Being Young Women" pp. 198–214 in *Feminism and Youth Culture* (2nd ed.). Houndmills, Basingstoke, Hampshire: MacMillan.

McRobbie, Angela. 2004. "Post-feminism and popular culture" *Feminist Media Studies* 4(3): 255–264.

McRobbie, Angela and Jenny Garber. 1976. "Girls and Subcultures" pp. 209–222 in S. Hall and T. Jefferson (eds.) *Resistance through Rituals: Youth Subculture in Postwar Britain*. London: Hutchison.

Meadows, Susannah. 2002. "Meet the Gamma Girls" *Newsweek*, June 3. Retrieved October 2, 2006, from Academic Search Primer.

*Mean Girls*. 2004. Directed by Mark Waters. Hollywood, CA: Paramount Productions.

Mercier, Emma M., Brigid Barron, and Kathleen M. O'Connor. 2006. "Images of self and others as computer users: the role of gender and experience" *Journal of Computer Assisted Learning* 22(5): 335–348.

Merskin, Debra. 2005. "Making an About-Face: Jammer Girls and the World Wide Web" pp. 51–67 in Sharon Mazzarella (ed.) *Girl Wide Web: Girls, the Internet, and the Negotiation of Identity*. New York: Peter Lang.

Merten, Don E. 1997. "The meaning of meanness: popularity, competition, and conflict among junior high school girls" *Sociology of Education* 70: 175–191.

Millar, Pamela and Sher Morgan. 1998. *Girlpower: A Research Report*. Ottawa: Status of Women Canada.

Milner, Murray Jr. 2004. *Freaks, Geeks, and Cool Kids: American Teenagers, Schools, and the Culture of Consumption*. London: Routledge.

Misciagno, Patricia S. 1997. *Rethinking Feminist Identification: The Case for de facto Feminism*. Westport, CT: Praeger.

Mitchell, Alysson, Lisa Bryn Rundle and Laura Karaian (eds.). 2001. *Turbo Chicks: Talking Young Feminisms*. Toronto: Sumach Press.

Moffatt, Lindsay and Bonny Norton. 2008. "Reading gender relations and sexuality: preteens speak out" *Canadian Journal of Education* 31(1): 102–123.

Mohanty, Chandra Talpade, Ann Russo and Lourdes Torres (eds.). 1991. *Third World Women and the Politics of Feminism*. Bloomington: Indiana University Press.

Moloney, Molly and Sarah Fenstermaker. 2002. "Performance and Accomplishment: Reconciling Feminist Conceptions of Gender" pp. 189–204 in S. Fenstermaker and C. West (eds.) *Doing Gender, Doing Difference: Inequality, Power, and Institutional Change.* New York: Routledge.

Morris, Helen. 2008. "Teachers' federation adopts policy to criminalize cyberbullying" *Montreal Gazette,* July 12. Available: http://www.canada.com/mon trealgazette/news/story.html?id=faff34b9-d856-454b-80e7-360bbd1574af

Moy, Lisa. 2008a. "Beyond 'bullying': get to the roots" *The Tyee,* February 27. Available: http://thetyee.ca/Views/2008/02/27/BeyondBullying/

Moy, Lisa. 2008b. Disrupting bully talk: Progressive practices and transformative spaces for anti-violence work in schools. Unpublished Ph.D. dissertation, University of British Columbia, Vancouver.

Moya, Paula M. L. 2001. "Chicana feminism and postmodern theory" *Signs: Journal of Women in Culture and Society* 26(2): 441–483.

Muncer, Steven, Anne Campbell, Victoria Jervis and Rachel Lewis. 2001. "'Ladettes,' social representations, and aggression" *Sex Roles: A Journal of Research* 44(1–2): 33–44.

Munro, Alice. 1968. *Dance of the happy shades: Stories by Alice Munro.* Toronto: Ryerson Press.

Narayan, Uma. 1997. *Dislocating Cultures: Identities, Traditions, and Third World Feminism.* New York: Routledge.

Neft, Naomi and Ann D. Levine. 1997. *Where Women Stand: An International Report on the Status of Women in 140 Countries 1997–1998.* New York: Random House.

Nelson, Lise. 1999. "Bodies (and spaces) do matter: the limits of performativity" *Gender, Place and Culture* 6(4): 331–353.

Nielsen, Harriet Bjerrum. 2004. "Noisy girls: new subjectivities and old gender discourses" *Young: Nordic Journal of Youth Research* 12(1): 9–30.

Nilan, Pamela. 1992. "Kazzies, DBTs and Tryhards: categories of style in adolescent girls' talk" *British Journal of Sociology of Education* 13(2): 201–214.

Orenstein, Peggy. 1994. *Schoolgirls: Young Women, Self-Esteem, and the Confidence Gap*. New York: Doubleday.

Ortner, Sherry B. 2002. "'Burned like a tattoo': high schools social categories and 'American culture'" *Ethnography* 3(2): 115–148.

Overbeck, Joy. 1993. "Sex, kids and the slut look" *Newsweek*, July 26. Retrieved November 30, 2006, from EBSCO data base.

Oxford English Dictionary. 2001. http://dictionary.oed.com/cgi/entry/00307048?single=1&query_type=word&queryword=girl+power&first=1&max_to_show=10

Paechter, Carrie. 2003a. "Masculinities and femininities as communities of practice" *Women's Studies International Forum* 26(1): 69–77.

Paechter, Carrie. 2003b. "Learning masculinities and femininities: power/knowledge and legitimate peripheral participation" *Women's Studies International Forum* 26(6): 541–552.

Pantin, Emily. 2001. "The Personal is Political" pp. 186–192 in A. Mitchell, L. Bryn Rundle and L. Karaian (eds.) *Turbo Chicks: Talking Young Feminisms*. Toronto: Sumach Press.

Parkins, Wendy. 1999. "Bad girls, bad reputations: feminist ethics and postfeminism" *Australian Feminist Studies* 14(30): 377–386.

Phillips, Louise and Marianne W. Jørgensen. 2002. *Discourse Analysis as Theory and Method*. Thousand Oaks: Sage.

Pikul, Corrie. 2005. "The girls are all right" *Salon.com*, April 20. Available: http://www.salon.com/mwt/feature/2005/04/20/stabiner/print.html

Pipher, Mary. 1994. *Reviving Ophelia: Saving the Selves of Adolescent Girls*. New York: Putnam.

Pollet, Alison and Page Hurwitz. 2004. "Strip till you drop" *The Nation*, January 12/19: 20–25.

Pomerantz, Shauna. 2007. "Cleavage in a tank top: bodily prohibition and the discourses of school dress codes"*Alberta Journal of Educational Research* 53(4): 373–386.

Pomerantz, Shauna. 2008. *Girls, Style and School Identities: Dressing the Part.* New York: Palgrave Macmillan.

Pomerantz, Shauna, Dawn H. Currie and Deirdre M. Kelly. 2004. "Sk-8ter girls: skateboarders, girlhood and feminism in motion" *Women's Studies International Forum* 27: 547–557.

Potter, Jonathan. 1996. *Representing Reality: Discourse, Rhetoric and Social Construction.* London: Sage.

Press, Joy. 1997. "Notes on girl power: the selling of soft-core feminism" *Village Voice*, September 23. Available: http://www.villagevoice.com/2005-10-18/specials/notes-on-girl-power/

Pyke, Karen and Tran Dang. 2003. "'FOB' and 'whitewashed': identity and internalized racism among second generation Asian Americans" *Qualitative Sociology* 26(2): 147-172.

Quartz, Alissa. 2006. *Hothouse Kids: The Dilemma of the Gifted Child.* New York: Penguin.

Ray, Sheri Graner. 2004. *Gender Inclusive Game Design: Expanding the Market.* Hingham, MA: Charles River Media Inc.

Reay, Diane. 2001. "'Spice Girls,' 'Nice Girls,' 'Girlies,' and 'Tomboys': gender discourses, girls' cultures and femininities in the primary classroom" *Gender and Education* 13(2): 153–166.

Reich, Dahlia. 2003. "Power play" *Owl Canadian Family*, September: 37–43.

Reid-Walsh, Jacqueline and Claudia Mitchell. 2004. "Girls' Web Sites: A Virtual 'Room of One's Own'?" pp. 173–182 in A. Harris (ed.) *All about the Girl: Culture, Power and Identity*. New York: Routledge.

Renold, Emma. 2002. "Presumed innocence: (hetero)sexual, heterosexist and homophobic harassment among primary school girls and boys" *Childhood* 9(4): 415–434.

Renold, Emma. 2003. "'If you don't kiss me, you're dumped': boys, boyfriends and heterosexualised masculinities in the primary school" *Educational Review* 55(2): 179–194.

Renold, Emma. 2006. "'They won't let us play...unless you're going out with one of them': girls, boys and Butler's 'heterosexual matrix' in the primary years" *British Journal of Sociology of Education* 27(4): 489–509.

Rimer, Sara. 2007. "For girls, it's be yourself and be perfect, too" *New York Times*, April 1: 10.

Ringrose, Jennifer. 2007. "Successful girls? complicating postfeminist, neoliberal discourses of educational achievement and gender equality" *Gender and Education* 19(4): 471–489.

Riordan, Ellen. 2001. "Commodified agents and empowered girls: consuming and producing feminism" *Journal of Communication Inquiry* 25(3): 279–297.

Risman, Barbara and Pepper Schwartz. 2002. "After the sexual revolution: gender politics in teen dating" *Contexts* 1(1): 16–24.

Roberts, Lynne D. and Malcolm R. Parks. 1999. "The social geography of gender-switching in virtual environments on the Internet" *Information, Communications, and Society* 2(4): 521–540.

Robinson, Kerry H. 2005. "Reinforcing hegemonic masculinities through sexual harassment: issues of identity, power and popularity in secondary schools" *Gender and Education* 17(1): 19–37.

Robinson, Kerry H. and Criss Jones Diaz. 2006. *Diversity and Difference in Early Childhood Education: Issues for Theory and Practice*. Berkshire, UK: Open University Press.

Rodino, Michelle. 1997. "Breaking out of boundaries: reconceptualizing gender and its relationship to language in computer-mediated communication" *Journal of Computer-Mediated Communication* 3(3). Available: http://ascuse.org/jcmc/vol3/issue3/rodino.html

Roediger, David. 1998. "What to Make of Wiggers: A Work in Progress" pp. 358–366 in J. Austin and M. N. Willard (eds.) *Generations of Youth: Youth Cultures and History in Twentieth-Century America*. New York: New York University Press.

Ross, Becki. 1997. "Destaining the (tattooed) delinquent body: the practices of moral regulation at Toronto Street Haven, 1965–1969" *Journal of the History of Sexuality* 7(4): 561–595.

Ross, Sharon. 2004. "'Tough Enough': Female Friendship and Heroism in Xena and Buffy" pp. 231–255 in Sherrie A. Innes (eds.) *Action Chicks: New Images of Tough Women in Popular Culture*. Houndmills, Basingstoke, Hampshire, UK: Palgrave Macmillan.

Ruditis, Paul. 2005. *Rainbow Party*. New York: Simon & Schuster.

Said, Edward W. 1985. *Orientalism: Western Representations of the Orient*. Harmondsworth: Penguin.

Said, Edward W. 1993. *Culture and Imperialism*. London: Chatto & Windus.

Sanford, Kathy and Leanna Madill. 2006. "Resistance through media game play: it's a boy thing" *Canadian Journal of Education* 29(1): 287–306.

Scheurich, James Joseph. 1995. "A postmodern critique of research interviewing" *Qualitative Studies in Education* 8(3): 239–252.

Schiano, Diane J. 1999. "Lessons from Lambdamoo: a social, text-based virtual environment" *Presence* 8(2): 127–180.

Schilt, Kristen. 2003. "'I'll resist with every inch and every breath': girls and zine making as a form of resistance" *Youth and Society* 35(1): 71–97.

Schlossman, Steven and Stephanie Wallach. 1978. "The crime of precocious sexuality: female juvenile delinquency in the Progressive Era" *Harvard Educational Review* 48(1): 65–94.

Sciadis, G. 2002. Unveiling the Digital Divide (research paper Catalogue No. 56F0004MIE, No. 7) Ottawa: Statistics Canada, Science, Innovation and Electronic Information Division.

Scott, Joan W. 1991. "The evidence of experience" *Critical Inquiry* 17(4): 773–797.

Scott, Kimberley A. 2002. "'You want to be a girl and not my friend?': African-American girls' play patterns with and without boys" *Childhood: A Global Journal of Child Research* 9: 397–414.

Scott-Dixon, Krista. 2001. "Girls Need Ezines: Young Feminists Get Online" pp. 302–308 in A. Mitchell, L. Bryn Rundle and L. Karaian (eds.) *Turbo Chicks: Talking Young Feminisms*. Toronto: Sumach Press.

Shaull, Richard 1989. "Foreword" pp. 1–15 in P. Friere *Pedagogy of the Oppressed*. Trans. M. Bergman Ramos. New York: Continuum.

Shaw, Gillian. 2004. "Messaging beats the mall: Internet has revolutionized teen socializing" *Vancouver Sun*, November 30: A1–A2.

Simmons, Rachel. 2002. *Odd Girl Out: The Hidden Culture of Aggression in Girls*. New York: Harcourt.

Skeggs, Beverley. 1997. *Formations of Class and Gender: Becoming Respectable*. London: Sage Publications.

Skeggs, Beverley. 2004. *Class, Self, Culture*. London and New York: Routledge.

Smith, Dorothy. 1980. "An Analysis of Ideological Structures and How Women Are Excluded: Considerations for Academic Women" pp. 252–267 in J. P. Grayson (ed.) *Class, State, Ideology and Change: Marxist Perspectives*. Toronto: Holt, Rinehart and Winston.

Smith, Dorothy. 1987. *The Everyday World as Problematic: A Feminist Sociology*. Boston: Northeastern University Press.

Smith, Dorothy. 1988. "Femininity as Text" pp. 37–59 in Leslie Roman, Linda Christian-Smith and Elizabeth Ellsworth (eds.) *Becoming Feminine: The Politics of Popular Culture*. London; New York: Falmer Press.

Smith, Dorothy. 1990a. *The Conceptual Practices of Power: A Feminist Sociology of Knowledge*. Toronto: University of Toronto Press.

Smith, Dorothy. 1990b. *Texts, Facts and Femininity: Exploring the Relations of Ruling*. London: Routledge.

Smith, Dorothy. 1999. *Writing the Social: Critique, Theory and Investigations*. Toronto: University of Toronto Press.

Smith, Dorothy, Paula Bourne and Liza McCoy. 1998. "Girls and schooling: their own critique" *Resources for Feminist Research* 26(1/2): 55–68.

Spencer, Renee, Michelle V. Porche and Deborah L. Tolman. 2003. "We've come a long way—maybe: new challenges for gender equity in education" *Teachers College Record* 105(9): 1774–1807.

Spender, Dale. 1980. *Man Made Language*. London: Routledge & Kegan Paul.

Spender, Dale. 1982. *Women of Ideas and What Men Have Done to Them: From Aphra Behn to Adrienne Rich*. London, Boston: Routledge & Kegan Paul.

Spivak, Gayatri Chakravorty. 1985. "Can the subaltern speak? speculations on widow sacrifice" *Wedge* 7/8: 120–130.

Spivak, Gayatri Chakravorty. 1987. *In Other Worlds: Essays in Cultural Politics*. New York: Methuen.

Stacey, Judith. 1988. "Can there be a feminist ethnography?" *Women's Studies International Forum* 11(1): 21–27.

Stacey, Judith. 1990. "Sexism by a Subtler Name? Poststructural Conditions and Postfeminist Consciousness in Silicon Valley" pp. 338–356 in Karen V. Hansen and Ilene J. Philipson (eds.) *Women, Class, and the Feminist Imagination: A Socialist Feminist Reader.* Philadelphia: Temple University Press.

Stack, Michelle. In press. "Video production and youth-adult collaboration: openings and dilemmas" *McGill Journal of Education.*

Stack, Michelle and Deirdre M. Kelly. 2006. "The popular media, education, and resistance" *Canadian Journal of Education* 29(1): 5–26.

Statistics Canada. 2004. Census at school. Retrieved November 14, 2004, from http://www19.statcan.ca/05/05_000_ehtm

Statistics Canada. 2007. Vancouver, British Columbia (table). 2006. Community Profiles. 2006 Census. Statistics Canada Catalogue no. 92-591-XWE. Ottawa. Available: http://www12.statcan.ca/english/census06/data/profiles/community/Index.cfm?Lang=E

Status of Women Canada. 2005. *Assessing Gender Equality: Trends in the Situation of Women and Men in Canada.* Ottawa: Status of Women Canada.

Stepp, Laura Sessions. 2002. "Alpha Girl in middle school, learning to handle the ABCs of power" *Washington Post*, February 23: C01.

Stoller, Debbie. 1998. "Brave new girls: these TV heroines know what girl power really means" *On the Issues* 7(4): 42.

Taft, Jessica K. 2004. "Girl Power Politics: Pop-Culture Barriers and Organizational Resistance" pp. 69–78 in Anita Harris (ed.) *All About the Girl: Culture, Power and Identity.* New York: Routledge.

Talbot, Margaret. 2002. "Girls just want to be mean" *New York Times Magazine*, February 24. Available: http://query.nytimes.com/gst/fullpage.html?res=9C05E5D81E3FF937A15751C0A9649C8B63

Talbot, Margaret. 2006. "Little hotties: Barbie's new rivals" *New Yorker*, December 4: 74–83.

Tamake, Mariko. 2001. "Robin and Me" pp. 27–32 in Allyson Mitchell, Lisa Bryn Rundle and Laura Karaian (eds.) *Turbo Chicks: Talking Young Feminisms*. Toronto: Sumach Press.

Tanenbaum, Leora. 1999/2000. *Slut! Growing Up Female with a Bad Reputation*. New York: Seven Stories Press/HarperCollins.

Tasker, Yvonne and Diane Negra. 2007. "Introduction: Feminist Politics and Postfeminist Culture" pp. 1–25 in Yvonne Tasker and Diane Negra (eds.) *Interrogating Postfeminism: Gender and the Politics of Popular Culture*. Durham, NY: Duke University Press.

Thiel, Shayla Marie. 2005. "'IM Me': Identity Construction and Gender Negotiation in the World of Adolescent Girls and Instant Messaging" pp. 179–201 in Sharon Mazzarella (ed.) *Girl Wide Web: Girls, the Internet, and the Negotiation of Identity*. New York: Peter Lang.

*Thirteen*. 2003. Directed by Catherine Hardwicke. Hollywood, CA: Fox Searchlight.

Thomas, J. J. and K. A. Daubman. 2001. "The relationship between friendship quality and self-esteem in adolescent girls and boys" *Sex Roles* 45(1/2): 53–65.

Thorne, Barrie. 1993. *Gender Play: Girls and Boys in School*. New Brunswick, NJ: Rutgers University Press.

Tolman, Deborah L. and Tracy E. Higgins. 1994. "How Being a Good Girl Can Be Bad for Girls" pp. 205–225 in Nan Bauer Maglin and Donna Perry (eds.) *"Bad Girls"/"Good Girls": Women, Sex, and Power in the Ninties*. New Brunswick NJ: Rutgers University Press.

Underwood, Marion K. 2003. *Social Aggression Among Girls*. New York: Guilford Press.

Underwood, Marion K. 2004. "Glares of contempt, eye rolls of disgust and turning away to exclude: non-verbal forms of social aggression among girls" *Feminism and Pschycology* 14(3): 371–375.

Valentine, Gill and Sarah L. Holloway. 2002. "Cyberkids? exploring children's identities and social networks in on-line and off-line worlds" *Annals of the Association of American Geographers* 92(2): 302–319.

Valverde, Mariana. 1991. "As if subjects existed: analyzing social discourses" *Canadian Review of Anthropology and Sociology* 28(2): 173–187.

Walby, Sylvia. 1997. *Gender Transformations*. London: Routledge.

Wald, Gayle. 1998. "Just a girl?: rock music, feminism, and the cultural construction of female youth" *Signs: Journal of Women in Culture and Society* 23(3): 585–610.

Walker, Rebecca (ed.). 1995. *To Be Real: Telling the Truth and Changing the Face of Feminism*. New York: Anchor.

Walkerdine, Valerie. 1990. *Schoolgirl Fictions*. London: Verso

Walkerdine, Valerie. 1997. *Daddy's Girl: Young Girls and Popular Culture*. Cambridge, MA: Harvard University Press.

Walkerdine, Valerie. 2003. "Reclassifying upward mobility: femininity and the neo-liberal subject" *Gender and Education* 15(3): 237–248.

Walkerdine, Valerie. 2006. "Playing the game" *Feminist Media Studies* 6(4): 519–537.

Walkerdine, Valerie and Helen Lucey. 1998. *Democracy in the Kitchen: Regulating Mothers and Socializing Daughters*. London: Virago.

Walkerdine, Valerie, Helen Lucey and June Melody. 2001. *Growing up Girl: Psychological Explorations of Gender and Class*. London: Palgrave.

Wallace, Claire and Sijka Kovacheva. 1995. *Youth and Society*. London: Macmillan.

Ward, Jane Victoria and Beth Cooper Benjamin. 2004. "Women, Girls, and the Unfinished Work of Connection: A Critical Review of American Girls' Studies" pp. 15–28 in Anita Harris (ed.) *All About the Girl: Culture, Power, and Identity*. New York and London: Routledge.

Weedon, Chris. 1987. *Feminist Practice and Poststructuralist Theory*. New York: Basil Blackwell.

Weeks, Jeffrey. 2003. *Sexuality*. London, New York: Routledge.

Weeks, Kathi. 1998. *Constituting Feminist Subjects*. Ithaca, NY: Cornell University Press.

Weir, Sara and Constance Faulkner. 2004. *Voices of a New Generation: A Feminist Anthology*. Boston: Pearson.

Weitz, R. 2001. "Women and their hair: seeking power through resistance and accommodation" *Gender and Society* 15: 667–686.

Weller, Susie. 2006. "Skateboarding Alone? Making Social Capital Discourse Relevant to Teenagers' Lives" *Journal of Youth Studies* 9(5): 557–574.

West, Candice and Don. H. Zimmerman. 1987. "Doing gender" *Gender and Society* 1: 125–151.

White, Emily. 2002. *Fast Girls: Teenage Tribes and the Myth of Slut*. New York: Scribner.

Willis, Paul. 1977. *Learning to Labour*. New York: Columbia University Press.

Wiseman, Rosalind. 2002. *Queen Bees & Wannabes: Helping Your Daughter Survive Cliques, Gossip, Boyfriends & Other Realities of Adolescence*. New York: Crown Publishers.

Wolf, Naomi. 2006. "Young adult fiction: wild things" *New York Times*, March 12. Available: http://www.nytimes.com/2006/03/12/books/review/12wolf.html?ei=5070&en=1e1b857b94888c40&ex=1148702400&pagewanted=print

Woolley, Pieta. 2006. "The myth of promiscuity" *Georgia Straight*, August 31–September 7: 45–46.

Worrall, A. 2004. "Twisted Sisters, Ladettes, and the New Penology: The Social Construction of 'Violent Girls' " pp. 41—60 in C. Alder and A. Worrall (eds.) *Girls' Violence: Myths and Realities*. New York: State University of New York Press.

Wyn, Johanna and Rob White. 1995. *Rethinking Youth*. Sydney: Allen and Unwin.

Yates, Simeon J. 1997. "Gender identity and CMC" *Journal of Computer Assisted Learning* 13: 281–290.

Yon, Daniel A. 2000. *Elusive Culture: Schooling, Race, and Identity in Global Times*. Albany: State University of New York Press.

Young, Iris Marion. 1989. "Throwing Like a Girl: A Phenomenology of Feminine Body Comportment, Motility and Spatiality" pp. 51–70 in Jennifer Allen and Iris Marion Young (eds.) *The Thinking Muse: Feminism and Modern French Philosophy*. Bloomington: Indiana University Press.

Young, Iris Marion. 2000. *Inclusion and Democracy*. New York: Oxford University Press.

media literacy, 204, 205—6, 221n2
mediation, xviii, 189, 201
Misciagno, Patricia, 130—3,
  168—9
moral panics, 3, 37, 38, 40—1, 47,
  48, 187, 194

name-calling, 91—93
  by boys, 92, 108n15, 134n2, 155
  online, 137
  sexual, 92—93, 96—97
  Also see meanness
neoliberal Subjects, 18, 202
  girls as, 25—26n25, 42
neoliberalism, 175, 202—3
normality, as a construction, 47—48
  *Also see* heterosexual matrix

ollie, defined, 134n5
online communication,
  effects, 150, 151—3, 157
  as teaching venue, 213—5
  *See under* computer
Online girls, 139
overachieving girls,
  debates, 39—42
  as middle-class, 41
  *Also see* gamma girls

Paechter, Carrie, 14, 95, 143
Park Gang, 113, 122—6, 132, 140,
  162, 167, 169, 211
  members, 122
  and transformative agency, 169
participants, in *"Girl Power"*,
  78—79n15, 85, 223—31
  Skater girls, 113
  Online girls, 142

peer cultures, 58, 208—9
  as communities of practice, 14
  as mediation, xviii
peer groups, *See* communities of
  practice, youth groups
peer influences, 101
peer pressure, 95, 186
*Perfect Girls, Starving Daughters,*
  the book, 41—42
performativity, 11—12, 23n7,
  24n19, 53, 97, 129
  of gender, 97, 157—8
physical violence, by girls, 106n10
Pipher, Mary, 6, 33, 54, 103
pole dancing, 37—38
political engagement, of youth,
  39, 51n3, 221n4
  *Also see* transformative agency
popular culture,
  girls as critical consumers of,
  29, 208
  as knowledge, 47—48
  relevance to *"Girl Power"*, xvi, 29
  as a resource for girls, 49—50
  as a teaching resource, 215—6
popular girlhood,
  as idealized femininity, 94
  as a moral imperative, 96, 97
  and racialization, 106n7
  rejection of, 114—5
Popular girls, 105n3
  as conformists, 170
  described, 86, 94
  as mean, 88—89
  as powerful, 89
popularity, 80n22, 83
  "good" versus "bad," 83
  as meanness, 32

**mediated youth**

Sharon R. Mazzarella
*General Editor*

Grounded in cultural studies, books in this series will study the cultures, artifacts, and media of children, tweens, teens, and college-aged youth. Whether studying television, popular music, fashion, sports, toys, the Internet, self-publishing, leisure, clubs, school, cultures/activities, film, dance, language, tie-in merchandising, concerts, subcultures, or other forms of popular culture, books in this series go beyond the dominant paradigm of traditional scholarship on the effects of media/culture on youth. Instead, authors endeavor to understand the complex relationship between youth and popular culture. Relevant studies would include, but are not limited to studies of how youth negotiate their way through the maze of corporately-produced mass culture; how they themselves have become cultural producers; how youth create "safe spaces" for themselves within the broader culture; the political economy of youth culture industries; the representational politics inherent in mediated coverage and portrayals of youth; and so on. Books that provide a forum for the "voices" of the young are particularly encouraged. The source of such voices can range from in-depth interviews and other ethnographic studies to textual analyses of cultural artifacts created by youth.

For further information about the series and submitting manuscripts, please contact:

SHARON R. MAZZARELLA
Communication Studies Department
Clemson University
Clemson, SC 29634

To order other books in this series, please contact our Customer Service Department at:

(800) 770-LANG (within the U.S.)
(212) 647-7706 (outside the U.S.)
(212) 647-7707 FAX

Or browse online by series at WWW.PETERLANG.COM